Mairéad Conneely

Between Two Shores /
Idir Dhá Chladach

Writing the Aran Islands, 1890–1980

PETER LANG

Oxford • Bern • Berlin • Bruxelles • Frankfurt am Main • New York • Wien

Bibliographic information published by Die Deutsche Nationalbibliothek.
Die Deutsche Nationalbibliothek lists this publication in the Deutsche
Nationalbibliografie; detailed bibliographic data is available on the Internet at
http://dnb.d-nb.de.

A catalogue record for this book is available from the British Library.

Library of Congress Cataloging-in-Publication Data:

Conneely, Mairéad.
  Between two shores = Idir dhá chladach : writing the Aran Islands, 1890-1980 /
Mairéad Conneely.
    p. cm. -- (Remagining Ireland ; 32)
  Includes bibliographical references and index.
  ISBN 978-3-0343-0144-2 (alk. paper)
  1. National characteristics, Irish, in literature. 2. Aran Islands (Ireland)--In litera-
ture. 3. English literature--Irish authors--History and criticism. 4. Irish literature-
-History and criticism. 5. National characteristics, Irish. I. Title. II. Title: Idir dhá
chladach.
  PR8722.N24C66 2011
  820.99417--dc22

                              2011019216

ISSN 1662-9094
ISBN 978-3-0343-0144-2

Cover image: 'Looking Eastward: Inis Oírr and the Burren, from Inis Meáin'
(John Cleary, 2010)

© Peter Lang AG, International Academic Publishers, Bern 2011
Hochfeldstrasse 32, CH-3012 Bern, Switzerland
info@peterlang.com, www.peterlang.com, www.peterlang.net

Printed in Germany

Do Mhama, John, Nóirín agus John
Le grá mór millteach

&

I ndil chuimhne ar
Mo Dhaide
Seáinín Bheachla Bán Ó Conghaile
1937 – 1986

"*Ár gcara, ár gcompánach, bhíodh i gcónaí ag spraoi linn,*
Beidh tú go deo a'inn mar ár n-aingeal aoibhinn".

Contents
Clár na n-Ábhar

Acknowledgments
Buíochas

This book began life as a PhD thesis, supervised by Dr Patricia Lynch and Dr Seosamh Mac Muirí. The encouragement, belief and insight which they provided then continue to this day and I am so fortunate to have them as friends. Buíochas ó chroí libh beirt.

I have also been very fortunate to receive advice, support and counsel from colleagues, scholars and friends from all corners of the world while researching both my thesis and book. Dr Anne Burke, Dr Brent MacLaine, Dr Caitríona Ó Torna, Dr Christina Gillis, Prof. Declan Kiberd, Dr Deirdre Ní Chonghaile, Dr Eugene O'Brien, Frank Ledwell (RIP), Prof. Godfrey Baldacchino, Dr Heidi Hansson, Dr Irene Lucchitti, Dr John Logan, Laurie Brinklow, Prof. Lyman Tower Sargent, An tOll. Máirín Nic Eoin, An tOll. Mícheál Mac Craith, Dr Michael Griffin, Dr Michael Kelly, Niamh Sheridan, Prof. Phil Hayward, Dr Riana O'Dwyer, Prof. Stephen Royle, Tim Robinson and Prof. Tom Moylan have all contributed to aspects of this work, and have provided me with a wealth of ideas throughout. Mo mhíle buíochas libh go léir.

I also wish to sincerely thank Eamon Maher and Christabel Scaife for their professional and perceptive treatment of this manuscript and for their enthusiasm throughout.

Máirín Pháidín Shaibhín Uí Chonghaile (Inis Meáin) and Sr Mary Lyons (Tuam), both inspirational teachers, supported my love of reading and the Aran Islands from an early age and encouraged me to follow this path.

I am honoured to have fantastic friends, who have supported me throughout the writing of this book and beyond and I thank them wholeheartedly: Jenny Ahern, Eileen and Mike Aylward, Mike Carey, Eimear Conneely, Loraine and Ronan Daly, Fiona Earls, Eileen Faherty, Sarah Faherty, Áine Folan, Sinéad Giblin, Denise Griffey, Louise Keane, Maria

Keane, Oonagh and John Maguire, Máiréad Moriarty and Lorcan Murphy, Máiréad Moriarty (Eile!), Susan Mulcahy, Aislinn and Ray Murphy, Karen Ní Chlochasaigh and Nicky Dowling, Máire Ní Ghráda, Deirdre Ní Loingsigh, Alan O'Callaghan, Ailbhe O'Flaherty, Aoife O'Grady, Íde O'Sullivan and Jim Murphy, Emily Anne Rennison, Lorraine Ryan, and Eimear Spain.

Ann and John O'Callaghan have kept a loving eye on me and I am so grateful to them.

Mom and John's love and faith are unstinting and their belief in anything I turn my hand and heart to has reassured me at every step. Maidir leis an leabhar seo, d'éist Mama le mo chuid ceisteanna, agus d'fhreagair sí iad; thug sí spreagadh dom nuair nach raibh mé in ann mo bhealach a fháil agus chuir sí ar bhóthar mo leasa mé arís. John provided unique insights, read passages and suggested improvements and took the photo for the cover of this book. I am truly blessed.

Nóirín makes me proud to be her sister, and keeps my feet on the ground and my heart in the right place.

John O'Callaghan has read every word and has always believed in me. He has made all the difference.

Mairéad Conneely
March 2010

CHAPTER I

Introduction
Réamhrá

> From Connemara, or the Moher clifftop,
> Where the land ends with a sheer drop,
> You can see the three stepping stones out of Europe.
> [...]
> And on Galway Bay, between shore and shore,
> The ferry plunges to Aranmore.
> — SEAMUS HEANEY, "The Evening Land" (in O'Sullivan, 1976: 6)

Inis Mór, Inis Meáin and Inis Oírr, the three Aran Islands[1], lie across the mouth of Galway Bay, some 50 kilometres from the city of Galway, "resembling a group of stranded whales" (O'Sullivan, 1976: 7).[2] The Islands' bedrock of grey-black limestone gives them their visually arresting appeal. Though some (see Robinson, 1986; Waddell *et al.*, 1994) agree that their collective name *Árainn*, or Aran, derives from their similarity to the shape of a kidney, or *"ára"*, O'Sullivan offers the Irish expression *"'Ard-Thuinn'*, meaning 'the height above the waves'" (1976: 7) as an alternative suggestion. The Islands have been populated for four thousand years (Robinson, 1986: 1; Ó hEithir, 1991: 1) and are perhaps Ireland's greatest (re)discovered,

---

1   "Aran" or "the Islands" will be used throughout this book to connote The Aran Islands, and the capital "I" will indicate the Aran Islands as opposed to other Irish islands.

2   Hugo Hamilton's *Hand in the Fire* also uses the imagery of the Islands as whales: "I was probably not the first person to think of this, but it felt to me like an original way of describing them because it was my first time seeing them. Whatever way the light falls, they keep moving a little, dipping and coming up again" (2010: 173–174).

recovered and uncovered landscapes. They are regarded as "Ireland raised to the power of two" (Robinson, 1992: xvii); their magnetic pull upon tourists and scholars alike is well documented and has been continually employed by advertising campaigns and tourism brochures to attract people to the Islands' shores.

The Islands are variously described on tourist websites as: "rugged, wild and beautiful" (<http://www.irelandsislands.com>), "unique and timeless [...] where one day is never enough" (<http://www.visitaranis-lands.com>) and "difficult to describe, and difficult to forget" (<http://www.discoverireland.ie/WEST/where-to-go/islands>). Though such descriptions contain elements of truth, island life is a complex phenomenon: for instance, I once observed a day-tripper to Inis Mór, the largest and most visited of the three Islands, swiftly demand her money back from the ferry company who had sold her a return-ticket to the island when, to her horror, she discovered that a Supermac's fast food restaurant had been opened there.[3] The tourist could not reconcile the presence of this latter-day symbol of mainland modernity with her utopian expectation of how the Islands should be, and what the islanders should be embracing and preserving. Tourist websites, however, are not the only sources for these kinds of idealised descriptions. Guide books and travel literature offer similar, overly romanticised interpretations of life on the Islands, and when Aran Island literature is used to supplement these pen-pictures, selected, familiar, passages are included for apparently more authentic effect. Passages from John Millington Synge's *The Aran Islands* are regularly found on Island websites, as are some texts by Liam Ó Flaithearta, and, though not as frequently, the poetry of Máirtín Ó Direáin. Perhaps the most essential information imparted by these sites relates to the physical features of the Islands. In terms of size and population Inis Meáin (5km

3   Supermac's, an Irish-owned fast food restaurant chain, opened in Inis Mór on 19 June 2005. The Tidy Towns Competition Report of 2007 noted that "Supermacs (sic) does not fit in well with the rest of the island streetscape" (<http://www.tidytowns.ie/u_reports/2007/2007%20COUNTY%20GALWAY%20INIS%20MOR%201173.pdf>). One islander labelled the fast-food outlet "vulgar" (<http://www.msnbc.msn.com/id/29603410/>).

by 3km; 154 in 2006) and Inis Oírr (2.5km by 2.5km; 247 in 2006) are much smaller than Inis Mór (12km by 3km; 824 in 2006), but in terms of tourist figures, the middle island of Inis Meáin remains the least visited. Inis Mór enjoys over 70 per cent of the total tourist influx to the Islands, with Inis Oírr getting a further 20 per cent, and Inis Meáin receiving the remaining 10 per cent.

Inis Meáin's lower volume of tourists is accounted for by the fact that it attracts long-stay visitors more so than day-trippers, who are more likely to frequent Inis Mór. The greatest foot-fall on the Islands is provided by ferry services from Ros a' Mhíl, in County Galway. There are usually four daily sailings to Inis Mór, whereas there are only two daily sailings to both Inis Meáin and Inis Oírr, thereby enticing people to travel to the larger island while also allowing them to leave earlier in the day.[4] However, this comes at a cost. Inis Mór's economy has suffered in recent years because of what has become known as the "tinfoil brigade", the day-trippers who come armed with their own food and supplies, and who leave very little in the way of spare change on the island itself. However, people come to Aran for all kinds of reasons; many come in search of peace and quiet, others come looking for somewhere different, and some arrive to seek out places for inspiration for writing and composition. There may be historical reasons for this; Inis Mór and Inis Oírr were considered to be of more strategic importance than Inis Meáin during the period of English ownership and occupation of the Islands, and as a result, Inis Meáin became associated with the less-contaminated essence which cultural and political national-ists have sought out in the West of Ireland.

One example of this is found in Patrick Pearse's decision, in 1898, to establish a branch of *Conradh na Gaeilge*, the Gaelic League, on the middle island at the expense of Inis Mór (Dudley Edwards, 1977: 27), which is often considered the capital of the three Aran Islands.[5] The British flag had

---

4   During the summer season, the Islands are also serviced by sailings from Doolin in County Clare. Daily year-round flights with Aer Arann also service the Islands.

5   As Irish was not part of the school curriculum at this time, the Aran Islanders could speak Irish but had no formal education in the reading or writing of the language. *Conradh na Gaeilge* saw its role as promoting Irish in English-speaking areas but also

never flown over Inis Meáin and this was particularly important to Pearse, as it further emphasised the purity of Inis Meáin's history.[6] Throughout the nineteenth century, scholars and sojourners visited Inis Meáin in various groups and with varied intentions, congregating in a cottage which was known as *Ollscoil na Gaeilge*, or the University of Irish. The cottage is now knows as *Teach Synge*, or Synge's Cottage. As Robinson notes, "Douglas Hyde, Eoin MacNeill, and the young Patrick Pearse [were] all looking for Ireland in Inis Meáin" (1986: 9). Indeed, in 1898 Synge left Inis Mór for Inis Meáin: "[the men from Inis Meáin] seem a simpler and perhaps a more interesting type than the people here [on Inis Mór] […]. I have decided to move on to Inishmaan, where Gaelic is more generally used, and the life is perhaps the most primitive that is left in Europe" (Synge, 1992: 10). It is interesting to note that Synge found that "it gave [him] a moment of exquisite satisfaction to find [himself] moving away from civilisation" (1992: 12) on his journey to Inis Meáin; perhaps the civilisation he was referring to was that of both Inis Mór and that of the mainland.[7] However, Synge was not the first of the literary set to land on Inis Meáin's shores; Father Eoghan O'Growney and Lawless had visited Inis Meáin as early as 1885, and W.B. Yeats visited in 1896. Emily Lawless's novel *Grania: The Story of an Island* (1892) was to become somewhat akin to "required reading" for visiting members of the literary community (Robinson, 1995: 130), as both Synge and Yeats read it on their way to Aran. It is revealing, however, that this novel is largely unknown among islanders today while

----

as preserving Irish in Gaeltacht areas. See Sisson (2004: 15, 36) for information on Pearse's desire to establish St Enda's school on Inis Meáin, thereby strengthening the learning, writing and reading of Irish on the island. A further connection between the island and the Pearse family lies in the fact that Pearse's father, James, carved the altar for the church in Inis Meáin.

6   Thomas MacDonagh also spent time on Inis Meáin, organising rifle practice (see Robinson, 1992: xvi–xvii, and Norstedt, 1980: 28).

7   In the "Introduction" to *The Aran Islands* Synge writes: "Kilronan […] has been so much changed by the fishing industry, developed there by the Congested Districts Board, that it now has very little to distinguish it from any fishing village on the west coast of Ireland. The other islands are more primitive, but even on them changes are being made […]" (1992: 3).

the relationships of Synge, Yeats, and Gregory *et al.* with the Islands are famed and revered.

The Aran Islands were, and continue to be, a Mecca for tourists, writers and artists, and most recently, for eco-friendly and spiritually-inclined individuals who are drawn to a retreat established by Celtic priest Dara Molloy on Inis Mór.[8] However, when Leon Ó Broin enquired of Breandán Ó hEithir: "[d]id you ever ask yourself why so many people find those three limestone rocks in the Atlantic so terribly interesting?" (Ó hEithir, 1991: 3), he inadvertently signalled the predominant motivation behind this book. Aran islanders very rarely question their place in the world, or indeed the importance of their island homes in the larger scheme of things. Islanders are aware that *strainséirí*[9] find both the Islands and their inhabitants of interest, but only occasionally consider why they might actually be of interest to these tourists, as well as writers. It is even more exceptional to find Island authors writing about what outside or mainland authors have been writing about for years, namely the significance of the Aran Islands and their inhabitants. When my grandmother, Máire Bean Uí Fhátharta, passed away on 6 January 2005, an obituary in the *Irish Times* marked it as "the passing of a cultural moment" (O'Grady, 7 March 2005). Bean Uí Fhátharta's grandparents Bríd and Páidín Mac Donnchadha, were J.M. Synge's hosts, and her uncle Máirtín[10] was Synge's guide and language teacher during his time on the island. Bean Uí Fhátharta was of a similar generation to novelist and short-story writer Liam Ó Flaithearta[11] and poet Máirtín Ó Direáin, both Inis Mór men, and though she herself was

8   "Aisling Árann" could be described as an "intentional community" (Sargent, 1994: 4).
9   *Strainséir*, or *strainséara*, pl. *strainséirí*, is the most commonly used word on the Aran Islands for a tourist or visitor to the Islands. *Strainséir* means "stranger", but can also connote "outsider" or "alien". It is also generally used to describe tourists or visitors. This may extend as far as estrangement, and may perhaps explain the feeling of being outside of current reality that many associate(d) with being on the Islands.
10 Máirtín Mac Donnchadha appears as "Michael" in Synge's *The Aran Islands*.
11 I will refer to the author as Liam Ó Flaithearta. The Irish form of the author's name will be used in favour of Liam O'Flaherty. However, when and where critics and other authors refer to Ó Flaithearta as O'Flaherty, the English form of his name will remain unchanged.

not a writer, she had an immense store of folkloric, literary and historical knowledge. The tribute afforded to her in the *Irish Times* reminded many islanders of both her individual contribution to island life, and also her generation's crucial role in safeguarding and promoting the literary and geo-cultural significance of the Aran Islands.

This book extends an examination through the past, present and possible future of the Islands, in search of other salient moments in the literature and culture of the Aran Islands. Aran's past has been mythologised, re-discovered and "raised to the level of national ideal" (Gibbons, 1996: 23); Aran's present is heavily reliant on its past, especially from an economic point of view, while trying to forge its way into the future. Aran's future, however, is uncertain in terms of whether it will press ahead with a more modern understanding of its own culture and heritage or whether it will remain faithful to its past, even in the face of huge changes on the Islands. Some predict, based on past events, that continued adherence to traditional values will preserve Aran from the doom of depopulation and geographical and cultural erosion, while others argue that the Islands must engage with mainland Ireland's progressive doctrines to some extent if they are to survive and prosper. Consideration is given throughout this book to Aran's past, present and future, as seen through literature and more recently, through cultural and social changes on the Islands themselves.

This study focuses primarily on Aran Island writing, and principally on Emily Lawless's *Grania: The Story of an Island* (1892), J.M. Synge's *The Aran Islands* (1992 [originally published 1907]), Liam Ó Flaithearta's *Dúil* (1953) and Máirtín Ó Direáin's *Dánta 1939–1979* (1980). Some translated examples of Ó Direáin's poetry from Mac Síomóin and Sealy's *Tacar Dánta / Selected Poems* (1984) will also be used in this work, as will work from Ó Direáin's autobiographical essays found in *Feamainn Bhealtaine* (1961). Translations of Ó Flaithearta and Ó Direáin's work are provided as appropriate and were carried out by this author unless otherwise stated.

Lawless and Synge were authors from outside the Islands, and yet *Grania* and *The Aran Islands* show levels of personal and communal intimacy which contradicts their supposed exteriority. While Lawless's *Grania* was widely read following its publication, it was quickly, and somewhat harshly, discredited by some of her fellow authors following their own visits to the Aran Islands. Synge was especially, and uncharacteristically, aggrieved by Lawless's novelistic treatment of Inis Meáin; however, his principal criticism of Lawless pertained to the amount of time she had allegedly spent on the island prior to writing *Grania*. Though Lawless does appear to exaggerate some elements of island life, and portrays her chief protagonist Grania as being closer in spirit to the warrior pirate queen Grace O'Malley, or Granuaile as she was more commonly known, than to any recognisable female islander, there are aspects of *Grania* that could only have come from Lawless's personal observations.[12] Synge carefully avoided charges of inauthenticity by writing a first-person travelogue about his four stays on Inis Meáin. However, both *Grania* and *The Aran Islands* share many common images and insights, and thus Synge would appear to have been slightly disingenuous in some of his criticism of Lawless's novel.

Ó Flaithearta and Ó Direáin, on the other hand, were insider-island authors, though both left Inis Mór in their teens. Ó Flaithearta received a scholarship to attend secondary school in Co. Tipperary and Ó Direáin left to seek employment in Galway city. Ó Flaithearta's relationship with the island of his birth and adolescence was complex and coloured significantly by his linguistic binarism, his fraught relationship with the Catholic priest on Inis Mór, and by the economic difficulties of writing in Irish in the mid 1920s and 1930s. Ó Direáin's association with Inis Mór was less complicated. His emotional relationship with the island centred on his remembrances of youth, and his early and middle poetry emphasised his imaginative re-creation of his island home. His later poetry, however, reflected his growing awareness that the island of his poetry and memory was incongruous with the realities of his former home.

---

12   Lawless's intricate descriptions of the limestone landscape, and of Inis Meáin's topography in particular, further reinforce this: "Inishmaan is divided into a succession of rocky steps or platforms, the lowest to eastward, the highest to westward, platforms which are in their turn divided and subdivided by innumerable joints and fissures. This, by the way, is a fact to be remembered, as, without it, you might easily wander for days and days over the islands without really getting to know or understand their topography" (1892: 58).

This book examines and treats of all four texts, and also all four authors, exploring the island(s) and the concept of islandness as it or they appear in the chosen works. Using postcolonial, utopian and island studies theories, this work investigates the literary, cultural and personal moments which emanated from the writing of Lawless, Synge, Ó Flaithearta and Ó Direáin. In doing so, this study considers how best to appreciate this writing, as well as present-day writing on and about Aran. This book exemplifies the seminal importance of the power of language, Irish and English, the authority of the island as a literary place of production – an interior labyrinth – and as a space of conception – an exterior mirror – and also the magnitude of the island as a metaphor and arena of tradition and memory in Irish literature. This book also proposes the wide-ranging significance of an Irish Islands Literature canon.

CHAPTER 2

Writing Aran
Ag Scríobh Árainn

> Aran, it is said [...] is the strangest place on earth. Sometimes for an
> hour you are, the rest is history: sometimes the two floods culminate
> in a dream.
> — AIDAN HIGGINS, *Balcony of Europe* (in Ó hAnluain, 1984: 20)

Introduction

The writings of Emily Lawless, John Millington Synge, Liam Ó Flaithearta
and Máirtín Ó Direáin explored in this book share a common literary point
of origin. This unifying heritage had its inception in the Aran Islands and
developed over time in an organic process as their respective constructions of Aran incorporated strong elements of continuity. This connecting
thread becomes most clearly visible by concentrating primarily, though not
exclusively, on Lawless's *Grania: The Story of an Island* (1892),[1] Synge's *The
Aran Islands* (1992), Ó Flaithearta's *Dúil* (1953) and Ó Direáin's *Dánta,
1939–1979* (1980). Each of these works has performed a seminal role in
creating and shaping both artistic interpretations and popular images of
the Aran Islands. Fundamental to any assessment of their influence must
be a study of the authors' biographical and linguistic backgrounds. The
critical reception of and response to these texts is also considered here

1   Lawless's *With the Wild Geese* (1902) will also be referred to alongside the study of
     Grania as some of this poetry collection was written while on Aran.

in conjunction with their canonical credibility. A re-evaluation of the significance and meaning of the above works in terms of our understanding of Aran will be offered in this chapter and subsequently in light of the dominant critical discourses. Central to this reassessment will be the contribution of Ó Flaithearta and Ó Direáin's Irish-language offerings to the overarching body of Aran Island literature and their many uses of the island as both source material and symbolic structure.

Emily Lawless

Emily Lawless is considered by some to be a "forgotten writer" (Grubgeld, 1983: 9). Born into an aristocratic family in 1845, Lawless was the fourth of nine children and the eldest daughter of the Third Baron Cloncurry. The future botanist, author and poet had a fondness for the outdoors, and at an early age "developed an interest in natural history which led her to collect moths" (Linn, 1971: 6). However, the spectre of mental illness hung over the family home, and, through suicide, claimed the lives of her father Edward and her sisters Rose and Mary. It is perhaps understandable then that Lawless would have found solice in the natural world and in books. The Lawless family home was at Lyons in Co. Meath. However, during the summers, the family stayed at Castle Hackett, Co. Galway. Castle Hackett was her mother's homestead and it was from there that Lawless was first introduced to the landscapes of the Burren and the Aran Islands.[2] This introduction was crucial, as William Linn explains:

> Emily loved these regions, and her creative imagination was fired by them, for the outstanding features of both her verse and prose are her descriptions of these

---

2   Lady Cloncurry, Lawless's mother, was a member of the Kirwan family, and was by all accounts a famously beautiful woman; see Robinson, L., ed. (1947) *Lady Gregory's Journals: 1916–1930*, pp. 218–219.

varied landscapes and her semi-romantic depiction of the hard lives which their inhabitants led (1971: 10–11).

Lawless was accustomed to travelling, and spent time in France, Italy and Spain throughout the period 1869 to 1895. She began her European travels after her father's suicide in 1869 and accompanied her mother on many trips on the continent until her mother's passing in 1895. Following Lady Cloncurry's death in May 1895, Lawless settled in Surrey, England, where she lived until her death in 1913 (see Linn, 1971: 13–44). In an article published prior to the release of her biography of Lawless, Heidi Hansson provides us with much interesting biographical and historical detail. Lawless, "[was] a member of the Anglo-Irish aristocracy and even though the family had a complex history, [...] most family members were Unionists by the end of the nineteenth century" (Hansson, 2003: 122). However, "Lawless's politically ambiguous writing began to be dismissed as conservative or even anti-Irish" (Hansson, 2003: 122) and was thus often ignored for failing to align itself with any one political orthodoxy. This was to prove ultimately detrimental to the reception which Lawless's work was to receive, as Irish literary criticism took on a more nationalist slant. For failing to advance the cause of either nationalist or unionist thought in her work, many viewed Lawless's writing as ambiguous and trivial. Moving beyond the confining categories of political belief and religious doctrine, Lawless sought instead to discover Ireland as a nature-based entity, a place capable of allowing her to be who she wished to be. Her journeys to the West of Ireland, in Connemara and The Burren in Co. Clare in particular, provided Lawless with the perfect backdrop for her novels and poetry, as well as providing her with the freedom to examine her own beliefs and ideas. Lawless was amongst the first of her generation to investigate the possibility of an Irish identity based on communion with the land and with the people rather than on any political or religious grounds. Lawless's early writing created an Ireland that was

> fundamentally unknowable and therefore uncontrollable, [critiquing] nationalist and colonialist rhetoric as well as masculine scientific norms and conveying a particularly feminine, if not explicitly feminine sense of nature (Hansson, 2003: 122).

In imagining such a fragmentary place and in disrupting the predictable course followed by much of the literature of the time, Lawless demonstrates how a strange and new landscape can provide an identity all of its own, one which allows people to know that landscape but never to own it (Hansson, 2003: 122). Further complicating Lawless's literary standing, however, is her own reserved nature: "I have a relish, I might almost say a passion for obscurity" (from *A Garden Diary*, 1906: 123). This obscurity was not limiting, however, but liberating:

> it means that you belong to yourself; that you have your years, your days, hours, and minutes undisposed of, unbargained for, unwatched, and unwished for by anybody. It means that you are free to go in and out without witnesses; free as the grass, free rather as the birds of the air (1906: 123).

It is of no small significance that such personally-liberating obscurity would eventually lead to her being so little appreciated or studied today. However, the current obscurity of her work was aided, to a large extent, by Lawless's own wishes upon her death. She had stipulated that only a few personal papers should remain after her passing, and her will instructed that the rest of her personal effects be burned. It is difficult to decide if her wishes were as a result of the diffculties which her work had posed for critics, who saw much of her writing as politically insignificant, or if her own mental instability also played a role in her decision to exorcise her own work and her voice from literary history following her death. It may, however, also be possible that she simply wished to die free of any worldly records of her achievements or disappointments. She may have been unaware that her legacy would require any anciliary documentation; nonetheless, her obituary in the *Irish Times* noted the passing of "perhaps, the most distinguished literary Irish woman of her time" (23 October 1913: 7).

Her desire for obscurity aside, Lawless was to become the author of fifteen novels, one biography, several essays and three collections of poetry. The most famous of these works were often the ones which brought her most critical scorn, as they dealt with subjects that critics such as Yeats and contributors to *The Nation* deemed unsuitable for a woman to discuss and describe. Her biography of *Maria Edgeworth* (1904) was well received, as were her historical novels *Hurrish: A Study* (1888) which detailed the relationship between landlords and farmers in Co. Clare during the Land League, *With Essex in Ireland* (1890) and *Maelcho* (1894). However, the novel which caused the most critical controversy was *Grania: The Story of an Island* (1892).

Grania: The Story of an Island

The landscape of the west of Ireland provided the most wide-ranging interspace possible for Lawless. The "interspace", a concept first coined by Lawless in "North Clare – Leaves from a Diary" (1899: 604) will be fully considered and examined in chapters 3 and 4 of this book. Completely unlike the restricted and constricting nature of urban life and social order, the West of Ireland seemed limitless in geographical and artistic terms. In writing *Grania: The Story of an Island* (1892) Lawless gave full voice to her own personal interspace, as well as that of Grania's. Telling the story of Grania O'Malley and her life on Inishmaan, Lawless's apparently straightforward form and plot serve to highlight the more powerful undertones of the novel. Though *Grania's* plot is uncomplicated, Lawless's depiction of the Islands and of her main protagonist, Grania, won her praise and guaranteed a successful reception from the critics; complimentary reviews appeared in the *Spectator*, the *Antheneum*, the *Bookman*, and the *Nation*. *Grania* was also critically well received in America and England (Hansson, 2007: 74). Reviews focused predominantly on Lawless's vivid descriptions of land and seascapes, on the harshness of life on the island and on the difficulty of gaining access to either mainland or island in unfavourable weather. Speaking to a close friend, Lawless confirmed that "the weather there [Aran] plays, as it does in my story, the part of Fate in a Greek tragedy" (Grant Duff, 1904: 82). Very little was made of the protagonist's powerful struggle with the ineptness of the male characters in her life, namely her strained relationship with her ever-absent father Con, and her lover Murdough Blake. It would appear that these kinds of themes were either deemed unsuitable for discussion or ignored completely. It may also have

been the case that Grania's rejection of male superiority and failure to conform to her assigned role in the island's community related more to Lawless
herself, and this would have proved to be an inappropriate association to
construct or critique at the time.

However, Lawless was herself very aware of the dangers of what we
may today call the tourist's gaze and of staking a claim to a land that does
not belong to either native or foreigner. She rejects the attempts by many
to "pluck out the whole heart of its mystery within a space of twenty-
four hours" ("Iar-Connaught: A Sketch," 1882: 319). Synge's criticism of
Lawless's novel, then, must seem rather ill-founded, given Lawless's clear
understanding of the processes of getting to know certain landscapes and
their people. What Lawless does advocate, however, is

> the possibility of a space which does not replicate the exclusions of the Same and the
> Other, or, in other words, an interspace. Whether geographically, socially or cultur-
> ally defined, this more modern concept of space allows the presence also of those
> who do not fit the prevailing systems (Hansson, 2003: 130–131).

However, in isolating herself from the male-dominated literary circles,
and by

> proposing an identity based on a geography in opposition to imperialist and nation-
> alist discourses of control and definition, [Lawless] thereby denies any possibility of
> a collective identity that could power political action, because political activity to a
> great extent "depends on concepts of territoriality", as was the case during the Land
> War. This is both the most radical and the most limiting aspect of her vision, since
> on the one hand, the absence of a group identity precludes the logjam of sectarian-
> ism, on the other, social change is only really possible when many work to instigate
> it – which requires a sense of commonality (Hansson, 2003: 136).

Considering Hansson's use of the interspace as a method by which to
analyse Lawless's bifurcated views and literary position, it is useful to also
link this with Kathleen Leonard's unpublished M.A. thesis (1990), "Emily
Lawless's View of Ireland: Gleams at Times of Sudden Light", which dedi-
cates a chapter to *Grania* and notes that Lawless's "desire to find a middle
way, to avoid the polarities is already clear from the setting – Inishmaan,
the middle one of the three Aran islands (sic)" (1990: 85). Synge's presence

on Aran suggests an awareness of a space between himself and the islanders and indeed the island itself. His rejection, therefore, of Lawless' creation, and the spaces she had designated for her protagonist, seems ill-founded. However, in writing a "direct account" (*The Aran Islands*, 1992: 3), Synge perhaps thought that the reality of his portrayal would in many ways protect him from criticism and from charges of cold, fictional distance. In *The Aran Islands* we find, nonetheless, a correlation between the mood expressed by Grania in wanting to be both insider and outsider with that of Synge's, frustrating though it must have been.

> In some ways these men and women seem strangely far away from me. [...] On some days I feel this island as a perfect home and resting place; on other days I feel that I am a waif among the people. I can feel more with them than they can feel with me, and while I wander among them, they like me sometimes, and laugh at me sometimes, yet never know what I am doing (1992: 66).

Later, while assisting a young island girl to light a fire, Synge compares her to a Parisian, and she reacts by suggesting that both she and the French gentleman are alike. Synge's disappointment at the distance between himself and the islanders at certain times is palpable, though completely natural, both on the part of the islanders and Synge himself. Lawless' Grania, however, "[i]n her neighbours' eyes was a 'Foreigner', just as her mother had been a foreigner before her [...] out of touch and tone with her neighbours" (1892: 104, 108). Grania's interspatial identity, then, is constant. Synge's is natural, and with time, becomes less of a marker of difference, and more of a necessary artistic viewpoint.

Synge and Lawless: Grania's difficulties

One of the most interesting comments on *Grania* came from John Millington Synge. Synge criticised Lawless for writing a novel based on only a brief visit to the island and thus on only a scant knowledge of the place and its people. He wrote:

> I read *Grania* before I came here, and enjoyed it, but the real Aran spirit is not there. [...] To write a real novel of the island life one would require to pass several years among the people, but Miss Lawless does not appear to have lived here. Indeed it would be hardly possible perhaps for a lady for more than a few days (Synge made this remark in an unpublished notebook, which later appeared in Greene and Stephens, *J.M. Synge, 1871–1909*, 1959: 95–96).

Basing his critique more on Lawless than on *Grania*, Synge says much about how women were viewed at the time. Though he himself would spend only a few weeks each summer on the Islands, he found it almost incomprehensible that "a lady" would attempt to write a novel based on a short visit. Perhaps pre-empting such a response, Lawless subtitled her novel *The Story of an Island*, and admitted in the preface to changing some aspects of character and place to better suit her thematic structure. Synge chose not to write what Declan Kiberd has called "a full blown novel" (2000: 108), perhaps wary of the brevity of his visits to Inis Meáin.[3] Kiberd also notes that, in Synge's judgement "to write a novel of such a life would necessitate years spent among the people, as well as a deeper recognition of Aran's *strangeness*" (italics are Kiberd's, 2000: 108). Besides the sexist overtones of Synge's critique, one may also detect a level of protectiveness in his notes: "you cannot make a pet book of a book everybody reads [...] and you cannot make a pet place of a place everyone visits" (Price, ed., *Collected Works II*, 103).

It is productive to consider Synge's critique of Lawless in the light of Mary Banim's journey to Inis Mór in 1885. Synge dismisses Lawless's novel on the grounds that she did not have sufficient experience to comment authoritatively on island life. As Tim Robinson has noted, Mary Banim, prior to departing for the Islands, left behind her dress improver – "four iron bars that gave a skirt a fashionable outline" (1995: 127) – so as not to appear disrespectful of the customs and simple style of island dress. However, upon arriving in the Atlantic Hotel in Inis Mór, Banim was shocked to find an improver used in the residence. Banim was also shocked to find that people on the island were hungry. Following the famine of 1885, many people on

3   Inis Meáin is referred to as Inishmaan by both Synge and Lawless.

Aran were forced to work on the construction of a pier at Cill Rónáin in order to make ends meet; Banim records seeing young women carrying huge stones from the nearby beach up towards the pier. Lawless's visit to Inis Meáin is thought to have taken place in 1885; one poem, "Looking Eastward" in *With the Wild Geese* is given as "Written in 1885" and would seem to place Lawless on the island at the time of writing. Though she was criticised for portraying Grania as having strength and stamina which would have been unlikely in those times, Banim's account would seem to confirm that many women on Aran were forced, mainly through economic necessity, to carry out work which would have been very physical in nature. Also, given Banim's account of the hunger and deprivation which was rampant on the Islands at the time, the descriptions in *Grania* of the sick and dying Daly family are more realistic than previously thought. Though Synge thought it next to impossible for a lady to survive the crossing to, and life on, the Islands at the time of his own visits (1898 to 1902), it would appear that both Banim and Lawless had achieved the impossible over a decade before his own arrival there.[4] To support this point, perhaps, Lawless wrote two English women tourists into *Grania*, who are quite taken aback at Grania's unconventional dress and attitude. The women had a chaperone on their visit; the inclusion of an escorting male figure only serves to highlight Grania's symbolic invocation of modernity, although the two ladies are initially thought to represent such difference. In defying "the tourists' expectations and [in] her achievement of a self-assurance, an independence that many women of the nineteenth century could only dream of attaining" (Edwards, 2008: 421), Lawless draws attention to Grania's position as representative of the emerging New Woman in British and American literataure. Though Synge would later become famous for celebrating the traditions and unique dress of the islanders, Lawless pre-figured the reality that the island women were far ahead in terms of adapting to modern

4   B.N. Hedderman (1873–1943) was the first district nurse appointed to the Aran Islands in 1903. Experiences from her time spent attending to her patients on both Inis Oírr and Inis Meáin are recorded in her book *Glimpses of My Life in Aran* (1917). Many of Nurse Hedderman's observations on the hardship of life on the Islands sit well with descriptions given by Lawless, Banim and Synge.

ways and styles. Edwards proposes that "Lawless's novel suggests what Synge observed but was unable to fully articulate: that Inishmaan was a geography characterized by its own particular modernity, one that could produce modern women" (2008: 422).

Of course, Lawless's own biographical information may also provide an important segueway at this juncture. When asked by her close friend Sir M.E. Grant Duff if "she had ever known an Honor in real life", Lawless replied that she had, indeed, known many people like the character of Honor, Grania's sister. Lawless commented that she "[had] known four or five. [...] No refinement, no purity which can be met with in the higher ranks is even equal to what may now and then be found in a West of Ireland cabin, amidst the most squalid surroundings. You come across people who are not merely fit for heaven; they are in heaven already" (Grant Duff, 1904: 82). Lawless's characterisation of Honor as saintly and frail contrasts perfectly with her sister Grania's strength and brashness. These latter characteristics may have been autobiographical to an extent, as descriptions of Lawless herself reveal a formidable and often difficult personality. It is highly probable that Lawless suffered from a similar psychological melancholy as other members of her family did; however, her death was not self-induced. Lawless did, nonetheless, suffer from both real and psychosomatic pain for much of her adult life, as well as being in "a constant state of nervous tension" (Linn, 1971: 45). These details may have more in common with Lawless's portrayal of Honor's anguish, yet they also relate to Grania's inate potency in the face of strife and upheaval.

The most striking theme or symbol in all of Lawless's poetry, and prose for that matter, is that of separateness and isolation. Whether commenting on human, nature-based or man-made separation, Lawless's work is preoccupied with the notion of divisions, splits, antitheses and separate spheres of life and natural order; this can be seen in her diary entries and newspaper articles[5], in her poetry (especially in *With the Wild Geese*), and in her novels, especially in *Grania*. In a style similar to that of Ó Direáin

---

5   "Iar-Connaught: A Sketch", 1882, "North Clare – Leaves from a Diary", 1899, "Wide is the Shannon", 1906.

and Ó Flaithearta, Lawless concentrates for most of her writing career on the distinct (metaphorical and actual) divisions between worlds, places and people. In fact, in Lawless's nature-based poetry, her work has much in common with many of Ó Flaithearta's short stories, reflecting as they do the harshness of life on the edges of Ireland and the isolated nature of both human and animal on Ireland's westernmost islands.

Lawless's poetic contributions

Lawless's three volumes of poetry, *With the Wild Geese* (1902), *The Point of View* (1909), and *The Inalienable Heritage and Other Poems* (1914, published posthumously) were well received, though they did not attract as much critical attention as her prose offerings. In 1965 Padraic Fallon compiled and edited *The Poems of Emily Lawless*, marking the first time that Lawless's poetry was collected together since her death. In the preface to *The Inalienable Heritage*, Edith Sichel writes that Lawless was "before all else, a poet and a seeker after truth – and in her the two were one. Before all else, also, an Irish poet" (1914: v).[6] However, Hansson's recent biography (2007) of Lawless is the first publication since then to consider the poetry to any notable extent. Hansson points out that Lawless's relative poetic success avoided the criticism which her novelistic efforts had received due to the fact that poetry was a more suitable vehicle for the Celtic mentality espoused by Irish literary revivalists (2007: 149). Poetry was considered a safer and ultimately a less politically dangerous medium of artistic expression. However, some critics, most notably the ardent Sinn Féin supporter, Arthur Clery, writing in the nationalist newspaper the *Leader*, regarded poetry as a poorer art form than that of the novel (Hansson, 2007: 149–150).

Perhaps the most interesting aspect of Lawless's poetry and its subsequent critical appraisal lies in the fact, as Sichel pointed out, that it was

---

6   Edith Sichel was a lifelong friend and companion of Emily Lawless's, and was herself a talented writer.

considered as identifiably Irish in nature. Given that Lawless's novels was severely criticised by Revivalists such as Yeats, and by nationalists and fellow writers of the time for failing to engage with Irish or patriotic concerns, it is fascinating to observe how her poetry seemed to satisfy her audience and detractors alike. Hansson notes that "[t]he verses that correspond to popular sentiment in the early twentieth century were indeed widely appreciated" (2007: 150). However, "[i]t is doubtful whether the poems would have had the same popular appeal if Lawless's questioning attitude to Ireland and the past had been fully appreciated" (Hansson, 2007: 150). Lawless's ambiguity towards debates on national politics or on aspects of her own feelings towards British and Irish relations remained a difficult issue, both for the author herself as well as for her many reviewers and critics. It could be argued that Lawless's poetry reflects love and admiration for her Ireland, but it stops short, at least overtly, of siding with any political or national subject matters. Many critics, among them Chanel (Clery's pseudonym), Yeats, Lady Gregory, and particularly those who were incensed with Lawless's politically and culturally detached novels, welcomed her poetic works. However, they may have chosen to ignore the fact that the Ireland which Lawless commonly describes in her poetry is not much different from the one which she used as backdrop to her novels and historical monographs, in order to strengthen their own opinions on her non-commital response to the political and social debates of the time. The Ireland of Lawless's poetry may seem to be a less confused country than that of her novels, but it is far removed from being a symbol for a politically-united and nationalist entity. Lawless may have been fortunate that critics such as Clery in the *Leader* (1902) and an anonymous *Times Literary Supplement* reviewer (1914) did not recognise this, choosing instead to highlight the cogency and descriptiveness of the verses she produced. Hansson (2007: 149–165) has noted that the female figures in her poems are often representative of Ireland itself; however, should this be the case, the Ireland of these poems is a fragmentary, frail and isolated figure. Unlike her fiction, the females in Lawless's poetry are rarely linked to the writer herself (Hansson, 2007: 36). However, this is somewhat ironic in that Lawless's most intimate portrayals of her own sense of gender and artistic freedom are given fuller exposition in her poetry than in her novels. Chapter 5 of this book will consider the relation between Lawless and her protagonist Grania, in order to illuminate Lawless's complex and multi-faceted understanding of both her background and her position as a female author. The importance of the Irish landscape and of the power of nature over all things, are themes which are much in evidence in Lawless's poetic contributions and are particularly significant when considering Aran Island literature. Her use of the uninhibited landscape of the West of Ireland, her employment of imagery that suggests both containment and freedom and her interweaving of the personal and the political represents some of her poetic symbolism. As we shall see, both her West of Ireland poetry and prose marries much of this symbolism and gives Lawless her greatest vehicle for self- and nation exploration. Elizabeth Grubgeld's article "The Poems of Emily Lawless and the Life of the West" (*Turn-of-the-Century Women*, 1986), begins in similar fashion to Hansson's essay on Lawless by questioning the reasons behind the "present obscurity" (1986: 35) of Lawless's work. As her poetry was "printed privately in limited numbers and only after her withdrawal from public life" (1986: 35), Lawless's poetic talent was "felt in moments of highly wrought intensity, unsuitable and unsustainable in the three-volume historical novel" (1986: 35). However, Grubgeld maintains, the greatest obstacle which Lawless had to surmount, and which led to the author's obscurity, lay in the "unfortunate disregard for women's writing which has characterized much study of Irish literature" (1986: 35). As a consequence of this, Grubgeld suggests, "Emily Lawless's voice, like many others, has not been heard" (1986: 35).

J.M. Synge

Unlike Lawless, John Millington Synge's literary career and biographical detail is widely known and well documented. Explaining his poem "*Ómós do John Millington Synge* / Homage to John Millington Synge" Máirtín Ó Direáin comments that *[n]í dóigh gur gá inseacht d'aon duine ar an saol seo cé hé Synge. Léigh muid a bheathais-néis, na leabhra go léir a scríobhadh air, agus tá a fhios againn gurb é Yeats a thug com-hairle dó nuair a bhí sé i bPáras na Fraince agus é ag scríobh léirmheastóireachtaí anseo agus ansiúd ar irisí fánacha, gur dhúirt sé leis glanadh leis 'and seek a life that has never found expression', nó rud éigin den tsaghas sin (Ón Ulán Ramhar Siar, 2002, 55).*[7]

Born into a wealthy Anglo-Irish family in Rathfarnham, Dublin, in 1871, Synge's early years were dominated by religious and patriotic influences such as those of his uncle, Rev. Alexander Synge, who had been a Church of Ireland minister in the Aran Islands in the 1850s. As a sickly child, suffering from asthma and related bronchial illnesses, Synge spent much time at home. Perhaps it was this claustrophobic environment that led him to question his beliefs and his family's strict religious adherence, much to his mother's annoyance. As Tim Robinson explains in his introductory essay on Synge in *The Aran Islands*:

> [w]ithin a few years he no longer regarded himself as a Christian but as a worshipper of a new goddess, Ireland. His disbeliefs and beliefs formed rift-valleys of incompre-hension between himself and his relatives, though he always preserved his status as a member of the family household. He gulped the patriotic balladry published in a nationalist newspaper, *The Nation*, and scoured the countryside in search of the Irish antiquities he read about in the writings of George Petrie (Robinson, 1992: xviii).

Early years and beliefs

Synge lost his father when just a year old (Tóibín, 2005: 4). Unsurprisingly, then, Synge's relationship with his mother was central to the formatoin of his character and was to impact heavily on both his writing and personal

---

7   "I do not think that anyone needs to be told who Synge is. We read his biography, all the books that were written about him, and we know that it was Yeats that gave him the advice while in Paris, France, while Synge was writing reviews here and there in various magazines, that [Yeats] told him to clear off 'and seek a life that has never found expression', or something like that".

relationships.[8] The memoirs of Synge's nephew Edward depict a home in which the matriarch figure was dominant and religion was pervasive (*My Uncle John*, 1974: 53). Despite Synge's own determined rejection of faith and his turn to agnosticism, he did maintain close relations with his family (Grene in Tóibín, 2005: 6). Synge later marveled at the closeness of family ties on the Aran Islands, and in particular with the connections between sons and their mothers. In *Riders to the Sea* and in *The Aran Islands* Synge draws on these relationships to create an atmosphere of close familial and communal ties. While his mother made efforts to bring her youngest son back to the faith, by age seventeen Synge was happy to write:

> [s]oon after I relinquished the Kingdom of God I began to take a real interest in the Kingdom of Ireland. My patriotism went round from a vigorous unreasoning loyalty to a temperate nationalism and everything Irish became sacred (in Tóibín, 2005: 9).

This abandonment of faith in favour of fatherland was to prove highly significant, not least in Synge's dramatic work. However, in *The Aran Islands*, Synge's own notion of a type of religious communion with land and with nature is seen to develop and to enhance his appreciation for the islanders and their home. It was, as Colm Tóibín notes, the case that Synge's religious faith appeared to be replaced by his growing interest in the world of music and languages (2005: 9). As Tóibín goes on to write

> [l]ike Lady Gregory who began to study Irish in these years, Synge and his fellow students used an Irish translation of the Bible to help them. Like Lady Gregory too, some magic came to Synge from the language he was learning, or some set of emotions which were part of that decade. Both he and Lady Gregory, in the same years, and through the same influences, slowly began to love Ireland, as though Ireland were a person. They loved its landscape and its ancient culture; they loved the ordinary people they met in cabins or on the roads. It was as though their own dying power in Ireland, the faded glory of their class, gave their emotions about Ireland a strange glow of intensity (2005: 10).

---

8   Joseph O'Connor's *Ghost Light* (2010) casts a fictionally-based eye over Synge's relationships with his mother and his lover, Molly Allgood.

In similar fashion to Lady Gregory, Synge was hesitant to take the political path (Tóibín, 2005: 10), and remained relatively quiet on issues which concerned Ireland's political relationship with Britain. However, both Lady Gregory and Synge were aware that their work was tied up in politics (Tóibín, 2005: 11). It would seem that Synge in particular was interested in the power which the country had upon him as a writer, and would later compare this power with the strong hold that Ireland had upon her patriots and rebels. Synge wrote that "[t]he Irish country rains, mists, pale insular skies, the old churches, manuscripts, jewels, everything in fact that was Irish had charm human nor divine, rather perhaps as if I had fallen in love with a goddess" (in Tóibín, 2005: 11). This goddess was to entice Synge, as it did more militant patriots, to create and write about an Ireland that was in danger of being lost.

Synge and Yeats

In a comparative piece on Synge and W.B. Yeats's important relationship when they first met in Paris in 1896, Roy Foster ("Good Behaviour: Yeats, Synge and Anglo-Irish Etiquette" in *Interpreting Synge*, Grene, 2000) points out that, though Yeats was six years Synge's senior, the former's background "was an important notch or two down that carefully defined ladder" (Foster, 2000: 44). Foster continues

> Synge's ancestors were bishops, while Yeats's were rectors; Synge's had established huge estates and mock castles, while Yeats's drew the rent from small farms and lived in the Dublin suburbs. Yeats had no money, while Synge had a small private income. Yeats had no university education, whereas Synge had been to Trinity [...] Another important difference between them, which reflects upon background and education, is that Synge, for all his unpretentiousness, was really cosmopolitan; whereas Yeats when they met, was desperately trying to be (Foster, 2000: 44).

Though older and more highly regarded in literary circles at the time, it is unusual to consider Yeats as having lower or lesser status than someone who would go on to become one of his contemporaries. However, it is fascinating, in the light of Foster's comments, to begin a reconsideration of the advice given to Synge by Yeats in relation to going to the Aran Islands. Though Synge attended Trinity College Dublin to study music, Irish and Hebrew (see Kiberd, 1979: 19), and although his interest in European literature brought him to Germany, and later Paris, it is important to note that his earliest encounters with stories and tales from the West of Ireland, coupled with an interest in antiquarian discoveries on the Aran Islands, were to prove his most vital source of artistic inspiration and focus. While in Paris, in 1896, Synge met with Yeats and Maud Gonne, both there to establish the *L'Association Irlandaise* ("the Irish League") as an outlet for Irish nationalists based in France. Synge initially joined the League, but subsequently resigned from the association, explaining that "I wish to work in my own way for the cause of Ireland and I shall never be able to do so if I get mixed up with a revolutionary and semi-military movement" (Robinson, 1992: xx). In much the same way as James Joyce shunned the cause of Irish republicanism and fled to the continent to escape what he perceived to be stifling conditions for an artist who did not wish to engage with the nationalist debate, Synge, it seems, was an artist with little interest in furthering the cause of Ireland's struggle in his work. Rather, he was insistent only upon producing art that showed the best of Ireland's people and places. It is clear, nonetheless, that this meeting with two of Ireland's most influential authors and nationalists left an indelible impression on the young writer. It appears from both Synge and Yeats' accounts of this time spent together that Synge showed a marked interest in Yeats' work on Celtic studies, particularly in his work on fairies and the West of Ireland's brand of mysticism (Robinson, 1992: xx).

Synge and Aran: Heading that way all along

Synge was personally and professionally focused upon returning to Ireland in 1897. Having engaged with both ardent nationalists and more pacifist artists independent of national trappings in Paris and at the Sorbonne in particular, Synge had no doubt begun to realise and recognise the type of artist he wished to be. Though Yeats is often credited with providing the initial encouragement to Synge to abandon his life in Paris and to return to Ireland in order to become a better writer, it should not be forgotten that from his earliest years Synge was accustomed to hearing about the Irish countryside and its allure and artistic riches. Advising Synge to "[g]o to the Arran (sic) Islands. Live there as if you were one of the people themselves; express a life that has never found expression" (from Yeats's Preface in *J.M. Synge, Collected Works III*, 1968: 63), Yeats is often misrepresented as Synge's sole inspiration to travel to the West of Ireland. The ambiguity of Yeats' advice to Synge is important. Kiberd (1996 and 2000), Foster (2000) and Tóibín (2005) investigate the possibilities of what Yeats may have actually meant by this expression. Noting that the latter part of the famous advice contains sentiments similar to Karl Marx's famous lines on the French peasantry "and applied by Edward Said as an epigraph to *Orientalism*: 'They cannot represent themselves, they must be represented'" (Kiberd, 2000: 90), Kiberd highlights the fact that "[i]n truth, of course, the people of Aran had been expressing their values through Irish for over a thousand years" and then revealingly adds that: "Yeats's sentence might be more tellingly read as applying to Synge, whose struggle for self-expression through the 1890s had been doomed to incoherence and mawkish sentimentality" (2000: 90–91). Kiberd's observation sheds light on two highly important, though often completely ignored, facts about Aran, its people and the growing cultural significance which their lives symbolised for the Irish literary revival writers. Whilst many believe (see Chapter 1; Sheeran (1976, 1994), Waddell *et al.* (1994), Robinson (1986, 2000)) that the *discovery* or *rediscovery* of the Islands from the 1800s onwards by antiquarians and historians alike was the first real or significant exploration of the Islands, accounts from Giraldus Cambrensis in *Topographia Hiberniae* (1220)[9] show the religious and geographical interest in the Islands, long

9   "There is an island in the sea west of Connacht which is said to have been consecrated by Saint Brendan. [...] Here men see with some wonder and recognize their grandfathers, great-grandfathers and great-great-grandfathers and a long line of ancestors. There is another remarkable thing about this island: while the whole of Ireland is infested with mice, there is not a single mouse here. For no mouse is bred here nor does one live if it be brought in. If by any chance it is brought in, it makes straight for the nearest point of the sea and throws itself in; and if it be prevented,

before the arrival of antiquarians O'Donovan, Wilde and Petrie in the 1860s. Clearly the Islands were well known to writers and travellers well before the 1800s. However, the second part of Kiberd's observation shows that it was mainly through Irish that the islanders would have expressed themselves and this, quite possibly, would have been the reason why many considered the largely Anglophone *rediscovery* of the Islands from the 1850s onwards as the first instance of dialogue and communication with the islanders themselves.

Key to the West: Synge, Yeats and language

Yeats had been to the Islands in the summer of 1896, in the company of Arthur Symons and Lady Gregory, and "as the strategist of the Irish cultural revival, he realised the islands' symbolic importance, but knew that the new recruit would be better equipped than himself for their retaking" (Robinson, 1992: xxi). Recognising both the cultural importance of the Islands and Synge's ability to best capture the essence of the Islands, Yeats was most prudent in realising that Synge's quiet nature, unobtrusive manner and linguistic ability would allow him to fit in with the way of life in Aran in ways which Yeats and other, more militant Revivalists could not. The idea of "retaking" the Islands, however, speaks to many different issues, some of which will be discussed in subsequent chapters. For the purposes of this chapter, however, the focus will remain on Synge's own decision to go the Aran, his experiences there as captured in *The Aran Islands*, and the critical reception afforded to Synge and this work in particular.

Though Yeats noted that in 1898 Synge "fled to the Aran Islands to escape the squalor of the poor and the nullity of the rich, there to find among forgotten people a mirror for his bitterness" (*Explorations*, 1962: 418), there is little evidence that this was Synge's main motivation, or that his alleged bitterness was evident and fostered during his time on the Islands.

---

it dies on the spot" (From *Gerald of Wales: The History and Topography of Ireland* (1982: 61) translated by John J. O'Meara).

The interest surrounding Synge's decision to go to Aran and the desire that fuelled this decision in the first place has spawned many myths; Yeats was among the first to create an image of Synge as some type of tormented artist seeking the path of inspiration. Donna Gerstenberger noted that *The Aran Islands* has been "persistently misread as a document of discovery of attitudes and themes" (1964: 16), rather than as a documentary of Synge's observations of island life and culture. Gerstenberger points to the fact that Synge's attitudes were quite probably already well established by the time he set foot in Aran, aged twenty-seven, and that if anything, "[w]hat the Islands did provide, in a more realistic appraisal, was a means to expression – a setting and an idiom – for attitudes already formed" (1964: 16). The importance of setting here should not be underestimated or ignored as both Kiberd (1996, 2000) and Grene (2000) have noted. The Islands functioned perfectly as a cultural and linguistic backdrop to much of Synge's already-formulated opinions and ideas about Ireland and her heritage; the idiomatic language Synge found there was one which he felt best suited and mirrored the qualities and distinctiveness of the Ireland he wished to dramatise and record.

Synge, Aran and The Aran Islands

Synge, the man and the artist, in Gerstenberger's opinion

> had acquired before his journey to the Islands the habit of isolation – physical, spiritual, and social – which enabled him to record and evaluate the lives of a people physically isolated from the rest of the world, spiritually and socially cut off from the world beyond the separating sea, a separation which Synge was ideally equipped to observe and understand (1964: 17).

This understanding of social and personal isolation would undoubtedly have allowed Synge to immerse himself quite inconspicuously into the way of life on the Aran Islands; unlike most of the previous artists, writers and other tourists, "Synge's creation of literature from his visits to the Aran Islands resulted not so much from what he found in the islands as from what he brought to them" (Gerstenberger, 1964: 20). Gerstenberger

sees the Islands' and Synge's relationship as symbiotic, if somewhat unbal-
anced; Synge investing more than he received from the association and in
turn giving more back to the Islands than many who went before and after
him. Gerstenberger considers that the Islands

> provided for Synge a stage free of the complexities and false props of "civilization",
> and against this stark background he saw enacted patterns of reality he had previ-
> ously observed – a conception of life which is completely and explicitly expressed
> in a (perhaps imaginary) sketch written in his notebooks before the Aran venture
> (1964: 20).

It is, perhaps, Gerstenberger's greatest failure that she refuses to acknowledge that the Islands were much more than a stage or a cultural backdrop. However, in separating out the myth that surrounds Synge's decision
to go to the Islands from that of some sort of Yeatsian-inspired mission,
Gerstenberger's work paved the way for a clearer, more informed investigation of Synge's own personal motives in making the fateful journey. As
Robinson (1992) and Kiberd (2002) have noted, Synge's uncle, the Rev
Alexander Synge had been stationed on Inis Mór in the 1850s and wrote
home on a regular basis, recounting stories of the islanders and, as he saw
it, their religious laxity.[10] Most of these letters are between Reverend Synge
and his brothers John (John Millington Synge's father) and Edward and
date from June 1851 to December 1852. Synge's own interest in the West
of Ireland was awakened most notably by the writings of George Petrie
in the *Nation*. Petrie's "patriotic balladry" (Robinson, 1992: xix) would
have doubtlessly enticed the young writer, particularly his description of
the Islands:

> The Araners are remarkable for fine intellect and deep sensibility [...] If the inhabit-
> ants of the Aran Islands could be considered as a fair specimen of the ancient and
> present wild Irish [...] those whom chance has led to their hospitable shores to admire
> their simple virtues, would be likely to regret that the blessings of civilization had
> ever been extended to any portion of the inhabitants of this very wretched country.

10 From "Letters of the Reverend Alexander Synge, June 1851–December 1852", Trinity
College Dublin.

But, fortunately for them, they cannot be so designated; much of their superiority must be attributed to their remote, insular situation, which has hitherto precluded an acquaintance with the vices of the distant region (quoted in Stokes, *Life and Labours in Art and Archaeology of George Petrie*, 1868).

In his most detailed analysis of *The Aran Islands* and of Synge's travels there, "Synge's *Tristes Tropiques:* The Aran Islands", Declan Kiberd's essay looks at the inspiration(s) behind Synge's decision to go to Aran and also details the style and content of *The Aran Islands* itself. Though Kiberd is arguably Synge's most prolific and insightful critic and though more substantial publications by Kiberd which dissect and evaluate Synge's work have appeared, "*Tristes Tropiques*" engages with a broad range of ideas.[11] Fintan O'Toole (1998, 2000) and Nicholas Grene (2000) have both commented on the documentary style of *The Aran Islands*. In Kiberd's essay, however, he takes the book's style one step further and examines both the society that Synge found on the Islands and the society which he came from and returned to after his sojourns there. Kiberd calls upon postcolonial literary criticism to highlight the importance of Synge's use of binaries and his understanding of the influence of the colonisation of Ireland on the west of the country in particular. In seeming agreement with Gerstenberger, Kiberd immediately acknowledges the "personal documentary" (2000: 82) which Synge composed in *The Aran Islands*. However, though Kiberd writes that Synge the narrator is not always present in the text itself, he does not go as far as Gerstenberger, who notes that "the Synge who appears in *The Aran Islands* is really a character anonymous" (1964: 23). Instead, Kiberd asserts that there is a more discernibly autobiographical underpinning to the book than may at first seem apparent to the reader. Kiberd also detects a certain "anthropological thrust" (2000: 82) to the work, reminding us that Synge had read Pierre Loti's *Pêcheur d'Islande*[12] the summer previous to his first journey to Aran and found in Loti's work "a terrified search for some

---

11   *Synge and the Irish Language*, London: Macmillan, 1979; *Inventing Ireland*, London: Vintage, 1996.
12   Translated as "Iceland Fisherman".

sign of the persistence of the person" (Price, ed., *J.M. Synge: Collected Works II*: 395). Given Synge's own illness and his documented obsessive interest in matters concerning mortality, it is fascinating to note that in *The Aran Islands* Synge may have been searching for a way to express his own life and to represent the life of the people there. Leaving a culture of "mass-produced types" which he detested, it must have come as a welcome surprise to Synge to find in Aran a race of people which thrived on individuality supported by community; "[h]is visits to Aran, ostensibly to study the island culture, will prompt him to deliver a fierce critique of a mainland which is losing contact with its own dynamic traditions, to make way for a double-chinned bourgeois vulgarity" (Kiberd, 2000: 82–83). Before long it became apparent that Synge's being on the Islands was more than a mere anthropological exercise, however, and signified a greater project, both personal and cultural. Though Synge's uncle arrived in Aran to convert the people there to Protestantism and to combat the "dirt and ignorance" (in Kiberd, 2000: 83), Synge himself set out "not so much on a mission as on a pilgrimage" (2000: 83). Though Synge was very familiar with previous anthropological expeditions to Aran, and would undoubtedly have read accounts of these trips, his mission was personal: he wanted to practice and improve his Irish and to surround himself with the Islands' culture (2000: 84).[13]

Synge, it thus appears, was much more interested in the people of Aran rather than in the more familiar representation of Aran as some sort of refuge for cultural nationalists. Rather than talking about Aran, Synge went to live in Aran, and for Kiberd, this is what marks Synge out from his contemporaries. In the place of patriotic rhetoric, Synge sought to immerse himself in the language and culture of Aran, and, it would appear, rather by chance came to find his greatest artistic inspiration there.

13   Sir William Wilde, O'Donovan and O'Curry's trip in 1857 was one of the most famous of these. Wilde proclaimed in Dún Aengus that "[i]t has been one of my fondest hopes to render Aran an object of attention, and an opposition shop, if I may say so, to Iona" (Stokes 1868: 376–377; also quoted in Kiberd, 2000: 84). Ó hEithir regards this gathering as signaling Aran's "'coming-out' into the modern academic world" (1991: 13).

Choosing the pastoral mode with which he was comfortable and which he promoted, Synge merges two types of pastoral writing in *The Aran Islands*: "the first [...] in which a leisured aristocracy plays at being poor in a spurious attempt to wish real class differences away [...] the second [...] in which a real peasantry may be depicted as having qualities often thought peculiar to aristocrats" (Kiberd, 2000: 84–85).

In utilising the first box-camera to capture Aran, Synge "runs the obvious risk of exposing him as a mere tourist in other people's reality and one, moreover, who may have the effect of reducing the islanders to tourists in their own" (Kiberd, 2000: 85). Synge's awareness, then, that he was in danger of misrepresenting those he wished to best represent, is counterpointed with his own desire to possess (in the most non-threatening of ways) and understand these mysterious places and people, recording them and their way of life for posterity and for the book which he would eventually write about his time there. However, Synge does not further isolate the figures in his photographs or the photographs themselves from literary or cultural history, and chooses to include them as contextualising pieces in the book. Wary, Kiberd imagines, of writing and photographically recording these people and this time, Synge refuses to "record in order to forget" (2000: 86) and instead records in order to remind and remember. What the camera did allow Synge to do was to "register that mingled sense of intimacy and estrangement" (2000: 87) which he, "a mere interloper among a welcoming people" (2000: 87) would have felt intimately. In fact "[h]e seems to have taken few, if any, photographs in Paris; and his object on the Aran Islands was to share with the people those pictures of them that he had made. Far from surveying them, he wished to help them survey themselves" (2000: 87). Though this may have resonances with Yeats's advice to Synge with regard to representation and the Islands, it must be understood from Kiberd, as Synge himself states in his foreword, that seeing and representing are two very distinct and potentially very deceptive things. Extending Kiberd's logic, it appears that representation may inevitably require an element of invention – often simply for artistic purposes – whereas seeing requires merely looking and recording, without having to foreground, background or embellish the scene at hand.

Synge, style and form

Gerstenberger differentiates between the styles represented in *The Aran Islands*, and suggests that his vision of Aran was both complicated and complemented by his own sense of simultaneously being an outsider while still being a welcome member of the community. Suggesting that the camera which Synge used on the Islands was an apt symbol for the author's own dual sense of being both insider and yet outsider, Gerstenberger points to the cameraman's position as both a voyeur and an active proponent of the action he depicts and captures. Indeed, as Gerstenberger and Kiberd both point out, the snapshot qualities of some of the writing in *The Aran Islands* may well be indicative of Synge's own preference for glimpses of life on the Islands rather than giving a more detailed and in-depth depiction of the place. His snapshot style in both prose and photography may also reveal much about Synge's own shy nature as well as his understanding of the importance of an unobstrusive approach in such small communities. The short, yet revealing passages are also mirrors for Synge's own brief visits to the Islands and may also point towards the author's foreword which illustrates the directness and truthfulness of the accounts given: "I have given a direct account of my life on the islands, and of what I met among them, inventing nothing, and changing nothing that is essential" (*The Aran Islands*, 1992: 1). Thus, by insisting on the "reality of the world found in these outlying Islands – a world not perceived in romanticized Irish terms, but one complete and meaningful to the observer willing to accept reality as it exists" (Gerstenberger, 1964: 21–22), Synge avoids suggestions of misrepresentation and further mythologisation of the Islands themselves. In fact, as Gerstenberger writes, "[the] key to the accomplishment [of *The Aran Islands*] which may best be explained as his ability to capture the essence of the Islands and to organize highly selected impressions and incidents into a meaningful pattern of reality" is found in the realisation of the kind of book *The Aran Islands* represents. As suggested by Gerstenberger and hinted at much earlier by Corkery (1931), *The Aran Islands* is a work akin to that of a documentary, much like that carried out by Robert Flaherty years later in *Man of Aran*. Flaherty credited Synge as having "taught him what to see" (Gerstenberger, 1964: 21–22).

Gerstenberger is correct in noting that "Synge himself does not attempt to define a genre for his book; his form is with reality and the service of truth, a concern endorsed by the form he has chosen for his work" (1965: 21–22). However, in his criticism of Lawless's *Grania*, he was unhappy with Lawless's use of the novel form. This may indicate the reverence and duty Synge felt in portraying as accurate as possible an account of the Islands and the islanders, and may hint at his dislike of fictional accounts of the reality of the world he found there and sought so passionately to protect from the exaggeration of such fictions.

Though his five visits to the Islands may seem unsubstantial, it is, nonetheless vital to understand the levels of familiarity and communication which Synge enjoyed while resident on the Islands, and in particular Inis Meáin. It is also to his credit that *The Aran Islands* is regarded as being as complete a picture of many facets of island life as was possible at the time; "[t]hat reality as it exists can be organized, without benefit of 'invention', to present a coherent view of *a* world, (and, by extension, of *the* world) is Synge's accomplishment in *The Aran Islands*" (Gerstenberger, 1964: 22). It is the method by which he does this, however, that has interested critics and readers alike, and indeed enriched the ways in which individuals receive the work itself. Synge's documentary-style writing coupled with his own unobtrusive manner and preference for listening and observing, are complemented by the many photographs which are included in most editions of *The Aran Islands*.[14] Synge mentions throughout the book that he remained on the periphery of many of the happenings and occurrences on the Islands: the wakes, attending Mass and staying in his room when certain visitors were in the McDonagh house. Noting that "his relationship to his material is essentially that of the cameraman – invisible, perceiving, objective, and amoral" (1964: 22), Gerstenberger preempts the many critical discussions and various portrayals of Synge's own character which have appeared since that time onwards.

On the whole, Synge's own presence on the Islands is less important to the overall content of *The Aran Islands* than the events, stories and

14   See Synge (1971) *My Wallet of Photographs: The Photographs of J.M. Synge.*

the people whom he encountered there; "Synge, who is not interested in writing his spiritual autobiography, states only 'I am in Aranmor'; and it is only as the recording ('listening') presence that [he] generally enters into the book" (Gerstenberger, 1964: 22). Giving precedence therefore to the scenes and the occurrences that he records in the book, Synge simultaneously creates and distances himself from his creation, in a fashion similar to the photographer who takes the shot but is never seen in the frame himself. Synge's combined absence from the predominant action of his book along with his creative presence in documenting the action itself is one of the most interesting facets of his work and has much in common with Lawless's creation of the artistic and personal *interspace*, as well as with Ó Flaithearta and Ó Direáin's employment of between or liminal spaces in their work.

Liam Ó Flaithearta

Liam Ó Flaithearta (1896–1984) courted much controversy and critical challenge throughout his writing career. Born in Gort na gCapall, Inis Mór, Liam was a brilliant student and won scholarships to Rockwell College in Co. Tipperary and to University College Dublin. However, upon arriving in Dublin, he quickly joined the Irish Volunteers:

> *[I]s mó dúthracht a chaith sé le polaitíocht ná le staidéar [...]. Ach níor fhan sé i bhfad sa Choláiste Ollscoile ach an oiread mar liostáil sé in Arm Shasana [don Chéad Chogadh Domhanda] faoin ainm Bill Ganly, rud atá thar a bheith spéisiúil ann féin* (Ó hEithir, in *"Liam Ó Flaithearta agus a Dhúchas"*, 1977: 72).[15]

15   "His commitment to politics was greater than to his studies [...]. But he didn't spend much time in UCD either because he joined the British Army [First World War] under the name Bill Ganly, which is very interesting in itself".

This particular biographical detail seems relevant for two reasons: Ó Flaithearta's family background was nationalist and his joining of the British Army came as a surprise, if not a disappointment, to his family. Secondly, Ó Flaithearta's determination to turn his back on this aspect of his upbringing shows his mentality of individual independence and also his deliberate attempt to alienate himself from a cause he would have been expected to support. Having been injured in Langmarck, Belgium, following an explosion, Liam returned to Ireland on a soldier's pension, suffering from *melancholia acuta*: *"níor tháinig sé ón úafás go hiomlán riamh"* (Ó hEithir: 1977: 72).[16] Though his novel *Return of the Brute* (1929) documents a soldier's experiences of war, it is in *Shame the Devil* that the author relates in the first-person that "[t]his was a far greater blow to my relatives than my refusal to become a priest [in Rockwell], and it was the event in my life most responsible for the outcast position in which I now found myself" (Ó Flaithearta, 1934: 17). In yet another change of allegiance, Ó Flaithearta went on to join the anti-treaty side during the Irish Civil War of 1922–23. Ó Flaithearta's ostensibly chameleon-like nature reflects a duality of mind and of action common in both his literary output later in his career and his divided loyalty to both linguistic codes as shown throughout his body of work. His short stories, particularly those in *Dúil* (1953), highlight this division of mind and language perfectly, showing Ó Flaithearta's ease in depicting conflicting layers of existences and personality traits, and also the islands' function as a place and as a zone of artistic imaginary freedom. This illustrates how Ó Flaithearta's personality benefits, and is reflected in, his work. In addition, in portraying existences on the edge, or liminal to the centre, Ó Flaithearta is perhaps mirroring his own divided images of the exiled islander, caught on the margins of his old island home and the margins of his lived existence in the city of Dublin. His own stated darkness of mind, coupled with his experiences of war may also be of significance here; Ó Flaithearta has been accused (Denvir, 1991) of being too brooding and fatalistic about the lives of others, but this is perhaps simply a

16   "He never fully recovered from the horror".

reflection of his own failure to settle anywhere successfully since leaving Aran. Comparisons with Ó Direáin abound here; however, Ó Direáin's "rose-tinted romance with Aran" (Collinge, 1985: 122) could not allow him to critique or in any way bleakly regard his home until his return in later life.

Ó Flaithearta authored twelve collections of short stories, seven novels and two volumes of collected letters, as well as numerous newspaper and journal articles. Some of his most famous and influential work includes: *Two Years* (1930), *Shame the Devil* (1934), *The Short Stories of Liam O'Flaherty* (1937), *Dúil* (1953), and *The Wounded Cormorant and Other Stories* (1973). Breandán Ó hEithir, Ó Flaithearta's nephew, provides a number of useful insights into his uncle's childhood (*"Liam Ó Flaithearta agus a Dhúchas", Willie the Plain Pint – agus an Pápa*, 1977). From a family of ten children, of which Ó Flaithearta was the second son, his older brother, Tom (sometimes referred to as Tomás) would also become a writer, but due to his commitments within the republican movement in the United States, his authorial career was rather curtailed. Tom's book *Aranmen All* (1934) provides details of Ó Flaithearta family life, and his second book, *Cliffmen of the West* (1935) outlines the backgrounds to some of Liam's short stories (O'Brien, *Liam O'Flaherty*, 1973: 16). Ó Flaithearta's three older sisters had emigrated to America before he was born. This was not unusal, of course, but it might, however, provide an interesting insight into Ó Flaithearta's own understanding of exile, isolation and living in a foreign land. It also makes stories such as "Going into Exile" all the more poignant (Ó hEithir, 1977: 159). The family, then, was accustomed to thinking about life outside of Inis Mór and the heartache and adventure this exterior way of life entailed for those left behind. It is worthwhile to consider at this juncture a number of other observations and stories which Ó hEithir gathered both from family members, and from his personal recollections of living and working with Ó Flaithearta. In Ó hEithir's portrayal of Ó Flaithearta's childhood, there are echoes of Ó Direáin's fascination with solitude and creation:

*Buachaill thar a bheith socair, staidéarach ba ea Liam Ó Flaithearta a bhí thar a bheith
tugtha don léitheoireacht agus do bheith ag spaisteoireacht leis féin timpeall Ghort na
gCapall (1977: 160).*[17]

However, even as a young boy, Ó Flaithearta was made aware of the strangle-hold which both religion and the land had over his small island community and he would later use these experiences in *Skerrett* and *Shame the Devil.* Ó hEithir was keen to point out throughout his own writing career and when commenting on that of his uncle's, that David O'Callaghan's influence on Ó Flaithearta's generation on Inis Mór was the most important intervention by an outsider on the island. O'Callaghan, a Limerick school teacher who taught Ó Flaithearta to read and write in his native tongue, and who would later provide Ó Flaithearta with his central hero-character in *Skerrett* (1932), was an essential figure in the young islander's educational upbringing. O'Callaghan appears to have gained the unwanted attention of the parish priest for his troubles. Ó Flaithearta could never reconcile the priest's treatment of the teacher who had taught him so much with the doctrine of the Church, and so regarded their presence in Aran, and the regard with which the clergy were held on the Islands, as utterly shameful. From Ó hEithir's perspective:

*[m]íníonn na nithe seo, maille le cúlra na muintire féin, cén chúis a raibh claonadh
láidir chun an tsóisialachais agus an chumannachais i Liam Ó Flaithearta agus ina
dheartháir Tomás. Míníonn sé freisin cén fáth a raibh an náisiúnachas sa mbeirt acu
[...]. [...] Mura míníonn sé go hiomlán – agus ní mhíníonn – dílseacht na beirte dá
dteanga dhúchais is ann atá síol an mhínithe. Táim féin suite de anois nach dóigh go
mbláthódh an Ghaeilge in Inis Mór ar chor ar bith murach teacht an fhir cheanndána,
chrosta úd as Iarthar Luimnigh, Dáithí Ó Ceallacháin (1977: 162).*[18]

17   "Liam Ó Flaithearta was a very docile, steady boy, who was very interested in reading
     and wandering on his own around *Gort na gCapall*".
18   "These things explain, along with the family's background, the reasons why Liam
     and his brother Tomás had a strong inclination towards socialism and communism.
     It also explains the reason why both were nationalist [...]. [...] If it does not fully
     explain, and it does not, the loyalty of both brothers to their native tongue, the seed
     of meaning is there. I am certain of it now that the Irish language would never have

Tom O'Flaherty's *Cliffmen of the West* (1935) explains another element of O'Callaghan's influence, whereby he encouraged islanders to remain faithful to their own language:

> At that time Aran was being Anglicised, and but for the work of the school teacher, David O'Callaghan, the people would have been ashamed to be heard speaking their own language in ten years' time (1935: 275).[19]

While Gaelic revivalists portrayed the Aran Islands as linguistically pure areas of Ireland, the reality was that the English language was slowly gaining sway in Aran throughout the last decades of the 1800s. As both Tom O'Flaherty and Liam Ó Flaithearta have testified, there was a growing distrust of the native tongue of Irish, and little emphasis placed on the learning of its basic elements. In the national shift from Irish to English, Aran was not exempt from this linguistic mindset, and the emphasis placed upon English as the medium of communication was growing. Ó hEithir spoke about this linguistic situation:

> *Ní fuláir a thuiscint go raibh Béarla ar an oileán le beagnach cead bliain. Ón mbliain 1840 nó mar sin bhí 'póilíos' in Árainn; bhí coastguards in Árainn; ba é an Béarla teanga na hEaglaise agus bhí beirt shagart ar an oileán; bhí scoil náisiúnta ar an oileán ón mbliain 1845 nó mar sin. Dá bhrí sin bhí Béarla ar an oileán. Dá bhrí sin bhí Béarla ag Liam Ó Flaithearta sular fhág sé Árainn. An rud iontach faoi ná go raibh Gaeilge aige freisin, is é sin go raibh sé in ann Gaeilge a scríobh, agus a bhuíochas sin don mhúinteoir seo as Luimneach a thosaigh ag múineadh scríobh na Gaeilge do dhaoine tar éis na scoile tráthnóna* (Mac Con Iomaire, 2000: 24).[20]

---

blossomed in Inis Mór at all without the coming of that headstrong, cross man from West Limerick, David O'Callaghan".

19   Tom O'Flaherty (Tomás Ó Flaithearta) was also editor, whilst in the United Sates, of *An tÉireannach* in the 1930s, a nationalist newspaper (see *An Chaint sa tSráidbhaile*, 1991: 13).

20   "It is important to understand that there was English on the island [Inis Mór] for nearly a hundred years. From 1840 or so, there were police in [Inis Mór]; there were coastguards in [Inis Mór]; English was the language of the Church and there were two priests on the island; there was a primary school on the island from 1845 or thereabouts. As a result, there was English on the island. As a result Liam Ó Flaithearta had English before he left [Inis Mór]. The fantastic thing about it was that he also had

It might seem unlikely, yet many of Ó Flaitheartaʼs generation had better
written and practical English than Irish upon leaving school. However,
having availed of David O'Callaghan's classes, many Inis Mór children
left school well versed in both linguistic codes. In Ó Flaitheartaʼs case,
nonetheless, there was always a strict emphasis on English. His father,
Maidhc Mhicil Phádraig Ó Flaithearta was a Fenian and was politically
active. The Fenians conducted their business in English, and thus helped
the spread of English throughout Gaeltacht areas (Ó hEithir, in Mac Con
Iomaire, 2000: 24–25). His mother, Maggie Ganly, influenced Ó Flaithearta
greatly, especially with regard to storytelling. Liam's maternal grandfather,
a Northern Protestant, had come to Inis Mór to work on the construction
of the Aerach lighthouse and Kilronan Pier (Ó hEithir, *Over the Bar*, 1984:
15). Liam Ó Flaitheartaʼs daughter, Pegeen O'Flaherty-O'Sullivan, revealed
that "the charm came from his mother and [...] the gravitas, the seriousness
came from his father [...] English came from his mother, and Irish from
his father" (*Ár nOileán: Tuile 's Trá*, 2004: 35).

The link made between militant and revolutionary nationalism
and the English language within the Ó Flaithearta household is important; the nexus between language and power was clearly demonstrated.
However, though Ó Flaithearta himself, in response to Una K. Dix's letter
castigating him for not writing in Irish, stated that "at the age of seven I
revolted against my father and forced everyone in the house to speak Irish",
Ó hEithir concluded that this was exaggeration (in Mac Con Iomaire, 2000:
25). Indeed, as Liam Mac Con Iomaire highlights, Ó hEithir frequently
acknowledged the tendency to exaggerate which Ó Flaithearta possessed:
*"Tá sé ráite níos mó ná aon uair amháin ag Breandán nach féidir brath i
gcónaí ar gach ar scríobh Liam Ó Flatharta (sic.) mar go raibh an áibhéil ag
baint leis na Flathartaigh. Thugtaí 'Flathartaigh na háibhéile' orthu, a dúirt
sé"* (2000: 25).[21] Regardless of this tendency towards exaggeration, however,

---

Irish, that is to say that he could write in Irish, thanks to this teacher from Limerick
who began teaching the writing of Irish to people after school in the afternoon".

21 "Breandán has said on more than one occasion that you cannot always rely on everything that Liam Ó Flatharta (sic.) wrote as the Ó Flathartas (sic.) were prone to
exaggeration. He said they used to be called 'The Exaggerating Ó Flathartas'".

Ó Flaitheartaʼs influence on Ó hEithir was immense and the latter made it
a personal goal of his to enhance peoplesʼ appreciation and understanding
of Ó Flaitheartaʼs literary contributions.

Breandán Ó hEithir: a view from the inside out

In *Breandán Ó hEithir: Iomramh Aonair* (2000), Liam Mac Con Iomaire
provides an insightful portrayal of the writer and his relationship with
his island identity as well as with his famous uncle, Liam Ó Flaithearta.
Mac Con Iomaire charts Ó hEithirʼs early introduction to the literary and
cultural importance of his heritage and that of his islandʼs, and his gradual
move away from Inis Mór, seeking his education and his fortune in Galway,
Dublin and London. Mac Con Iomaire observes that *"Árannach a bhí i
mBreandán Ó hEithir a raibh meascán mór de mhianach Éireann agus Árann
ann"* (2000: 15).[22] Though this may appear largely self-evident, given the
adult Ó hEithirʼs somewhat cosmopolitan existence, it is, nonetheless, significant that his biographer would remark upon the islanderʼs dual identity:
an Irish man and an island man. For just as Ó Direáin and Ó Flaithearta
saw themselves as islander first, and Irish second, so too, a generation later,
did Ó hEithir. Of note also is Ó hEithirʼs life-long fascination with his
home-place, and, most importantly, with the preservation and promotion
of Aranʼs literary traditions and heritage. Tomás de Bhaldraithe would
later introduce Breandán as *"Árannach a tháinig go hÉirinn"* (2000: 88).[23]
In a talk which Ó hEithir gave in Inis Mór two years before his untimely
death in 1990, serendipitously recorded by Raidió na Gaeltachtaʼs Máirtín
Jaimsie Ó Flatharta, Ó hEithir spoke for over an hour to a small gathering
of fellow islanders about the rich and important heritage which had been
passed down to their generation, and the influence which this heritage could
have for both present and future writers. Ó hEithirʼs main preoccupation

22 "Breandán Ó hEithir was an Aran Islander who had a considerable mix of Irish and
    Aran qualities in him".
23 "An Aran Islander who came to Ireland".

during this talk, and indeed in much of his own writing on Aran's literary history, was of course his uncle Liam Ó Flaithearta's contribution. Having lived with Ó Flaithearta in Dublin during the period when the latter was writing *Dúil*, Ó hEithir had an unparalleled view into the notoriously difficult writer's world, and also had some interesting opinions to contribute to the production himself. Following the publication of *Dúil* in 1953, Breandán Ó hEithir noted that his uncle was *"tosaithe ar cheann [úrscéal] i lár na gcaogaidí ach gur éirigh sé as nuair a léigh sé an léirmheastóireacht ghéar a rinneadh ar Dhúil"* (2000: 32).[24]

Nonetheless, Ó hEithir's early career corresponds more closely to Ó Direáin's than Ó Flaithearta's. Ó hEithir noted in an RTÉ interview in 1990 that *"[a]n ghreim is mó atá ag cathair na Gaillimhe ormsa, ar mo shamhlaíocht agus ar mo chuimhne, gur ann a d'fhás mé suas i m'fhear"* (in Mac Con Iomaire, 2000: 94).[25] In much the same way as Ó Direáin saw Galway as his first introduction to Ireland, or at least the world outside of Inis Mór, Ó hEithir associated Galway city with his own maturity and social education. The most essential aspect of Galway for both Ó Direáin and Ó hEithir was its proximity to the Aran Islands and the shared linguistic code of both island and city. In an essay entitled *"Cathair na dTreabh / City of the Tribes"* (ed. C. Nic Pháidín, in *An Chaint sa tSráidbhaile*, 1991) Ó hEithir remarks that *"[i]s cuid shainiúil de shaol na Gaillimhe a gcloistear de Ghaeilge á labhairt ar a sráideanna agus ina tithe óil. An té a shiúlfadh sráideanna na Gaillimhe oíche ar bith sa tseachtain chloisfeadh sé allúntas Gaeilge [...]"* (1991: 125).[26]

It is interesting that both Ó Direáin and Ó hEithir seem much more aware of the cosmopolitan nature of their situation and the differences between this and their homeplace than Ó Flaithearta. It is perhaps as a

24   "He [Liam Ó Flaithearta] had started one [novel] in the mid-fifties but he threw in the towel when he read the cutting reviews written about *Dúil*".
25   "The largest hold that Galway city has upon me, on my imagination and my memory, is that I grew into a man there".
26   "It is characteristic of Galway life that Irish is spoken on her streets and in her public houses. Anyone who walked Galway's streets any night of the week would hear a share of Irish".

result of this self-consciousness that Ó Direáin and Ó hEithir used the metaphor and the image of the island throughout their careers to punctuate their writing narratives and to illustrate their awareness of the island identity which shaped their world-view. For Ó Flaithearta, who seemed to initially shun his island background in favour of a life in metropolitan cities, the island did not initially offer a welcome retreat for the weary writer, but instead represented the narrowness which he wished to escape. Much of this bitterness was fuelled by the harsh intervention by Fr Farragher (thinly veiled as Fr Moclair in *Skerrett* and as Fr O'Reilly in *Thy Neighbour's Wife*) into the teaching of David O'Callaghan. However, once his editor Edward Garnett advised Ó Flaithearta that the island would be central to his career, his attitude to Inis Mór changed markedly. Garnett's advice to "keep it short and tell the truth" signalled Ó Flaithearta's return to the island of his youth, at least in the literary sense, and from 1923 onwards, his short stories began to detail the small, yet essential events of rural life (Cahalan, 1999: 48).

Happily for Ó Direáin, he revelled in the positive and overtly romantic attributes of his memories of Inis Mór. Liam Mac Con Iomaire, in an introductory essay to the collected writings of Ó hEithir in *An Chaint sa tSráidbhaile* writes that

> *[b]a mhicreacosma nó mionsamhail den domhan a bhí in Inis Mór, [...]. Cé go raibh an fharraige ina bac ar thaisteal, go háirithe sa ngeimhreadh, is fíor a rá freisin gur tharraing an fharraige chéanna gach cineál duine ó chian is ó chóngar chuig an oileán, [...] [a]ntraipeolaithe, lucht scannán agus scríbhneoirí ó na ceithre cearda. Scríobh 'file mór Árann', Máirtín Ó Direáin, [...] gur 'cúinge cathair ná oileán'. Scríobh Breandán féin faoi Ghaillimh níos deireanaí: 'Is oileán gach cathair agus is cathair gach oileán'* (1991: 14).[27]

---

27 "Inis Mór was a microcosm or miniature of the world [...]. Though the sea was an obstacle to travel, especially in winter, it is also true to say that the same sea brought every sort [of person] from near and far to the island, [...] anthropologists, film crews and writers from the four corners of the world. 'Aran's Poet' Máirtín Ó Direáin wrote [...] that 'a city is narrower than an island'. Breandán [Ó hEithir] later wrote about Galway: 'every island is a city and every city is an island'".

It is salient that for both Ó Direáin and Ó hEithir the island is the yard-stick for the city's scale, and even though Galway and Dublin are infinitely larger than Inis Mór, the cities are measured in relation to the island. However, though the city is a wide-sprawling vista, Ó Direáin still finds it more confined than the smaller island of his youth and imagination. For the poet, the city is narrow on a number of levels: culturally, linguistically, scenically and also thematically; Ó Direáin felt that the city offered him much less poetically than the smaller island in the West. The island, though small, offered vast amounts of poetic inspiration.

What all three Inis Mór writers have in common, however, is their understanding of the power of language, and none more so than Liam Ó Flaithearta. However, Ó hEithir also recognised the struggle inherent in choosing one language over another, and wrote in both languages in a similar fashion to his uncle. Writing in his diary while working in London, Breandán Ó hEithir explained that *"níl gníomh is réabhlóidí ar bhealach ná cloí le Gaeilge amháin, ach an gníomh réabhlóideach é a mbeidh toradh air? Sin í m'fhadhb"* (entry dated 13 September 1978, quoted in Mac Con Iomaire, 2000: 461).[28] Ó hEithir's relationship with the Irish language was not as fraught as Ó Flaithearta's; however, both writers clearly saw that writing in English was a financially healthier option. Writing in Irish was viewed by others as a form of lip service to their heritage rather than as any revolutionary departure in literature. Though Ó hEithir was more fortunate in finding outlets and funding for his work in Irish, Ó Flaithearta's relationship with the language was coloured by many factors which were of their time but also intricately linked with the writer's own truculent attitude towards certain language organisations in both English and Irish. Nonetheless, in an interview with RTÉ in July 1980, Ó hEithir was asked whether his proposed biography of Ó Flaithearta would appear in English or Irish, and the former replied that

[t]á mé ag iarraidh ceann a scríobh agus a fhoilsiú i nGaeilge ar dtús agus ansin beathais-néis níos iomláine agus níos faide b'fhéidir, i mBéarla. Ba mhaith liom ceann a bheith

28 "There is no more revolutionary an action that to adhere to Irish only, but is it a revolutionary action that will have a result? That is my difficulty".

amuigh i nGaeilge ar dtús [...] é a bheith ar fáil i nGaeilge ar dtús, ar ndóigh (in Mac Con Iomaire, 2000: 507).[29]

It is significant that Ó hEithir would want to publish Ó Flaitheartaʼs biography in Irish first, given that its audience would be smaller, and also that Ó Flaitheartaʼs greatest literary successes were in English. However, Ó hEithir mentioned in the interview that the Irish-language publisher Sáirséal agus Dill, who also published *Dúil*, had shown an interest in publishing a biography, and it would appear that no interest was immediately forthcoming from any English-language publishers. In Ó Flaitheartaʼs case, the underlying economic factor of literary production had raised its head again. Ó hEithir never completed the biography, and, at time of writing, no complete biography of Ó Flaithearta has appeared in either language.

Early life and language issues

Peter Costelloʼs *Liam O'Flaherty's Ireland* (1996) opens with a cogent depiction of Ó Flaitheartaʼs career and highlights the juxtapositions which marked the writerʼs life:

> Liam O'Flaherty was a child of the nineteenth century, and a man of the twentieth. Born in rural poverty, he died in urban comfort. Passionate in his love of nature, he abhorred everything brutish in man. [...] O'Flaherty was a strange, often contradictory man, unique among his contemporaries in Irish literature. In his writings we can see the beginnings of much that is now being done in both Gaelic and Irish literature. [...] From the dying remnants of an ancient culture, from the shattered fragments of a modern life, he composed the unities of his art (1996: 9).

It is important to consider, as James M. Cahalan does in *Liam O'Flaherty: A Study of the Short Fiction* (1991b), that "[a]n awareness of his peasant upbringing is central to understanding not only this authorʼs personality and

---

29   "I want to write and publish one in Irish first and then a fuller and longer biography perhaps, in English. I would like one [biography] to be out [published] in Irish first [...] for it to be available in Irish first, of course".

life but his short fiction." Cahalan goes on to suggest that Ó Flaitheartás
outwardly simple style often masked a much more complex view of the
world (1991b: 3). Cahalan also writes that it is his personal contention that
"his [Ó Flaitheartás] work and the experiences and convictions so deeply
ingrained in it were anything but simple, but rather were marked by a set
of interrelated, unresolved, often contradictory tensions and issues" (1991b:
3). The lack of an official biography has hampered a greater understanding of Ó Flaithearta and his art. It is interesting to note, however, that
Ó Flaithearta himself showed a degree of "scorn for such [biographical]
scholarship" (Cahalan, 1991: 4), commenting in his semi-autobiograph-
ical work *Shame the Devil* (1934) that "should I be considered worth a
biography, I have robbed grave-robbers of their beastly loot" (1934: 284).
There are, however, autobiographical details and descriptions to be found
in many of his short stories, even though "O'Flaherty's stories are not
generally assessed as directly autobiographical" (Cahalan, 1991b: 4). One
aspect of Ó Flaitheartás biographical detail which, though all important,
is very often glossed over without much explication, concerns the writer's
bilingual upbringing and his complex attitude towards both the Irish and
English languages. With regard to Irish in particular, "[i]n his personal
outlook on the language, as with other cultural concerns, he tended to
be a shifting extremist – at some points adamantly in favour of using the
language, at others bitterly convinced of the futility of any such attempt"
(Cahalan, 1991b: 14). Considering a chronology of Ó Flaitheartás Irish
language career, as Cahalan has done, one finds that

> [a]s a schoolboy he won a prize for his writing in Irish; in 1925 he wrote a play in
> Irish; in 1946 he declared that Irish should be made compulsory; and in 1953 he
> published a volume of stories in Irish. Yet when he made no money from his play, he
> bitterly vowed never to write in Irish again, and indeed he continued to write mostly
> in English and to make his name as a writer in English (1991b: 14).

Cahalan offers an interesting rationale for Ó Flaitheartás problematic
relationship with both linguistic codes. Considering Conrad Arensberg's
(1959) work on the "tenacious cultural conventions of Irish peasant society"
(1991b: 14), Cahalan writes that Ó Flaitheartás linguistic dualism may be
reflective of his position as both a peasant (how Ó Flaithearta described

his own upbringing) and also as a "cunning type of peasant [who] rises out of this hellish life, using his cunning and rapacity and his shameless indifference to honour and decency in order to succeed" (Ó Flaithearta, *A Tourist's Guide to Ireland*, 1929). Seeing himself as having a foot in both types of peasant-based identity, and as "a writer exiled from his native peasant society, he rationalized that he must be a chameleon in order to succeed" (Cahalan, 1991b: 14). Thus, Ó Flaithearta's identity and his personality are considered as dualistic, or in some way double or shifting. This duality also resonates on planes relating to island identity, and these will be more fully discussed in later chapters.

Ó Flaithearta's relationship with Pádraic Ó Conaire is of interest in this linguistic dialogue, and speaks to ideas relating to poverty, readership and location. Ó Conaire had a significant influence on Ó Flaithearta's writing, but also advised the young writer on the dangers of art for art's sake, and suggested to Ó Flaithearta that he should make sure he had a home to live in and a comfortable income in order to survive as an artist. Ó Flaithearta seems to have registered the advice, although he continued to write some stories and one play in Irish in the following years. However, Breandán Ó hEithir provides another interpretation of his uncle's gradual retreat from the Irish language, one that does not engage with monetary reasons, but instead suggests that distance from the language on a daily basis and a strong independent streak were the main reasons for Ó Flaithearta's decision to commit more earnestly to English than to Irish (Ó hEithir, *Willie the Plain Pint – agus an Pápa*, 1977: 76). However, money was to play at least one significant role in Ó Flaithearta's decision regarding which language to use; in 1925 his Irish language play "*Dorchadas /* Darkness" garnered him no income, while his English novel of the same year, *The Informer*, was to prove to be an economically fortuitous enterprise.

Short stories and translation

This linguistic debate may at first seem rather clear cut; however, if one considers the attention given to Ó Flaithearta's English short stories and the accomplishment he enjoyed as a result of their success, then one must

also consider, as Kiberd has commented, that Ó Flaitheartás short stories
are studied in either English or Irish but rarely examined contrapuntally
or as translations of each other (*Synge and the Irish Language*, 1979: 5).
Interestingly, in Irish-language criticism, the English versions of the short
stories are rarely considered; it would appear that Ó Flaithearta continues
to divide the masses and his critics, and indeed the languages which, ironically enough, he battled to reconcile during his own lifetime.

In 1927, Padraic Colum wrote an article in *The Saturday Review of
Literature* entitled "Letter from Ireland" in which he bemoaned the fact
that "no writer worth translating has appeared in Gaelic" (1927: 206). The
rest of his article went on to critique Liam Ó Flaithearta in particular,
writing that "it is disappointing to note that the one literary man who
has come out of the Gaeltacht, Liam O'Flaherty, writes in English, and in
an English which has not even a Gaelic flavour" (1927: 206). In the wake
of such claims, *The Irish Statesman* published a number of letters which
demonstrated that opinion was divided on Ó Flaitheartás literary achievement. The majority of letters in support of Ó Flaithearta focused on his
right to write in English because of either monetary needs or his desires
to find an appropriate vehicle of literary expression; Walter Chambers
wrote that "[t]he fact that a writer of O'Flaherty's unquestionable ability
[...] should write in English in preference to Irish is by no means surprising. [...] modern Irish is entirely inadequate as a means of literary expression [...]" (1927: 252). George Russell, editor of *The Irish Statesman*, also
noted that "Mr. O'Flaherty probably desired to be published and read.
[...] At present the books for schools are the only books in Irish sure of a
swift sale" (Chambers, 1927: 252). At the end of that year, Ó Flaithearta
himself joined the debate. He explained in almost explosive fashion that
he wrote in English because his particular audience at the time did not
speak Irish; he also notes that when he did write a play in Irish in conjunction with Pádraic Ó Conaire for the Gaelic Drama League, he did
not receive payment for it. Ó Flaithearta wrote: "I naturally swore that
I would never write another word in Irish. If I do write in Irish I'll take
good care not to publish it and place it at the mercy of those sows" (1927:
348). Having not received payment from the Gaelic Drama League and
having been castigated for an affair he had with Margaret Barrington,

wife of Professor Edmund Curtis, Ó Flaithearta completely abandoned writing in Irish and for the next twenty-five years, wrote only in English. Some years later, however, "to multiply the contradictions [...] he passionately denounced the English language as his chosen medium" (Cronin, 2003: 49). Theo Dorgan's essay "Twentieth-century Irish-language poetry" notes a similar language-switch made by poet Michael Hartnett (Mícheál Ó hAirtnéide) and comments, in a way which could perhaps explain some of Ó Flaithearta's decisions, that

> it was a gesture read in one of two ways: it was quixotic and arbitrary, or it was a choice made in the face of forces, ahistorical powers, he was helpless to resist. With the passage of time, and following his uncriticised and civilly-received return to English [not so for Ó Flaithearta], it is possible now to see that Hartnett's choice was made in response to a simple imperative: the words sought him out, and the words were in Irish (2002: unpaginated).

Brian Ó Conchubhair's important article *"Liam Ó Flaithearta agus Scríobh na Gaeilge: Ceist Airgid nó Cinneadh Chonradh na Gaeilge?"* (2000) is the first to examine the effects of the Gaelic Drama League's failure to pay Ó Flaithearta as well as the repercussions of this decision for the rest of Ó Flaithearta's career.[30] Ó Conchubhair finds that

> *[i]s léir ó chiúnas Liam Uí Fhlaithearta ar an ábhar seo i rith a shaoil gur chuaigh na heachtraí seo go smior ann. B'fhearr leis go gcuirfí saint ina leith ná go nochtfadh sé a shaol pearsanta agus go ngortófaí arís é féin, a bhean agus a leanbh. Ba é cinneadh Chonradh na Gaeilge agus ní cúrsaí airgid ba chúis do Liam Ó Flaithearta éirí as a bheith ag scríobh i nGaeilge sna fichidí* (2000: 140).[31]

---

30   "Liam Ó Flaithearta and Irish Writing: A Question of Money or Conradh na Gaeilge's Decision?"

31   "From Ó Flaithearta's silence on the matter throughout his life, it is clear that these events hurt him deeply. He would rather have been accused of greed than to have his private life exposed, and that he himself, his wife and his child would be hurt again. It was Conradh na Gaeilge's decision and not money matters that caused Liam Ó Flaithearta to stop writing in Irish in the 1920s".

In both languages, however, Ó Flaithearta quickly became a masterful short story writer. His most powerful stories are those which deal with nature, animals and the force of the elements, as witnessed in stories such as "*An Seabhac* / The Hawk", "*Bás na Bó* / The Cow's Death", "*Uisce Faoi Dhraíocht* / Enchanted Water" and "*An Scáthán* / The Mirror" (*Dúil*, 1953). Cronin notes that in his vivid descriptions and attention to minute detail, Ó Flaithearta is reminiscent of Synge (2003: 52). Liam Daniels (1988) quotes O'Faoláin's high praise of Ó Flaithearta's style:

> I know of very few instances in Irish writing, in either language, that welds the tender and the tough as consistently as O'Flaherty does [...] His stories, for all their pervasive hardness and occasional wildness, [are] shot through and through with [...] much elemental tenderness [...] (1977: 112, 116–117).

Daniels also points out that critics have underexamined the importance of setting of Ó Flaithearta's stories (1988: 128). Saul finds that the sea-cliffs in *Dúil* and in the *Complete Short Stories* (1937) are a "common locale for action" (1963: 101), and though Ó Dubhthaigh (1981) comments on the notion that Ó Flaithearta's island stories allow the reader a glimpse of the interiority of life there, very little work has been done since to analyse the importance of the island setting in Ó Flaithearta's work. This is surprising, to say the least, as almost each story in *Dúil* takes place either on the cliff-edge, on the sea-shore, in fields near the sea-cliffs and in homes near the pier. There has been little work done on how most of the characters (either animal or human) are caught in what seems like a middle space – an interspace – between staying and going (*"An Scáthán"*) between the island and the sea/mainland (*"Bás na Bó"*) and between humans and the land or the sea ("*Daoine Bochta* / Poor People"). This in-betweeness may also have something to do with, or be representative of, Ó Flaithearta's own linguistic dividedness or dualism, as well as his cultural binarism, living predominantly in Dublin throughout his writing career. Both of these aspects are also found in the work of Máirtín Ó Direáin; however, Ó Direáin did not translate his own work (Mac Conghail, 1988: 188) as Ó Flaithearta did, and so avoided much of the angst and debate surrounding this issue. As Cahalan notes, Ó Flaithearta's treatment of women is

also an understudied theme in his writing. In his autobiographical book
Shame the Devil, Ó Flaithearta admits that he "did not understand them
[women] very well" (1934: 77); Cahalan (1999), Kelly (1976) and Friberg
(1990) have carried out work on this matter. Though Ó Flaithearta is
keen to point out his strong and loving relationship with his mother, his
short stories and especially his novel *The Black Soul* (1924) highlight the
tension he senses in male and female relationships, and also the difficulty
with which he deals with that duality. Though the island (Inis Mór) of his
stories is often represented as feminine in nature and character, his per-
functory treatment of his female characters is perhaps one of his greatest
weaknesses. However, his handling of female animal characters is far from
mechanical, and by far surpasses his often two-dimensional characterisation of women.

Given Ó Flaithearta's own complex relationship with language, and
in particular his often outspoken critiques of both Irish and English as an
adequate medium for his work, it is not unsurprising to find that critical
work exists in both languages on Ó Flaithearta's *oeuvre*. However, in contrast with Ó Direáin, the majority of criticism available on Ó Flaithearta
is in English. Why these ratios are of interest and importance has more to
do with the scant treatment of Ó Flaithearta in critical circles than with
any linguistic one-upmanship. Having said that, however, it is clear that
to undertake any evaluation of Ó Flaithearta's work involves a measure
of linguistic flexibility, and also translation. That there has yet to appear
anything even approaching a bi-linguistically considered critical biography
of Ó Flaithearta attests to the fact that the variety and isolated schools of
opinion on the writer pose a challenge for any prospective biographer.

Dúil / Desire

Gearóid Denvir's work on *Dúil* is one of the most important developments
in the study of Ó Flaithearta's collection of short stories, primarily because
it is the only work of its kind that evaluates the stories in the language in
which they appeared. The word *"dúil"*, of course, has many different uses
and connotations, though it primarily relates to notions of desire; some

of these assocations have strong connections within utopian theory and these will be examined in Chapter 4. Placing Ó Flaitheartaʼs collection on a footing with Joyce, Denvir writes that *"Níl aon amhras faoi ach go bhfuil an cnuasach gearrscéalta Dúil le Liam Ó Flaithearta, a foilsíodh den chéad uair i 1953, ar cheann de na ráitis chruthaitheacha is suntasaí dá bhfuil againn i litríocht Ghaeilge na haoise seo"* (1991: 7).[32] Denvir traces the importance of the theme and presence of *dúil* or desire in the short story collection and also looks at the prominence given in the stories to seemingly ordinary occurrences concerning Ó Flaitheartaʼs outwardly simple people and animals. However, as Denvir demonstrates, many found his short stories all the weaker for this overt simplicity, often remarking that they were cold and content-wise, quite simple:

> *"Is dóigh gurb í an oibiachtúlacht seo is cúis le tuairim roinnt léirmheastóirí gur scéalta ʼfuaraʼ iad cuid mhaith de ghearrscéalta Uí Fhlaithearta agus nach bhfuil iontu ach* ʼlimited emotional rangeʼ *agus* ʼsimple characters, such as childrenʼ, *mar a dhearbhaigh A.A. Kelly (1976: 12)"* (Denvir, 1991: 27–28).[33]

However, as Denvir explains later, in the Irish language versions of these stories, there is a subtler, perhaps more sparse rendering of desire running through them, which is more overtly described in the English versions. The notable differences between both language versions still cause critics and students much consternation; there is often more emphasis or discussion on the differences between the stories in either language than there is on the stories themselves and their possible meanings (cf. Daniels, 1988 and de Bháldraithe, 1968 for examples). Quoting from Ó Flaitheartaʼs *The Black Soul*, Denvir points out that the character of Fergus

---

32   "There is no doubt but that Liam Ó Flaitheartaʼs collection of short stories *Dúil*, first published in 1953, is one of the most significant literary statements that we have in Irish language literature in this century".

33   "It is perhaps this objectivity that leads some reviewers to suggest that these short stories are ʼcoldʼ and that they only possess a ʼlimited emotional rangeʼ and ʼsimple characters, such as childrenʼ as A.A. Kelly asserted".

became intimate with every ledge and slit and boss and weatherstain on the cliffs, with every wave on the bay, with every rock that jutted from the water, with its wet red mane of seaweed floating around it. He even felt kinship with the fishes prowling in the depths [...] The tide going in and out was a living thing to him. He felt that he was a component part of this complex life, that he could rest in peace, that he was free from care and danger and sorrow, that even death could not touch him (1924: 212, in Denvir, 1991: 28).

This level of familiarity with the land and the island's geographical features would seem to resonate with much of Synge's work in *The Aran Islands* and also with many of Ó Direáin's poems. However, though the Irish short stories do not seem to offer the same level of intimacy and familiarity between land and human, it would seem from Denvir and Cronin (2003) that this has in fact little to do with poor translation on the author's part and rather more to do with the Irish language's nuanced relationship with nature itself. As Peter Costello recounts:

> Though O'Flaherty claimed that he wrote even his English stories in Gaelic first drafts, the evidence about this is not consistent, and the Gaelic stories are, it seems, his own translations of his work. [...] The publication in 1953 of *Dúil* was important for the Gaelic literature movement of the day. It was reviewed with appreciation, for instance, by Richard Power, himself an author of a powerful novel set on Aran.[34] Stories in English still appeared from time to time in *The Bell*, and in America Devin-Adair, the conservative Irish-American publishing house, brought out in 1956 *The Stories of Liam O'Flaherty* with an introduction with Vivien Mercier, an Irish-born literary critic of the new generation (Costello, 1996: 96).

Liam Ó Flaithearta, like Lawless, has not received the level of critical enquiry befitting a writer of his standard; this is attested to by frequent calls by academics and scholars (Cahalan, 1999, Costello, 1996 amongst others) in relation to the need for an official biography of Ó Flaithearta. Indeed Cahalan has drawn attention to the lack of scholarship on both authors, and seems almost incredulous at the fact that both Lawless and Ó Flaithearta have become so peripheral to the canon of Irish literature. Though Hansson's biography has satisfied the gap with regard to scholarship

34 *The Hungry Grass*, 1969.

on Lawless to a large extent, work on Ó Flaitheartaʼs literary legacy has
petered off in recent years. If we consider the importance of the short
story form in Irish at the beginning of the last century, particularly with
regard to the work of Pearse and Ó Conaire, it is difficult to believe that
Ó Flaitheartaʼs work in Irish continues to remain underexamined. He was
writing a novel at the time of his death which was to have been his first
in Irish. His daughter has commented that he was exceptionally sad at
the end of his life that he could not finish the book, as it was to detail his
childhood on the island (2004: 42).

Máirtín Ó Direáin

Máirtín Ó Direáin was born in Sruthán, Inis Mór, in 1910. He was the
eldest of four children born to Seáinín Mháirtín Thaidhg Ó Direáin and
his wife, Peige Tom Phait Mhóir. His father died of tuberculosis when
Máirtín was only seven years old, leaving his mother to raise himself, his
brothers Seán and Tommy and their sister Máire alone. His fatherʼs death
affected him enormously. In an interview with Muiris Mac Conghail for
Comhar, Ó Direáin recounted how he was frightened to touch his fatherʼs
hand while he was being waked, even though all the mourners were dong
so; *"[n]íor leag mé mo láimh ar a láimh [...] bhí faitíos orm roimh mʼathair
nuair a fuair sé bás: bhí faitíos orm breathnú síos air"* (1984: 4).[35] His motherʼs
first husband had drowned at sea. As a result of his fatherʼs passing, and
because of his quiet and shy nature, Máirtín spent considerable time in his
motherʼs company, helping her with her knitting and listening while she
and her neighbours talked at night. His poem *"Boige /* Softness" (*Dánta
1939–1979*, 1980: 143) reflects both the comfort and the difficulty of this
relationship:

35   "I didnʼt touch his hand [...] I was frightened of my father when he died: I was
      frightened to look down at him".

An té a thógann máthair   He who is raised by his mother
Gan athair ina dháil: With no father supporting:
Ní rí ar thada é   Is king of nothing;
Is mogha ar bhoige é.   He is slave to softness.[36]

Ó Direáin had little or no interest in farming, and even less in fishing, and so contented himself with the solitude he found in wandering, in hiding from the gossiping neighbours and creating little stone figureens for himself. While helping a neighbour with lifting creels of seaweed, Máirtín left the creel fall and his friend advised him: *"téirigh go Bleá Cliath!"* (1961: 33).[37] He left home to work in the post office in Galway in 1927. He considered himself exceptionally fortunate to get a job as an office clerk and delighted in being able to send money home to his mother and siblings, although as he admitted to Diarmuid Ó Gráinne in an interview just a year before he died, Ó Direáin hated clerical work (Ó Gráinne, 1989: 18). Ó Direáin met Liam Ó Flaithearta for the first time while working in Galway:

> *Fear breá dathúil a raibh cáil idirnáisiúnta bainte amach aige lena scríbhneoireacht Béarla [...]. [...] d'fhiafraigh sé dhíom cérbh mé fhéin. D'insíos sin dhó. D'fhiafraigh sé dhíom ar thaithin an áit liom. Dúirt mé nár thaithin. Chomairligh an Flaitheartach dhom a raibh d'airgead tirim in Oifig an Phoist a fhuadach agus é a ghearradh go Sasana. Lig sé scairt gháirí as agus amach an doras leis* (Ó Gráinne, 1989: 18).[38]

Galway opened Máirtín's eyes to drama and literature, and of course, to writers and poets. A few short months after his arrival in the city, *An Taibhdhearc*, Ireland's only Irish language theatre, was opened, and Ó Direáin took part in the theatre's inaugural performance, under the direction of Mícheál Mac Liammóir. Máirtín, though nervous, found the stage gave him a confidence in which he was lacking (Ó Gráinne, 1989: 19). In 1937, however, he moved to Dublin, securing a position as

---

36 Collinge's translation (1985: 263).
37 "Go to Dublin!".
38 "A fine handsome man who had achieved international acclaim with his writing in English. He asked me who I was. I told him. He asked me if I liked the place. I told him I didn't. He advised me to take all the cash in the Post Office and to leg it to England. He let out a roar of laughter and out the door he went".

a clerical officer in the Department of Posts and Telegraphs. Though Ó Direáin noticed that Dublin was not as friendly a city as Galway, there were more writers there, and this fact provided Máirtín with much comfort and community (Ó Gráinne, 1989: 19). He quickly joined Cumann na Scríbhneoirí, aquainting himself with many aspiring writers, and it was there that he heard Tórna's lecture on poetry. Ó Direáin recounted that it was *"[f]ilíocht na séú agus na seachtú haoise déag a bhí idir chaibidil aige. Chuaigh gach ar chuala mé go mór i bhfeidhm orm. Shiúil mé abhaile agus bhí 'coilleach' i mo cheann".*[39] It was from this time onwards that Ó Direáin began to write poetry in Irish, focusing on the island as his central theme and character. He funded and published his first collection, *Coinnle Geala* in 1942. In her meditation on the importance of space and place in the poetry of Ó Direáin, Isobel Ryan writes that:

> if [an individual] leaves their mountain or river or island, then the *geographical becomes imaginative* [my emphasis] and the heart begins to long for, imagine and recreate islands, rivers and mountains [...] Poetry written by immigrants is full of rocks and lakes and geographical references of all kinds (2002: 267).

Undoubtedly, Ó Direáin's poetry shows signs of the "geographical becoming imaginative" with the advent of his work-imposed exile in Dublin. There remain only two collections of translated work of Ó Direáin's poetry (Mac Síomóin and Sealy, 1984 and Collinge, 1985). However, the primary reasons for the paucity of publications on this subject are linguistically-based. As with Ó Flaithearta, though his poetry was highly praised and well-received, both in Ireland and internationally, Ó Direáin's work has remained significantly under-examined for the past two decades.[40]

---

39 "He was discussing the poetry of the sixteenth and seventeenth century. Every word I heard influenced me greatly. It was like a light went on in my head".

40 In 1977, Ó Direáin won the Ossian-Preis, the highest honour an individual could receive for working or writing on behalf of a traditional or minority culture; see Prút, *Máirtín Ó Direáin : File Tréadúil*, 1982: 20–21. In the same year, Ó Direáin was awarded an honorary D. Litt. from the National University in Ireland; see Prút, 1982: 20–21.

Ó Direáin the poet

The existing commentary does, however, confirm that Ó Direáin's craft and his poetic work was and continues to be highly regarded among his small circle of reviewers. As Mícheál Mac Craith comments: *"Nuair a smaoinímid ar Mháirtín Ó Direáin smaoinímid ar fhile a chaith beagnach leathchéad bliain i mbun a cheirde, scríobhréim fhada thorthúil a thuismigh aon chnuasach déag filíochta"* (1991: 1).[41] What for many sets Ó Direáin's work apart from all else, however, is the fact that *"thar aon ní eile smaoinímid ar an Direánach mar fhile Árann, file a chuir an t-oileán draíochta úd gona phobal agus a shaíocht ag rince ina steillbheatha os ár gcomhair"* (1993: 1).[42] Ó Direáin's connection with the Aran Islands and in particular with his native Inis Mór cannot be severed from his own poetic identity. Given that almost each of Ó Direáin's poems, at some level or other, talks directly about the island experience or uses the island as a metaphor, it is natural that both poet and place have become so intricately associated. What gives this connection or this creative relationship even more gravitas is the fact that, due to economic and artistic necessity, Ó Direáin left his island home for Dublin, a place where, as evidenced by many of his poems, he was almost completely unhappy in the early days of his life there. Following the drowning of his mother's first husband, and that of his inspirational teacher, Seosamh Ó Flanagáin some years later, Máirtín appears to have developed a fear of the sea, and a dislike of travelling. Though this would not be uncommon among island communities, where a healthy fear of the sea is often promoted, the poet's anxiety was heightened upon leaving Inis Mór.[43]

41 "When we think of Máirtín Ó Direáin we think of a poet who spent almost fifty years at his craft, a long and fruitful writing life that yielded eleven collections of poetry".

42 "Above everything else, we think of Ó Direáin as an Aran poet, a poet who put that magical island, with its people and its riches, dancing before our eyes".

43 In *Grania*, Lawless details the act of leaving an island: "it seems a far more startling piece of transplantation than any flitting can seem to one who merely shares a mainland dotted over with tens of thousands of homesteads more or less similar to one's

Unusually for an islander, Ó Direáin never rowed a currach, and never visited Inis Meáin or Inis Oírr (Ó Gráinne, 1989: 20). He told Mac Conghail
that his mother worried continuously about him being on or near the sea,
and so he did not go against her wishes, staying on dry land and thus, never
learning much of the rich vocabulary associated with the sea (1984: 5). He
also, as recounted in the poem "*Díomá* / Disappointment" never raided
a sea-bird's nest and never earned the "*toirtín*", the money received after
finding a new-born lamb (1980: 31). Once settled in Dublin, Máirtín found
travelling home a difficult and painful task; on the rare occasions that he
did return home, his poetry reflects his sense of confinement, estrage-
ment and confusion at the changes taking place on Inis Mór. Ó Direáin
explained that

> [c]huile uair dá ndeachaigh mé ar ais [...] bhraith mé sáinnithe cosúil le duine a bheadh
> i bpríosún. B'fhada liom go n-imínn as an áit. Ní raibh tada ag an oileán le tairiscint
> dom ach cuimhní. Bhí mé díphéamhaithe (sic.) más maith leat. Is ón tuairim seo go
> bhfuil tú scoite díphréamhaithe a d'fhás dánta cosúil le Árainn 1947 [...] (Ó Gráinne,
> 1989: 20).[44]

Ó Direáin and Synge

Although it may not initially seem like the most obvious of comparisons
to make, Synge and Ó Direáin's careers are juxtaposed in order to show
how the migration from city to island (in Synge's case) or from island to
city impacted upon their craft and their own personal lives. Mac Craith
writes:

---

own. To sail away, see it dimly receding behind you, becoming first a mere speck,
then vanishing altogether, must be a very serious proceeding" (1892: 104).

44   "Every time that I went back, I felt trapped, like someone would in a prison. I could
     not wait to leave the place. The island offered me nothing but memories. I was, if you
     like, uprooted. It is from the perspective that you are cut-off, uprooted, that poems
     like '*Árainn 1947*' grew".

Is dual do thráchtóirí liteartha comórtas a dhéanamh idir an Direánach agus Synge. B'éigean do Synge cathair Pháras a thréigean agus dul go hÁrainn le teacht in inmhe mar scríbhneoir. [...] B'éigean don Direánach ar an lámh eile an t-oileán a thréigean agus dul chun na cathrach i mBaile Átha Cliath chun a ghairm fhileata a aimsiú. Tá olldhifríocht mhór amháin le sonrú idir cur chuige na beirte áfach. Cuma cé chomh mór agus a d'fhéach Synge len é féin a thumadh i gcultúr an oileáin ba strainséir i gcónaí é, is ag breathnú ar an taobh istigh ón taobh amuigh a bhí sé, gan dul aige ón 'as if you were one of the people themselves' (1993: 1–2).[45]

The considerable difference between both writers, as Mac Craith has shown above, is that Synge could not achieve the total immersion into island life that he desired, whereas, given that he did not desire the same type of absorption or involvement in city life, Ó Direáin chose instead to remain imaginatively attached to the island while living away from it. Ó Direáin initially failed, or perhaps refused, to recognise the city where he lived and worked as anything even resembling a type of home place, whereas Synge, having abandoned city life for island life, possibly needed to establish the sort of roots in Aran which Ó Direáin would have never allowed himself to have in Dublin.

Árannach go smior ba ea an Direánach, áfach, gan aon chur i gcás ag baint leis. Oileánach cruthaithe ag scríobh faoin oileán agus é ar deoraíocht ón oileán. An teannas sin idir saol na cathrach agus saol an oileáin ar dlúth is inneach d'fhilíocht Mháirtín Ó Direáin é, [...] (1993: 1–2).[46]

---

45 "It is usual for literary commentators to draw comparisons between Ó Direáin and Synge. Synge had to leave the city of Paris and go to Aran to come into his own as a writer. [...]Ó Direáin, on the other hand, had to leave Aran and go to Dublin city to find his gift for poetry. There is, however, a huge difference between the approaches of both men. No matter how much Synge sought to immerse himself in the island's culture, he was always an outsider, looking at the inside from the outside [...]".

46 "Ó Direáin was an islander through and through, however, without any doubt whatsoever. A creative islander writing about the island while in exile from the island. This tension between city life and island life is central to the poetry of Máirtín Ó Direáin".

Displacement and exile

In a more recent article, "Home and Exile: A Comparison of the Poetry of Máirtín Ó Direáin and Ruaraidh MacThòmais" (2001), Mícheál Mac Craith and Michelle Macleod comment that

> [o]ne of the most dominant themes in the Gaelic literary tradition of the past one and a half thousand years is exile. [...] The study of exile in Gaelic literature need not be restricted to the study of physical displacement, however, for exile may also be noted in terms of internal disaffection. [...] there is more to the theme than lamentation of the homeland (2001: 72).

Both physical displacement and internal disaffection are themes which Máirtín Ó Direáin reflects on in his poetry. The uprootedness of Ó Direáin's existence in Dublin is perhaps his most powerful and personally painful thematic device; his poem "*Stoite* / Uprooted" highlights this perfectly. In *Ón Ulán Ramhar Siar* (ed. Eoghan Ó hAnluain, 2002), an invaluable source which has collected many of Ó Direáin's own thoughts on his poetic legacy, Ó Direáin talks about "*Stoite*" and his feelings about the subject of being uprooted from one's home.

> *Seo é an chéad dán a scríobh mé ar an téama sin. Deireann daoine go bhfuil baint ag mo chuid dánta le 'stoiteachas' nó 'díphréamhachas', más maith libh, 'uprootedness'. [...] Agus ag smaoineamh siar dom ar an gcaoi sa tseanaimsir a mbíodh daoine ag maireachtáil in áit ó shinsear go chéile, ó mhac go mac a mhic, go bhféadfá a rá san aird sin thuas go raibh a mhuintir, Clann Uí Chonghaile, abraimís, ann le ceithre chéad bliain, nó gur thosaigh daoine ag fágáil an áit. Agus anois, go mór mór ó shaol cathrach agus mar sin de, go bhfuil na fréamhacha briste* (2002: 43).[47]

---

47 "This is the first poem I wrote on this theme. People say that my poems have something to do with [...] uprootedness. And looking back on how, in the olden days, people would live in the same place for generations, so that you could say, in that village up there the Conneely family lived there for, we'll say, four hundred years, until people started leaving the place. And now, especially from the point of view of city life, the roots are broken".

In creating, or in some cases recreating, the island of his home and his youth, it was possible for Ó Direáin to physically live in one place but to live imaginatively in another place. The danger in this scenario was, however, that Ó Direáin's creation would one day become outdated, and having little real contact with the island during his time in Dublin that is precisely what happened. Effectively, the poet created two separate island-based entities, the actual or real island of Inis Mór and the less precise, yet more elaborate island of Árainn. For our purposes here, when referring to the more abstract and imagined island of Inis Mór in Ó Direáin's poetry, it will be described as Árainn, while the actual geographical island will be called Inis Mór to differentiate between both.

In his study of Ó Direáin's poetry, Mac Craith (1993) introduces the work of Iain Mac a'Ghobhainn, a Scottish poet and writer concerned with issues of uprootedness and dislocation for the island writer.[48] Quoting from Mac a'Ghobhainn's famous article "Real People in a Real Place" (Crichton Smith, *Towards the Human*, 1986), Mac Craith notes the distinctions which Mac a'Ghobhainn makes between the tourist who sees the island terrain as *"pharthas buan do-athraithe"* and the islander who returns from a period of exile in the city (1993: 2–3)[49]:

> The islander who is living in the city is like the tourist in that he does not want to acknowledge change either, he wants the islands to belong to the world which he too has created, one of happy boyhood, perpetual summers, nice, kind people, lack of ambition and adult emotions. He too wishes to return to a place where doors are never locked [...]. [T]he tourist and the exiled islander belong to a similar species, each deceiving himself, though the reasons are not exactly the same. For the islander, exile leads to bad poetry; for the tourist, who has no experience of real exile, it leads to a dream without substance. But the exile has in fact lived in the islands and his self-deception is the greater (1986: 17).

Mac a'Ghobhainn's comments are most enlightening, marking out as they do the distinctions between staying and going, between exile and return. However, in Ó Direáin's case, his exile did not lead to "bad poetry"; in fact

48 Also known as Iain Crichton Smith.
49 "... a permanent, unchanged paradise".

the opposite is the case. Ó Direáin's ability to create great poetry in exile
was due to two main factors: firstly, he did not return home to Inis Mór on
any regular basis and so would have been less aware of the changes that were
occurring there than a more regular visitor would comprehend; secondly,
because Ó Direáin was able to create a very palpable tension between his
imaginary island and his city life, there was ample poetic ground available
to plough and thus no shortage of artistic opportunities to exploit and
explore. Had Ó Direáin been a more frequent visitor to the island, as he
became in later life where a discernable change in his attitude to his home
place is evident, it is not difficult to imagine that his earlier poetry would
be quite different in content and theme. However, thanks to his disillusionment with city life, as well as a demanding job and countless lectures
and teaching responsibilities, Ó Direáin's poetry flourished while in exile,
even if the island of his poetry was eroding and changing in reality.

Speaking about his poem "*Ár nÓige* / Our Youth" (1980: 110), Ó Direáin
comments on the strangeness of the fact that although he spent most of his
life living in Dublin, he rarely, if ever, reflected on this in his poetry:

> *Ní mórán dánta i ndáiríre a scríobh mise ar shaol mo 'leathdhúchais', más maith leat*
> *é sin a thabhairt air, mo 'leathdhúthaigh' anseo i nGaillimh ná i mBaile Átha Claith.*
> *Is dóigh nach bhfuair sé greim cheart orm riamh, nach ndeachaigh sé i bhfeidhm ceart*
> *orm. Mheasfá go mba é sin an rud loighiciúil agus go leanfadh sé an rud eile, is é sin*
> *saol an oileáin. Ach níor lean sé ar an mbealach sin é ach amháin, b'fhéidir ó thaobh*
> *smaointe, rudaí a chuir isteach orm, ach níor lean sé ó thaobh an tsaoil féin, ó thaobh*
> *na rudaí a ndeachaigh mé tríd agus na rudaí a raibh cleachtadh agam orthu ó thaobh*
> *áiteacha, áiteacha a mbeadh dáimh agam leo* (Ó hAnluain, 2001: 155).[50]

---

50   "I did not write too many poems, in all honesty, about my 'half-heritage', if that is
     what you would like to call it, my 'half-heritage' here in Galway or in Dublin. I sup-
     pose it never got a proper hold on me, that it did not influence me in any real way.
     You would think that that would be the logical thing and that one would follow
     the other, that of island life. But things did not work out that way, except perhaps
     with the exception of the thought process, and with things that bothered me. It did
     not follow me through life, from the point of view of things I went through and the
     things that I was accustomed to from the point of view of places, places that I had
     affection for".

Noting that city life "never got a proper hold on him", Ó Direáin's poetry shows the extent to which the poet's seventeen years on Aran before exile to Galway and then to Dublin affected him and his subsequent work. It would appear that his native roots could not be severed by the distance of exile. However, he does acknowledge a "half-heritage" of sorts, suggesting a liminal or interspatial existence for himself in his dealings with his island and his city life.

Mac a'Ghobhainn's essay, however, sheds light on another very important element of the exiled islander's relationship with his/her home when he writes that

> [t]he islander has never had the chance of staying where he is: history has condemned him to departure, and afterwards to the choice of whether or not to return. Thus the home becomes far more important than it does for others and the temptation to idealise it immense and almost forgivable. When the home is shifting continually one feels compelled to name it, and sometimes to do so falsely. The fact of the exile leads to the lie which is intended to comfort and fix the home. [...] To be an exile is to be a double man, living in a new world while still enchanted by the fantasies of the old. [...] But it is always anachronistic, the home has left him behind, and this because it belongs to a real land in a real place. As he moves towards it, it recedes forever as the water did from Tantalus (quoted in Mac Craith, 1993: 4–5).

The *doubleness* or the duality inherent in the exiled artist forces him to imagine or create a stable and unfragmented home with which to fix his identity while he himself is in a situation of flux and change, becoming accustomed to a new life in a strange and busy city. By naming and by embellishing his home place, the poet can then have an assured locus of identity as well as an artistic base upon which to begin his career. However, creating two separate and often competing versions of the same place can inevitably lead to a dissonance between both and ultimately to the creation of a more myth-based vision of one in place of the reality of the other. A discussion of these issues, which have resonances within the disciplines of postcolonial and utopian theory, will be discussed in chapters 3 and 4 of this book.

Nostalgia for home

On 23 April 2008, Professor Gearóid Ó Tuathaigh of NUI Galway officially
unveiled a memorial plaque to Máirtín Ó Direáin on the Salthill Promenade
on the outskirts of Galway city. The poem which the organisers chose to
use for the plaque was *"Fear Lasta Lampaí – Gaillimh 1928 /* The Lamp
Lighting Man – Galway 1928" (1980: 97). The positioning of the commemorative inscription is important; it faces outwards towards the Aran
Islands, which are usually visible from the Promenade. However, it also
points to another direction, that of Galway city, where Ó Direáin first
began his literary education, and further still to the mainland of Ireland,
where the poet was to spend the rest of his career. Ó Direáin continually
looked to the West, predominantly to the Aran Islands, though he remained
in exile from that geographical location from the age of seventeen. The
poem chosen is not the most famous of Ó Direáin's, and yet it illuminates
perfectly the poet's own interest in both poetry and city life.

Ba dhraíodóir an fear beag	He was a magician, the little man
A raibh an solas ina ghlaic,	With light in his grasp,
É ag tabhairt na gile leis	Bringing the light with him
Ó lampa go lampa sráide.	From lamp to street lamp.

At the unveiling of the memorial, Professor Ó Tuathaigh referred to
Ó Direáin as *"duine de mhórfhilí na haoise seo caite"* ("Nuacht" TG4, 23
April 2008).[51] Writer Joe Steve Ó Neachtain said that *"is ceart ómós a thab-
hairt dá leithéid, a chaith a shaol ar fad leis an gcultúr agus leis an nGaeilge.
[...] Eisean agus a leithéid a choinnigh beo an cultúr agus an teanga agus an
fhilíocht"* ("Nuacht" TG4, 23 April 2008).[52] *"Fear Lasta Lampaí – Gaillimh
1928"* was published in *Ár Ré Dhearóil* (1962) but was clearly inspired by
Ó Direáin's first year in Galway city. Apart from the obvious references to

---

51   "... one of the leading poets of the last century".
52   "... respect should be given to his likes, who spent his whole life involved with cul-
      ture and with Irish. [...] It was [Ó Direáin] and his likes who kept the culture, the
      language and the poetry alive".

the night-time cityscape, and the lighting of the gas-lamps, there are other images at play in the poem which illustrate the poet's own understanding of his craft. Ó Direáin's admiration for the simple man, passing light between each solitary, unlit lamp, in many ways foregrounds the poet's movement from the initial under-development of his own maturing poetic imagination to the illuminating brightness of inspiration in subsequent years. However, though Ó Direáin does not see the lamp-lighter as extraordinary, the industry with which he carries out his work is much admired by the poet. Ó Direáin also sees that in the simple act of illumination, a certain magic occurs with the touch of the magician's hand. In the movements of the lamp-lighter, Ó Direáin notes that the magic of light is carried in his hands, is a transportable gift, but that the light and the man are co-dependent on one another in this action. To extend the imagery of the poem further, Ó Direáin is clearly interested in the transportability of action and inspiration. The fact that Ó Direáin carried his poetic gift with him from his childhood in Inis Mór to Galway and then Dublin, and that it strengthened and grew as time passed, illustrates this point. The lights that Ó Direáin refers to, one must also consider, were often visible to the islanders on Aran on bright nights, and thus created another link between mainland and periphery.

The notions of invention and of nostalgia are ones which critics have commented upon in Ó Direáin's poetry. In his idealisation of his island home, Ó Direáin creates *"dhá dhomhan ar leith"* (Ní Riain, 2002: 8);[53] one abstract and one physical, or one metaphorical and one actual. Mac Craith and Macleod note that "[a]lthough Ó Direáin paints a very pretty picture indeed, he does, nonetheless, view his home through the 'rose-tinted spectacles' of exile, for the islanders' harsh struggle for survival is almost romanticized out of existence" (2001: 73).[54] On the notion of invention, or artistic license, Mac Craith and Macleod write that "[i]n some of his earlier works Ó Direáin's striving for poetic and emotional effect occasionally

53 "... two distinct worlds".
54 A TG4 documentary, *An Charraig Stoite* (The Uprooted Rock) (2003), however, discusses that, as Ó Direáin was moulded by his island, he was an authentic witness to that time and place. The documentary was written by Alan Titley and produced by Mac Dara Ó Curraighín (1: 14 mins.).

leaves him at odds with reality and one can sense the poet struggling to achieve the balance between poetic quality and truthfulness" (2001: 74). This is because Ó Direáin is caught between his own creation and the reality of the situation, and it may also be that the often-idyllic upbringing which he had on the island is beginning to fade in his memory and he feels the need to recreate it once more.

In his PhD thesis, "Rock, Stone and Shore: The Poetry of Máirtín Ó Direáin, 1939–1979. A Translation and Critical Analysis" (1985), Declan Collinge focuses on Ó Direáin's island identity and on how this shaped his artistic vision. The most revealing section of the thesis is the author's interview with Ó Direáin. The section of the interview, "On Synge", gives us a very interesting insight into Ó Direáin's admiration for Synge as both a man and an artist. In the following excerpts, we see how Ó Direáin aligns himself with Synge's vision of the Islands:

> DECLAN COLLINGE: Both Synge and yourself greatly romanticise Aran, though Synge is prepared to point up the coarser aspects of life on the islands, (especially in *The Aran Islands*). Do you feel that you have been less than honest in this regard, notably in your earlier poetry?
>
> MÁIRTÍN Ó DIREÁIN: I think that I wrote of Aran at the time as a young exile. It struck me that way, and I can no more be faulted for this than Synge can be for neglecting the Catholic ethos [...] (1985: 361).
>
> D.C.: Like Synge, you were once of the opinion that the rich Irish of Aran was itself poetry. Do you still subscribe to this romantic notion, or have you since reconsidered?
>
> M.Ó.D.: I don't know. I haven't been back in a long time. I don't think the language is as rich, or as poetic, as it was then. [...] Maybe my original assumption was too modest. One is conditioned by one's society [...] (1985: 361)
>
> D.C.: Has your knowledge of the Gaelic tradition been attained as autodidact, or did you already have the music of tradition in your ears before you left Aran in 1927?
>
> M.Ó.D.: What I had on leaving Aran was no more than the songs and the aphorisms of the people. This, in itself, did not equip me with much in my poetic career. I have had to explore the greater part of the poetic tradition by constant reading (1985: 378).

Collinge's dissertation also provides a very interesting summary of the treatment afforded to Ó Direáin's work. He notes that no great body of criticism has been written on his poetry, although such critics as Mac Craith and Liam Prút have examined his works in depth (1985: 224). Writing in 1985, it is important to note that Collinge's statement continues, by and large, to apply; Ó Direáin's work still awaits a definitive treatment and comprehensive study. The Merriman Winter School, 2010, however, was dedicated to Máirtín Ó Direáin, marking the centenary of his birth. A number of other important events took place to celebrate Ó Direáin's important anniversary: an updated and illustrated edition of *Dánta 1939 – 1979* was published by Cló Iar-Chonnachta, An Post issued a commemorative stamp by Tom Ryan, showing Ó Direáin and Inis Mór, and an exhibition of new paintings inspired by Máirtín's poetry by the Inis Mór artist Seán Ó Flaithearta was unveiled. These are welcome and significant events, and yet, Collinge's assertion that "[a]t best, he is read superficially, at worst, he is ignored" (1985: 224) has some truth to it. It illustrates the slim examples of Ó Direáin's work that are offered for consideration and also shows the scant attention given to the work. It was perhaps to Ó Direáin's detriment that his poetry was used in such an isolated and codified manner (for the purposes of examination) as what emerges from this is an over-familiarity with his work and yet only a weak understanding of the actual artistic significance of the poetry at hand. Though generations of adolescents were undoubtedly given the opportunity to read Ó Direáin through this system, it was perhaps this system that would see his work become restricted to a small, and for the most part, uninterested audience. In allowing for only a small section of his work to be considered on the Intermediate or Leaving Certificate course, Ó Direáin's poetry was also consigned to the notion of passively *being learned* rather than actively being read and appreciated, while also giving the impression that what was offered on the course was the sum total of the poet's *oeuvre*. However, one wonders if Ó Direáin's words had not been obligatory reading material for state examinations, if his work would be even more tangential than it presently is? He was both fortunate and unfortunate to receive feedback on his poetry's impact on students on many occasions. Countless students would call him on the eve of the Irish exam to ask for his insight and advice; a surgery nurse whispered to him that she had never forgiven him for making her repeat her Leaving Cert (Sheridan, in *Ár nOileán: Tuile 's Trá*, 2004: 107).

Collinge also considers, as Mac Craith, Prút and, later, Ní Riain do,
that "[t]hrough his poetry, he articulated the trauma of cultural compromise, until such a time as he used his native Aran as the yardstick by which
the alien culture could be measured, and found wanting" (1985: 224–225).
However, with the passing of time, Ó Direáin began to realise that his
refusal to abandon his pursuit of home and his rejection of his urban existence was futile and painful. The island began to shift, and became associated
with pastness; Ó Direáin had to re-engage with his current reality in order
to prevent himself and his art from slipping through the creative veils he
had created for his own comfort and protection.

Synge and Ó Direáin shared a comparable artistic nature. Both authors
enjoyed quite solitary adolescences and sensed their marginality from the
societies around them keenly (1985: 242–243). Collinge pertinently notes
that both Synge and Ó Direáin's childhood was something that intrigued
people. However, both writers were, more often than not, misunderstood in
their artistic plights. Ó Direáin's poem "*Óige an Fhile* / The Poet's Boyhood"
(1980: 26) considers these themes and recalls that

Bhíodh na comharsain ag magadh fúm,	The neighbours would mock me,
Is mo mháthair de shíor ag bagairt orm,	And my mother would threaten me constantly,
Ach níor thuigeadar ar aon chor mé	and they never understood me at all,
An buachaill aisteach ciúin.	That strange quiet boy.
Ghreamaigh díom an galar úd	That affliction took hold of me
Is ní saor mé uaidh go fóill,	And I still am not free from it,
Is é a sheol ar bhóthar na n-aisling mé	It steered me on the road to vision
Is a dhealaigh mé ón sló.	And set me apart from the rest.[55]

It is Ó Direáin's youth which best explains his poetic inspiration as well as
best exemplifies the romantic or rose-tinted imagery which he used in his
work about Aran. His early poetry, as Collinge explains, is full of images
of colour, vibrancy, communal understanding and nature-based appreciation of his home place (1985: 246). There is little bitterness in this early
work, teeming as it is with examples of man's struggle to make a living

55   Collinge's translation (1985: 26).

from the soil or with the island's strength against tide and forces of nature. However, Collinge writes that much of Ó Direáin's middle poetry rebukes the Catholic middle class, and also highlights his bitter disappointment that the aspirations of Pearse and Connolly are being disregarded and unfulfilled (1985: 247). For Ó Direáin, during this poetic period, "[t]he island and its culture, then, is thrown into more striking relief against the background of the huckster city" (1985: 247), where, ironically, Ó Direáin himself must work as a clerk, and the sense of betrayal of kin and tradition gives his middle verse a greater poignancy:

Mo dhúil féin de ghnáth ní mór	Usually my own interest in paper work
I ngnó an pháir seach breacadh dán:	Goes no further than scribbling down a poem:
Ábhar priacáil dom gach lá	And all that comes daily to me
A dtagann i mo chomhair faoi iamh comhaid.	Enclosed in a file of agony.

A thuistí a chuaigh romham sall	O forebears who went before me
Sin bhur n-oidreacht chugam anall,	This is what you have bequeathed me,
Maithígí dom nuair is mó mo chás	Forgive me if my sorrow is greater
A mhalairt dá mb'áil liom de rogha.	I would choose another way.[56]

As Collinge goes on to explain, Ó Direáin's trauma, as expressed in the above lines, "is occasioned by his desire to cling to his native language and culture – he can trace his lineage back to his great-great-grandfather Domhnal of Sruthán – while being forced to communicate in a foreign language and forsake the role of farmer/fisherman, infinitely more romantic than the drudgery of Civil Service life" (1985: 247). Throughout this earlier writing period, Ó Direáin's image of Aran remained constant and unyielding to change. However, as Mac Craith and Macleod (2001) comment, his poem "*Árainn 1947* / Aran 1947" (1980: 34), symbolises the poet's best attempt to resolve the romantic dream of the island of his youth with the actual, often difficult, realities of that life now (2001: 74), though ultimately the poet is disappointed to see the disappearance of the Aran he once knew.

56   Collinge's translation of "*Gnó an Pháir* / Paper Work" (1980: 126), (1985: 247).

Liú áthais ná aitis	A shout of joy or pleasure
Ó chroí na hóige	From the heart of the young
[...]	
An tráth seo thiar	This time in the West
Níor chualas.	I heard not.

Ní don óige feasta	Not for the young any more,
An sceirdoileán cúng úd.	That narrow windswept island.[57]

In a significant departure for Ó Direáin, however, with the publication of *Ó Mórna is Dánta Eile* (1957), we find that the "disappointment evident in '*Árainn 1947* / Aran 1947' is replaced by a gentle affection; the island becomes his *oileán rúin*, his precious and secret island" (2001: 74). Thus, in order to reconcile both of the islands in his former poetry, the real and the imaginary, Ó Direáin now takes elements from both of these to create an island which would seem to allow him even greater imaginative scope and the freedom to create further work.

All through Ó Direáin's career, as evidenced by his elegy *"Ómós do John Millington Synge"* (1980: 55), Synge's stays on Aran and his influence on writers like Ó Direáin himself are considered as central points of comparison and interest.

An toisc a thug tú chun mo dhaoine	The impulse that brought you to my people
Ón gcéin mhaith don charraig ghabh	From the distant pasture to the harsh rock
Ba chéile léi an chré bheo	Was partnered by the living clay
Is an leid a scéith as léan is danaid.	And the imitations of loss and sorrow.
[...]	
Tá cleacht mo dhaoine ag meath,	The ways of my people decay.
Ní cabhair feasta an tonn mar fhalla,	The sea no longer serves as a wall.
Ach go dtaga Coill Chuain go hInis Meáin	But till Coill Chuain comes to Inis Meáin
Beidh na bréithre a chnuasaís tráth	The words you gathered then
Ar marthain fós i dteanga eachtrann.	Will live on in an alien tongue.[58]

---

57   Mac Síomóin and Sealy's translation (1984: 17).
58   Mac Síomóin and Sealy's translation (1984: 41).

Perhaps because both Synge and Ó Direáin were self-confessed men of words rather than of action, and because of their combined disdain for urban life in favour of a more pastoral existence, it is quite difficult to find an article or an appreciation of Ó Direáin that does not draw on similarities between both writers. In Mac Síomóin and Sealy's introduction to *Tacar Dánta* (1984), they quote a passage from Skelton's *J.M. Synge and his World* (1971) that could just as easily be said of Ó Direáin as it has been of Synge:

> He noted only those aspects of island life which fed upon his own imagination and supported his views [...] while he referred to the hardness of the islander's life he did so rather with the admiration of the romantic than with the concern of the sociologist [...] Haunted by the thoughts of mortality, he saw in the endless battle of the islanders with the elements and their constant nearness to sudden death a parable of the human condition [...]. In their ancient culture, their stories and mythic understanding of the natural world, he perceived a kind of knowledge that lay deeper than that of the intellect [...] (1971: 38).

Ó Direáin and language: power of place and power of tongue – Feamainn Bhealtaine

It would appear that the issue of language was not as contentious or as obvious for Máirtín Ó Direáin as it was for Ó Flaithearta, or indeed for Ó hEithir. Two factors could account for this: firstly, Ó Direáin, unlike both Ó Flaithearta and Ó hEithir, was in full-time employment (in the Civil Service, Department of Education) throughout his career; secondly, in the early 1940s and 1950s, the appreciation of Irish-language poetry, unlike that of prose, was in the ascent and a growing number of scholars and readers recognised the importance of the craft and the literary heritage it symbolised. In his essay "Twentieth-century Irish-Language Poetry" Theo Dorgan writes that

> [t]he first Gaelic poet of serious achievement in the new century, Máirtín Ó Direáin, [...] would say at the outset *"Níor chabhair mhór d'éinne againn san aois seo an aon uaill ná mac alla ó na filí a chuaigh romhain inár dteanga féin"* – No cry or echo from the poets who went before us in our own tongue would be of help to any of us in this time (2002: unpaginated).

In his conversation with Declan Collinge, Ó Direáin commented that "when all tangible things have been exhausted, you're left with the concept, the abstract" (1985: 369). This is one of the most revealing insights which Ó Direáin gave with regard to his own work, and his own perspective on the creative process in which he was engaged. It would appear that Ó Direáin was offering an explanation of how his vision of the tangible island eroded with time and of how the emptier shell of the abstract was all he was left with. However, as becomes apparent in a close reading of Ó Direáin's poetry, the abstract was the poet's primary tool throughout this exile in Dublin, and though he visited his island home on various occasions between 1922 and 1985, his understanding of the "real" island of Inis Mór was obfuscated by his more fully formed relationship with the conceptual, amorphous, island of Árainn.

However, during Ó Direáin's childhood on Inis Mór, it is clear that the young poet had begun to develop a simple imaginative style. In *Feamainn Bhealtaine*, a much-understudied book, Ó Direáin charts the vital and earliest relationship with the men and women of stone he fashioned to satisfy "the creative urge" (1961: 13). Though initially a child-like attempt at animating lifeless objects, before long it became clear to the poet, and his worried mother, that this relationship was a far more symbolic exercise than first thought.

> *Thosaigh mé ag déanamh 'fearachaí cloch'. Má ait leat an focal 'fearachaí' chuala mise é chomh minic is tá méar orm ag na daoine fásta is iad ag caint linne gasúir, sea! agus 'beannachaí freisin. Cineál Baby Talk, is dóigh. Rinne mé samhail de gach fear agus de gach bean ar an mbaile. Bhí samhail de gach teach agam freisin* (1961: 12).[59]

Upon making and creating likenesses, both accurate and imaginative, of each of his neighbours, Ó Direáin set about animating his characters, fully aware of his role as the puppet master. This game was not as facile as one

59 "I began making 'mens of stone'. If the word 'mens' is odd for you, I heard the grownups using it when talking to us children as many times as I have fingers, yes!, and 'womens' too. A kind of *baby talk*, probably. I made a likeness of every man and every woman in the village. I had an image of every house too".

might initially imagine, however, and Ó Direáin clearly understood this from an early age. He comments in *Feamainn Bhealtaine* that he had full power over the men and women of stone: *"bhí urlámh iomlán agam orthu"* (1961: 12).[60] Ó Direáin also explains his ability to enliven these characters, and also to put them under the trance of sleep as and when he wished. The future poet considered his power over them to be god-like: *"ba dia beag mé a raibh créatúirí cloiche i gcúl mo ghlaice agam"* (1961: 12).[61] This observation is vital and pre-empts much of what was to follow in Ó Direáin's artistic career. Ó Direáin's awareness of his creative abilities at such a young age is fascinating and it emphasises the association which he makes between the stones and his own imaginative growth. His imagination was moulded and invigorated through his delight in making the most rigid of subjects seem like creative clay in his hands and in his mind.

What also becomes apparent through Ó Direáin's comments on this phase of his creative development is his self-immersed isolation from his adolescent cohort. *"D'éalaínn liom ó chaidreamh is ó chuideachta daoine, ó chluichí mo chomh-ghasúr uair i ndiaidh uaire i mo shuí ar mo ghogaide"* (*Feamainn Bhealtaine*, 1961: 13).[62] Ó Direáin's decision to separate himself from his school friends and their games foregrounds an important feature of his own isolationist nature, one which was given fuller voice years later in his exile in Dublin. However, there is no associated pain or loss to be felt in his youthful isolation; Ó Direáin consciously moves away from the everyday pursuits of his fellow islanders and seeks out a private nook for his own imaginative games. He emphasises the urgency with which he focused on his creations and how this aroused much unwanted attention from his neighbours and his mother.

> *Bhí mé chomh práinneach i nithe neamhbheo nuair a bhí mé i mo ghasúr is go ndéarfá go raibh dáimh agam leo. [...] Tosaíodh ag caint orm. Ní raibh mé ceart. Chuala mo mháthair faoi. D'fhair sí mé. [...] ag iarraidh orm ligean as an nós clochaí, agus a*

---

60 "I had total control over them".
61 "I was a small god who had these creatures of stone in the palm of my hand".
62 "I would escape from friendship and from company, from the games of my fellow-children for hours on end, sitting on my hunkers".

bheith mar mo leithéid ar bith, ach ní raibh maith orm. D'éirigh mé ní ba fhaichillí, ní ba ghlice. D'athraigh mé mo chuid 'muiríneacha' go dtí buaile bheag éigin eile, áit ar cheap mé nach bhfeicfeadh deoraí riamh mé, ach thángthas orm. 'Caith uait iad sin feasta choíchin', adeir mo mháthair. 'Is beag a' dochar duit náire a bheith ort, is leath an oileáin a' magadh fút' (1961: 13).[63]

The "creative urge" referred to earlier was clearly in the ascent here, though Ó Direáin could not have understood that at the time. There is also a strong sense of desire apparent here, in that Ó Direáin's creation was about wanting a community to whom he could relate, as he was always considered to be *"an buachaill aisteach ciúin"* by the community in which he could not find his own voice.[64] The desire to create and to attempt to perfect that creation is potent throughout Ó Direáin's work, none more so than in his earlier collections. *"Ionracas /* Integrity*"* (1980: 69) is another of Ó Direáin's poems where there are visible signs of the essential quality of stone imagery in his work.

Coinneod féin an t-oileán	I will keep the island
Seal eile i mo dhán,	a little longer in my poem
Toisc a ionraice atá	because of the truth of
Cloch, carraig is trá.	Stone, rock and strand.

The *"file mór"* mentioned in the poem is Seán Ó Ríordáin, a contemporary of Ó Direáin's. Ó Ríordáin's admiration for his fellow poet's work "sprung from [Ó Direáin's] unceasing pondering on a little island in the sea" (in *Tacar Dánta*, 1984: xiv).[65] In response and in agreement with Ó Ríordáin's

63   "I was so taken with inanimate things when I was a child that you could say that I had a relationship with them. [...] They started talking about me. I wasn't right. My mother heard about it. She watched me. [...] wanting me to let go of the habit of the rocks, and to be like my kind, but it came to nothing. I grew even more circumspect, smarter. I moved my 'little shells' to another little field, somewhere I thought that I wouldn't be found by anyone, but I was. 'Throw away those [stones] for good' my mother said. 'You should be mortified, with half the island ridiculing you'".

64   "The strange, quiet boy" (*"Óige an Fhile /* The Poet's Boyhood").

65   Ó Direáin, on being asked what poetry was, stated that poetry is about words, but they must have some magic about them, or, in the words of Seán Ó Ríordáin, they

assertions, Ó Direáin wrote *"Ionracas"*.[66] While accepting that the island and love of women are the subject matter and reason for his poetry, Ó Direáin decides to continue to keep the island in his poetry for a while longer, as though it were a possession or commodity available to him. Ó Direáin seems to believe in the integrity of the island, and sees it as an amalgamation of stone, rock and strand. These three constituents are an interesting set of images in themselves; all three are prone to erosion and change. Yet, certainly for Ó Direáin, they appear timeless and represent the stalwart integrity of the island's domain. It is also important to note that the island in Ó Direáin's poetry remains intact over a long period of time, until the poet himself returns to the island years later, and from which point these images of erosion and decay enter into his poetry. It is unsurprising that the island does not erode in much of Ó Direáin's poetry; for it to have done so would have been detrimental to the poet's psychological and imaginative hold on the place of his birth. However, with the passage of time, and Ó Direáin's gradual acceptance of inevitable change, the island begins to fade from its position of strength and centrality in the poetry and becomes instead a metaphor for disillusionment, intangibility and deceit.

The poet's decision to cling to the stones of his youth, much as they clung to him (*"Óige an Fhile"*) for most of his exile in Dublin, represents a sustained bond between the inanimate and the imagination. Stone is both a geological and an imaginative subject matter for Ó Direáin, and he moulds both physical and mental objects into real and animate subjects. The poet comments in *Feamainn Bhealtaine* that *"caidreamh na gcloch"* (1961: 13)[67] was a sustaining relationship for him, even though he gradually grew out of making men and women of stone. Even a cursory review of Ó Direáin's poetry, however, reveals that while his physical relationship with the stones

---

must move you (*"geit a bhaint asat"*). From an interview collected in *An Charraig Stoite* (3: 40 mins., 2003).

66 Interestingly, Mac Síomóin and Sealy give three possible translations for "Ionracas": "Guilelessness, Integrity and Truth" (1984: xiv), whereas Collinge translates it as "Integrity" (1985: 412). Mac Craith and Macleod translate it as "authenticity" (2001: 75).

67 "The relationship of stone".

had ended, the mental grip of the stone on his mind would only increase with his departure for Galway. Ó Direáin later reflected on the creative urge and considered it as an ongoing process. What he was very aware of, nonetheless, was his need for community:

> If one hasn't community, one doesn't have neighbours. You don't work properly when it's missing. I feel I was at all times searching for it and even creating it for myself during my boyhood when I made "stone men" in the walls. [...] I believe [my mother] thought that I'd end up in Ballinasloe mental hospital (Collinge, 1985: 361–362).

In creating, then, a community of stone figures with whom he could share his thoughts and secrets, Ó Direáin was also fashioning a world around himself that would set him apart from his fellow islanders, and later, his colleagues in Dublin. Given that Ó Direáin's father, like Synge's, had died when the poet was very young, the poet was "isolated from male company and was never inaugurated into the traditions of physical labor on the island" (Mac Craith and Macleod, 2001: 72). Indeed, Ó Direáin states in *Feamainn Bhealtaine* that *"[n]í dhéanfainn aon mhaith ar an talamh, adúradh. [...] ní raibh aon luí agam leis mar thalamh, cé go ndearna mé roinnt giotamála, ach ní mórán a bhíodh i ndiaidh mo shaothair"* (1961: 28).[68] This strained relationship with the land might have been different had Ó Direáin's father lived. However, it is remarkable to note that Ó Direáin did not sense any level of longing for the land. For Ó Direáin it is the stone and the rock with which he seeks solidarity, not the soil or the poor terrain. It is noteworthy that the colder, most inanimate and impassive of all subjects is that which Ó Direáin cherishes and with which he forms the greater bond. One reason for the poet's failure to be captivated by farm work certainly pertains to the absence of his father's influence, but might also relate to the fact that his poetic faculties were keen enough to be aware of the reality that he needed isolation and separateness rather than connection to thrive as a writer. The land gains hold of the individual in ways which relate to responsibility

---

68 "It was said that I would never be any good working the land. [...] I had no inclination towards working the land, [and] although I did do some pottering around, there wasn't much to show after my work".

and service, and ultimately to staying put in one place. Stone, on the other hand, provides a very different form of attachment. Though it later came to represent the island for Ó Direáin, the stone, and his early relationship with it, represented a prior incarnation of isolation and alienation for the poet. It is clear that Ó Direáin was making islands long before he left his own island for the first time.

Micheál Ó Conghaile's *Conamara agus Árainn 1880–1980* gives an insight into the dexterous and enterprising character of Connemara and Aran people which is echoed in Synge's *The Aran Islands*. Ó Conghaile finds that, given the poor quality of land there, many people had to train themselves to be skilful in a variety of crafts and trades, in order to save their families and their homesteads from ruin. Though farming and fishing were the most obvious forms of income and exertion, families often had to be industrious in other modes (1988: 73). Synge found the islanders to be equally hard-working:

> [i]t is likely that much of the intelligence and charm of these people is due to the absence of any division of labour, and to the correspondingly wide development of each individual, whose varied knowledge and skill necessitates a considerable activity of mind. Each man can speak two languages. [...] His work changes with the seasons in a way that keeps him free from the dullness that comes to people who have always the same occupation (*The Aran Islands*, 1992: 84).

It could be said that the islanders were not only hard-working from an agricultural point of view, however, but that this diligence also extended to their deftness of mind and language. Though Ó Direáin and Ó Flaithearta did not fare well as farmers or fisherman, they did, nonetheless, cultivate the landscape of Aran for their own creative ends. Constantly digging, toiling and mining the Islands for themes, metaphors and images, both writers were aerating the soil and chipping away at the stones of their home place, in much the same way as their fellow islanders did with their shovels and picks in order to make fields and build houses.

Another factor, however, which must be considered here relates to comments made by Ó Direáin himself in *Ón Ulán Ramhar Siar* (2002). Talking of his childhood, Ó Direáin recounts that *[b]huel, deir siad gur domhan beag ann féin Árainn. Is fíor – domhan beag ann féin chuile áit chomh fada agus a bhaineann sé, is dóigh, leis an duine a tógtar ann. Ach ní amháin go mba domhan beag ann féin Árainn ach níorbh é an domhan amháin a bhí ann, bhí trí dhomhan, ceithre dhomhan, b'fhéidir, san oileán féin* (2002: 15).[69]

It is clear from this that Ó Direáin was aware that even within the micro-cosmic world of his own island, there existed many different definitions of that island, and also many different versions of the island. For the Ó Direáin family, their part of the island stretched out towards a jutting section of land and sea, and the poet notes that everything outside of that small village was like a separate entity, another island (2002: 15). This communal understanding of divisions and separateness must have impacted on the young poet, for he speaks about his own separateness of character and imagination immediately following his depiction of land divisions and villages. He understands his own isolation in much the same fashion as he comprehends how different parts of the island were owned and ruled by different families; Ó Direáin controls his own move away from his com-munity, pre-empting his separation from it and perhaps preparing himself for the severing of his island-ties in favour of his artistic exile in Dublin. Though it was through stone that Ó Direáin found his greatest link with his own island identity, stone also provided the poet with the quintessential symbol for isolation, alienation and resilience.

Tim Robinson's two books on Aran's unique geological and carto-graphical nature, suggest two productive ways in which to think about the Islands' stone and its relationship with the Islands and the islanders them-selves: *Stones of Aran: Pilgrimage* (1986), and *Stones of Aran: Labyrinth* (1995). The notion of the return or the religious nexus between the place and the person is suggested by the first book, *Pilgrimage*. However, the linked image of the *Labyrinth* is also important. One goes on a pilgrim-age to reconnect with spirituality, with self and with nature. One enters

69   "Well, they say that Árainn [Inis Mór] is a small world of its own. And it is true – every place is a small world, by and large, in the eyes of those brought up there. But it wasn't just that Árainn was a small world, but the island in itself represented, three, perhaps four worlds, maybe".

a labyrinth to embrace the sense of being lost but also of finding a way out. Pilgrimages often take place on islands (Lough Derg, for example), adding to the sense of escape from the humdrum of consumer-driven life-styles and hectic, rigidly-scheduled existences. Thus, the twin notions of clarity and confusion are conjured up by both pilgrimage and labyrinth. One may note in this respect that the islander's view of going to an island is described as going in, or in Irish, *ag gabháil isteach ar oileán*, whereas a mainlander describes the same process of going to an island as going out, *ag gabháil amach ar oileán*. The older Irish word for island, *inis*, still in petrified use in many of our place names, has within it the elements of *"in"* and *"seas"*, that is, to stand within (Buck, 1949: 29). The modern word of *oileán* is a compound of Old Irish *"ail"* and *"én"* or diminutive rock (Quin, ed., *Dictionary of the Irish Language*, 1984). The notion of absorption is important in this context, as if the Islands function as capsules or chambers which allow entry and expulsion. Mary Banim noted that her excursion to the Aran Islands begged the question:

> would the weather be fine? That, on such occasions, is the chief consideration, for there is this charm about these excursions to the Isles, – except in very fine weather you can't get in, and then it is a chance if you get out again (the natives never say "land on Arran", or "leave Arran" – it is invariably "come in" or "go out"). Therefore there is always a delightful uncertainty in a visit to these islands [...] (1896, in Ó hEithir, 1991: 74).

Adding to this sense of isolation or entrapment often encountered by those on an island is the significance of the encircling sea. As Robinson explains, "the ocean encircles Aran like the rim of a magnifying glass, focusing atten-tion to the point of obsession" (1986: 10). However, Robinson is also keen to emphasise that the Islands did not present themselves as "[Robert] Flaherty's pedestal of rock on which to strike a heroic stance" but instead as being places "on which one might flirt delectably with alternative futures" (1986: 10). If one considers this last observation of Robinson's in light of Ó Direáin's poetic (re)creation of both alternative pasts and alterna-tive presents, then a very powerful invocation of the Islands' potentiality is exposed. In "On the Shores of the Past" (*Pilgrimage*, 1986: 134–138) Robinson recounts how Ó Direáin's poetry often refers both to "back" and "west" when using the word *thiar*.[70] Robinson also notes how "the frictions of Irish history and geography have given the concept of 'the West' such a charge that *thiar* is almost as potent a word as *sean*, old, is in Irish" (1986: 135). Thus Robinson touches on a third strand in the conception of the West of Ireland, that of antiquity or ancientness, a notion of pastness. All considered, *thiar* incorporates ideas concerning direction ("back"), geographical location ("West") and also an understanding of time and historical legacy ("old"). It is as though the word itself, *thiar*, has gathered all three strands together, and can manifest one or more meanings in any given piece. This sense of a gathering together is also used by Robinson to explain Ó Direáin's fascination with symbols of the shoreline and of sea-weed collection. Robinson makes the point that "*Feamainn Bhealtaine*, 'Mayweed', could indeed be taken as symbolic of literature's gathering-in of the old shore-life, for it is the Aran term for the banks of redweed cast up by the gales of spring" (1986: 136). However, as Robinson also illustrates, Ó Direáin's main fascination lies in

> the moments of relaxation from toil, of stillness and contemplation, [and it is these moments] that shine most brightly in the memory of that child from Sruthán thought of as a lazy dreamer – while in fact he was already at work, picking up the whole village, its cottages, fields, shore and folk, to carry them across into our world (1986: 136).

What is most interesting about Robinson's reflection here is his comment about the transportational nature of the symbols Ó Direáin used in his work. Each one of these symbols can be picked up, transported and imaginatively transplanted because their basic element is that of the stone. Ó Direáin's familiarity with stone, and his obsession with its form and function, particularly during his childhood, represents a vital relationship between the poet and the inanimate object, between the poet and the island (the stone on a larger scale) and also between the poet and his craft. It suggests, above all other things, an understanding on the poet's part of

70 See "*An t-Earrach Thiar* / Spring in the West", "*Coinnle Ar Lasadh* / Lighted Candles", "*Faoiseamh a Gheobhadsa* / I will Find Solace" (1980: 33, 17, 19) for examples of the many uses of the words "*siar*" and "*thiar*" in Ó Direáin's early poetry.

the imaginatively transportable function of stone, and could perhaps be thought to pre-empt his need for a symbol, once in exile, that was poetically adequate in his urban predicament.

In contrast with Ó Direáin's idyllic, slow-paced representations of his life on Inis Mór, Robinson suggests that the poet's "nostalgic watercolours" (1986: 137) are far removed from the more "lurid oil-painting" of Liam Ó Flaitheartas's writing style. Ó Flaitheartas's stories are certainly more frenetic than Ó Direáin's poetry. Even when Ó Flaitheartas's characters are in situ, in bed or sitting by the fire, there is a clear urgency of mind or action foregrounded by the narrator of the story which infuses a constant energy throughout the tale. In the case of Ó Direáin, however, there is little urgency or rush apparent in his poems, and in *Feamainn Bhealtaine* there is more emphasis on stasis and tale-telling, than on manual work or labour. This may, of course, have more to do with Ó Direáin's own gentle nature, and his love of fire-side stories than with the external realities of island life at that time. However there is another crucial aspect to Ó Direáin's quiet and unhurried depictions of island life that remains understudied. The poet's core relational nexus with the island of his poetry and his birth centres on the symbolic and physical nature of stone and its power to encapsulate the twin concepts of erosion and permanence. However, what makes Ó Direáin's poetry effective is that it simultaneously reflects a gentle physical and imaginative erosion and also a strong and stoic permanence. It is as though the poet cannot accept that his intimate relationship with the stones of his youth is being corroded both by time and his own physical distance from the realities of life there. More than this, Ó Direáin cannot relinquish his own control over the stones of his childhood and so cannot imagine the loss of this bond. In many of the earlier poems, it is clear that the only erosion and/or attrition that Ó Direáin can imagine is that which his own poetry is creating. The exiled poet is conscious of taking from the physical island in order to construct his own imaginative island.

Bongie's *Islands and Exiles: The Creole Identities of Post/Colonial Literature* (1998) examines this creative erosion and the repercussions of such activity for both the mainland and the peripheral island. Citing Rousseau, Bongie emphasises how the small island "will be destroyed in the end because soil is constantly being taken from it in order to repair the damage made by waves and storms to the big island [...] the substance of the weak is always used for the benefit of the powerful" (1998: 21). However, in Ó Direáin's case, the situation is reversed in that, while he does take imaginative soil from the island, he replaces it with a creation of his own mental island, reversing the theft and giving the new island the weight and feel of the former. In Ó Direáin's poetry we do not find, as Rousseau does, that the mainland (big island) benefited from the substance of the small island. Instead we find that his exile in Dublin was the main catalyst in focusing Ó Direáin's attention on the microcosm, rather than inspiring him to explore his mainland sensibilities and discoveries. However, what is clear is that, in giving power and precedence to his imagined island Ó Direáin's grasp of the real island began to falter and so in this instance it could be argued that the real island was weak as it was more susceptible to change and time and was also used to form and fill the requirements of the created island of the poet's work.

Bongie's *Islands and Exiles* studies the role and function of real and literary islands in conveying the difficulties of identity formation and national selfhood. Although he deals predominantly with Caribbean and Pacific islands, his hypothesis could be employed for islands globally. Emphasising the inherent duality of the island figure in history, geography and literature, Bongie highlights the variety of methods used to explore this doubleness. He writes that:

> [t]he island is a figure that can and must be read in more than one way: on the one hand, as the absolutely particular, a space complete unto itself and thus an ideal metaphor for a traditionally conceived, unified and unitary, identity; on the other, a fragment, a part of some greater whole from which it is in exile and to which is must be related – in an act of (never completed) completion that is always also, as it were, an ex-isle, a loss of the particular. The island is thus the site of a double identity – closed and open [...] (1998: 18).

The images of abundance and loss are striking here, and apply to individual, communal and national identity. The image of completeness of the island, as compared with that of the fragmented and scattered island is also important, although it is a more common one. What is most remarkable about this argument, however, is Bongie's interpretation of the island as a fragment but also as a complete territory in its own right. The displaced islander, then, could be thought of in a similar vein, a fragmentary citizen, at odds with the confines and boundaries of the city, constantly seeking realignment with the home place, but out of sync, both psychically and psychologically, with that home place following years of exile and nostalgic remembering. Bongie notes that "because this loss of self cannot be fully recorded or even acknowledged, one returns, repeatedly and impossibly, to that which has been left behind and can never be truly recovered" (1998: 18). There is a sense here that the exile, or the ex-isled individual, is now an island him/herself and cannot fit back onto the map of his/her geographical island; the mainland, the city is in the way of the island and the islanded individual.

Ó Direáin's own realisation of the mainland was awakened by returning emigrants, and not by innate wonderment about the larger island of Ireland to the east of his island home. This in itself is not very surprising, given Ó Direáin's immersion in the interior life of his own consciousness and that of the island's character, and his isolation from the principal events on the island, concerning economic and communication difficulties. It is clear that Ó Direáin had no interest in the bigger picture which was ahead of him and slowly encroaching around him. His poetic career, nonetheless, would depend on that picture and on the realities of life on and away from his island home. He comments:

> [c]aithfidh sé gur cheapas tráth de mo shaol nach raibh aon áit eile ar an domhan ach an t-oileán sceirdiúil úd thiar ar ucht na mara inar rugadh agus inar tógadh mé. Má cheap féin ní fada a mhaireas amhlaidh, mar bhí an saol mór ag brú isteach orm de réir a chéile. [...] Chloisinn féin cuid mhaith cainte uatha ar Boston, ar Dorchester, ar Woburn agus ar áiteanna eile tráth a mbídís cruinnithe cois tine (*Feamainn Bhealtaine*, 1961: 27).[71]

71 "I must have thought once that there was no other place on earth other than that windswept island back on the crest of the sea where I was born and raised. If I was of this mind, it wasn't long before I realised that this was not true, because the real world was beginning to make itself known to me. [...] I heard a considerable amount of talk from them [returning emigrants] about Boston, Dorchester, Woburn and other places when they gathered around the fireside [to recount their stories]".

Conclusions

This chapter has introduced the four main authors and their work which the rest of the book will discuss and examine. In approaching the authors in a biographical and critically-based fashion, it was intended to highlight their contributions to the canon of Irish literature, in both Irish and English, and also to position each author chronologically and bibliographically for ease of study and so as to consider spheres of influence. Many issues are clear upon concluding this chapter; chief among these are the impact of critical attention on all of the work presented, the importance of the presence and/or absence of sufficient translations of Ó Flaithearta and Ó Direáin's work, the obscurity of Lawless's contribution to Aran literature matched with the fame achieved by Synge's and finally the diverse, yet interrelated pictures which all four authors have contributed to our vision of the Aran Islands and its associated literary role.

Between Two Shores
Idir Dhá Chladach

> Postcolonial theory approaches history, politics and culture not as the
> "clash of civilisations", a notion which relentlessly replays distorted stere-
> otypes, but as a dialogue among cultures. In this dialogue all sides need
> the permission to speak and be heard.
> — CLARE CARROLL (in Carroll and King (eds), 2003: 15)

Introduction

In utilising some of postcolonial theory's literary tools to examine and
evaluate the literature discussed in the previous chapter, the purpose here
is to fully explore issues pertaining to language, to insider and outsider
perspectives on *islandness* and the literary power of the island, as well as
issues that call into question the importance of the geographical location
and the geo-cultural significance of certain places, and in particular islands.
Instead of analysing the texts at hand in relation to their nationalist or non-
nationalist underpinnings, the focus will be on issues pertaining to postcolonial theory's core constituents, namely: language, geographical power and
influence, and issues of peripheral and dominant viewpoints and contested
dialogues (insider and outsider; male and female perspectives) as presented
by Synge, Lawless, Ó Flaithearta and Ó Direáin. In placing emphasis on
postcolonial theory's inner workings rather than on its more controversial,
often politically-charged, outward or public position, this chapter will draw
attention to the value of the theory itself, an aspect which is often danger-

ously overshadowed by the debate surrounding postcolonialism and *the postcolonial* as an historical and cultural framework.

While the Aran Islands may not seem immediately colonially-significant, they were in fact heavily garrisoned for most of the period from 1600 to 1922 and were considered as vital trading and entry points for the Irish nation on the Western seaboard.[1] Though the Islands may have been considered as havens out of reach of colonial interference, they are clearly not without their colonial history. Máirtín Ó Direáin comments on the presence of the Black and Tans in Inis Mór, for example, writing: *"tháinig scata acu i dtír i bPort Mhuirbhí [...]. Níor fhágadar aon teach ó Bhungabhla go ceann thoir an tSrutháin gan dul isteach ann"* (1961: 52).[2]

Further complicating the linking of the Islands with any colonial activity is the fact that it jars considerably with our more recent understanding and interpretation of what the Islands represented and continue, albeit on a reduced scale, to represent today. The Irish Literary Revival in particular perpetuated the image of the Islands as far-removed from the colonially-saturated East of Ireland as could be geographically possible.[3] Tim Robinson's account of the killing of Lawrence McDonogh by Black and Tans on 19 December 1920, however, reveals much about the Islands' interaction with Crown Forces. Fifty Black and Tans had come ashore in Inis Mór in search of three Irish Volunteers who had sought refuge on the island; many of the islanders were themselves members of the Volunteers and quickly hid to avoid capture. Lawrence McDonogh was on his way to mass when two Tans ordered the parishoners to turn back. Deciding to take a lower road to the church, he was spotted and shot. A stone plaque now marks the spot where McDonogh was shot (Robinson, 1995: 165–167).

---

1   As a result of the garrison presence, surnames and bloodgroups continue to reflect the "intermingling" (Robinson, 1992: xii) between soldiers and islanders. See also Hackett and Folan (1958) and Relethford (1988).

2   "A crowd of them came ashore in Port Mhuirbhí. They entered each house from Bungabhla to the most easterly point of Sruthán".

3   One could almost say here that the Islands were, for many, removed from not just the East but from all the rest of Ireland also. See Powell, *Oileáin Árann*, 1983: 45, 51 and Roderic O'Flaherty (1846) in Hardiman, 1978: 92).

However, some islanders were sympathetic to the Tans' difficulties; Ó Direáin noted that one soldier who visited their home was polite and asked for bread (1961: 52) and Robinson also writes that the islanders were aware that the men were just doing their duty (1995: 167). Synge also remarked on the islanders' inherent lawlessness, and found stories where people were given sanctuary of great interest, and would later them as the basis for plays such as *The Playboy of the Western World*.[4]

The Aran Islands: Historical, Geographical and Cultural Significance

Though many scholars will be intimately familiar with the cultural import of the Aran Islands as cultural and linguistic areas, a brief consideration and summary of the historical and geographical significance of the Islands is offered here in order to provide historical setting and to flesh out the broader picture of how the Islands came to acquire such a position of substance in the Irish psyche and in Ireland's political and strategic constitution. Although one could be excused for thinking that the Aran Islands only became known to the wider world, particularly within Ireland itself, from the late eighteenth century on, there are accounts to be found of the

---

4   "This impulse to protect the criminal is universal in the west. It seems partly due to the association between justice and the hated English jurisdiction, but more directly to the primitive feeling of these people, who are never criminals yet always capable of crime, that a man will not do wrong unless he is under the influence of a passion which is as irresistible as a storm on the sea. If a man has killed his father, and is already sick and broken with remorse, they can see no reason why he should be dragged away and killed by the law. Such a man, they say, will be quiet all the rest of his life, and if you suggest that punishment is needed as an example, they ask, 'Would any one kill his father if he was able to help it?'" (Synge, *The Aran Islands*, 1992: 50). See also Robinson, 1992: xi–xv for further information on the disregard for the law on Aran.

Islands' religious settlements and the many saints who had monasteries there from the eighth century onwards. From around the twelfth century we get a much clearer picture of the human history of the Islands and of the many overlords and owners who took possession of Aran throughout successive generations (see Powell, 1983: 43–52, 55). Even at this early stage in Aran's history, whenever ownership of the Islands was passed on either through title or through plunder, it was the strategic position of the Islands that was of utmost importance to the new owners.

   An essential geological fact pertaining to the Islands relates to their bedrock: the Islands are composed of the same Lower Carboniferous Limestone as the Burren (Feehan, in Waddell *et al.*, 1994: 18; see also Robinson, 1986, 1995), which indicates immediately that the Islands once belonged to County Clare. Although this may seem quite insignificant nowadays, it is perhaps worth noting that the Islands were contested areas well before the coming to Ireland of the Vikings (AD 800) or later the English (from the fifteenth century onwards). In almost each foreword or introduction to literature or tourist-oriented material on Aran, one will find descriptions which make reference to their geographical position at the mouth of Galway Bay.⁵ Though this cartographical feature is salient in that it points to the natural defensive function of the Islands, it also plays neatly into the hands of writers and artists who took the Islands to represents places outside of the larger island of Ireland and as places just beyond the eye's reach, though often just within the imagination's grasp. In *A World of Stone: Life, Folklore and Legends of the Aran Islands* (O'Sullivan (ed.), 1976) the legend relating to the Islands' formation is also mentioned: "the islands are the remnants of a rock barrier that once stretched from Galway to Clare, trapping the waters of the present Galway

---

5   Roderic O' Flaherty notes the Islands' strategic importance: "All the ships for or from Galway, must saile by the isles of Aran, in either of the four roads, viz., Bealagh-Lougha Lurgan (so called of old, Lough Lurgan) between the west continent and the great island. Bealagh-na haite (so called of Binnaite, the next land over it in the great island), between the great island and the midle island. Bealagh na-fearboy, so called of the land next it in the middle island and the east island. And Bealagh-na-finnis, between that and the county of Clare" (in James Hardiman 1846 [1978], p. 92).

Bay in a gigantic lake" (1976: 7). Though there is little actual geological evidence for this, it does, however, reinforce the idea that the Islands were regarded as having both a protective and preservatory function well before they acquired the more culturally-oriented aspects of these functions in the early eighteenth century.

Tim Robinson:
The Cartographer's Contribution to the Debate

> But at the very moment that I look at a map – when I follow with my finger the route of a road, a contour line, when I cross here and not there a frontier, when I jump from one bank of a river to the other – at this very moment, a figure is extracted from the map ground, the figure of a projected journey, even if it is an imaginary one, a dreamed one. With that figure a narrative begins, with a before and an after, a point of departure and a point of arrival, a happy coming-back or a final permanent exile. The locus has become space [...] space "awakens" to narrative [...] (Marin, 1993: 414).

The most prolific and informative cartographically-inspired writer on the Aran Islands has been Tim Robinson, who has carried out sustained investigations of Aran's geographical and folkloric history over a period of more than thirty years. Though his maps of Aran (1980, updated in 1996) are without question the most highly regarded cartographical representations of the Islands[6], it is his literary work, as gathered in *Stones of Aran: Pilgrimage* and in *Stones of Aran: Labyrinth* that best illustrates the Islands' intricate detail and marked significance. The following quote from *Pilgrimage* highlights the Islands' geographical distinctiveness and also both their shared and individual character:

6   The maps are often cited and quoted in anthologies on Aran as well as being included in many prefaces and appendices to books on or about Aran; see Waddell *et al.*, 1994.

And in fact the three Aran Islands are fragments of a single, long, low escarpment, a broken arm of the limestone uplands known as the Burren on the mainland to the East. They had been blocked out and given their individual existence by the forces [of nature] long before the onset of the Ice Ages two hundred thousand years ago, but it was the glaciers creeping across and around them from the north that gave them their fineness or finish, polishing them like lenses for the clearer reading of the past. By the time the last of the ice-sheets had melted away about fifteen thousand years ago, large areas of the islands had been stripped of soil and all other debris of previous ages of erosion and left blank for the inscription of subsequent time. [...] To this retentive nature of the terrain itself must be added the conservative effect of its situation just beyond the farthest reach of Europe, wrapped in a turn or two of ocean. The material destructiveness of modern life is only now beginning to impinge on Aran, and until very recently the sole custodian of this land of total recall has been a folk-mind of matching tenacity, focused by the limitations of island life and with the powers of memory of an ancient oral culture (1986: 3–4).

This excerpt foregrounds two signal aspects found in most literary and cultural representations of the Aran Islands; the *createdness* of the land-scape and also the *tabula rasa* quality of the Islands, clean and available for any and all forthcoming interpretations. For Robinson, it is clear that the Islands are primarily areas akin to naturally-produced and sculpted chronicles of time's passage and nature's craft. However, Robinson also relates to the literary value attached to the Islands and is interested in the ways in which this has shaped our understanding of the Islands for better and for worse. Robinson is also intrigued by the various owners of the Islands and the developments which changes in ownership brought about throughout history, and latterly, by his own process of acquaintance with the terrain, both imaginative and actual, of Aran. The author immediately introduces the former name of the Islands – *Ára na Naomh*, or Aran of the Saints, and thereby establishes the important role which the Islands had in providing shelter and refuge for their many Saints and monastic settlements in centuries past. Much is made by authors such as Feehan, O'Connell and Waddell (see Waddell *et al.*, 1994) of Aran's monastic and religious importance, which emphasise the regard in which the Islands were held from the fifth century onwards. The qualities of the Edenic which the Islands were regarded as possessing is important in relation to the quasi-utopian linking of spiritual islands with paradises outside of the realms of the great nation.

Gerry Smyth (2001) notes that "[a]lthough an 'outsider' by birth, Robinson's maps are an attempt to capture what William J. Smyth in a related context referred to as 'the rounded sense of place as experienced by an insider' (1985: 4)" (2001: 53). Robinson's challenge was to re-map the Islands, a process which had not been carried out since the 1830s and in turn, record the placenames and the specific geological and geographical features of the Islands. However, in doing so, Robinson also created another kind of map; though the maps and their accompanying essays were:

> conceived perhaps as exercises in reclamation and preservation, [they] paradoxically contribute to this modern sensibility, construing Aran, Connemara and the Burren as landscapes retaining a special significance which may still be accessed by those from less existentially enriched environments (Smyth, 2001: 54).

The "special significance" which Robinson finds in the West and in Aran in particular, does not relate to romanticised visions of the region; in fact Robinson is often at pains to portray these places as living, though desolate areas, rather than giving a picture of a more rose-tinted nature.[7] However, from the very first descriptions of Aran and the West, there has been a strong tendency to contrast these places with the rest of the country, and in so doing, a custom of embellishment and exaggeration has built up around the Islands, often to their detriment. Smyth comments on this comparative culture in Ireland, with particular reference to Robinson's maps and the tribulations of offering a picture of a landscape which will inevitably be used as a contrast with somewhere else, with that "somewhere else" never quite being as authentic or intrinsically all-enticing as that which the map shows:

> The danger is that the "primitive" landscapes of the West are romanticised *vis-à-vis* other, somehow more mundane, less human landscapes, thus contributing to the notion of that region as a haven of authenticity in a world swamped with simulacra.

7　Robinson does, nonetheless, see that "Aran, that forlorn outcrop of want, was to become one of the chief shrines of this Ireland of the mind" (1992: xv).

There should be no doubting Robinson's commitment to the landscapes he remaps/
renames; what happens to those texts when they escape the deeply personalised,
face-to-face context in which they are conceived and executed is another matter.
"Everyone should be the mapper/namer of their own environment" may be the
intended message; "Come to the West of Ireland and save your soul" may be how
the work is actually being interpreted" (2001: 54).

His comments on mapping and naming raise two salient points. The first
has to do with the process of naming or of intimately knowing your own
place, and by extension knowing yourself more fully as a result of your surroundings, history and geographical location in the world. The second point
speaks to the wider implications of this "naming" and "knowing" phenomenon; from a colonial standpoint it signifies the mapping processes used by
colonists which did away with the country's own maps and placenames and
enforced the colonisers' language and cartographical understanding upon
the original versions. However, a second strand of this plan is one which
is far more revealing: in having a map or a cartographical code to a given
place, you not only have an entry point to this area, but you also, symbolically, take up actual *and* physical ownership of the region. The landscape
becomes indecipherable, unknown and most importantly, translated from
under its true owners' feet.

The most explicit example of this "naming-taming" (Friel, "Extracts
from a Sporadic Diary" in Tim Pat Coogan (ed.), *Ireland and the Arts*, 1986:
58) exercise is given voice in Brian Friel's *Translations* (1980), an exposition of the power of language and of placenames within the national and
personal psyche. Friel's play foregrounds a very important strain of colonial
interference: the desire to translate a colony's placenames and to impose
the colonists' own language upon the colonised nation so that they have
both linguistic and geographical ownership of their subjects and their
associated lands. However, in *Translations*, it becomes clear that awareness
of landscape and of national language is often only awakened in a people
when they are most under threat; colonisation stirred and perhaps (re)
created a greater sense of Irishness in the Irish people than the Irish were
themselves aware of in the first instance. Of significance also is the fact that
throughout both *Translations* the play, and the actual translation of the
placenames of the Irish countryside by English cartographical engineers,

a reinvigoration of the power of language and the power of place occurs. Brian Friel has commented that in writing *Translations* he consulted very few other sources except the letters of John O'Donovan, Colby's *Memoir: A Paper Landscape*, *The Hedge-Schools of Ireland* by Dowling, Steiner's *After Babel* ("Sporadic Diary", 1986: 57). O'Donovan was the leading scholar of the Irish language of his age and was employed by the Ordnance Survey in the 1830s to investigate Irish placenames.[8] "He thus embodied the precarious ambivalence of the *traduttore traditore* (translator traitor)" (O'Malley, 2003: 72). Thomas Davis, a supporter of O'Donovan's work, argued vociferously for the value of investigating and reenergising the nation's interest in itself: "to be able to keep [Ireland], and use it, and govern it, the men of Ireland must know what it is, what it was, and what it can be made" (Davis, "The History of Ireland", *Essays, Literary and Historical*, 1914: 382).[9]

Owning Aran: Plunder, Profit and Protection

The Aran Islands seemed throughout the centuries to "drop out of history" (Robinson, 1986: 6) just as they reappeared at various intervals. Daphne Pochin Mould's *The Aran Islands* (1972) gives considerable attention to the landlords and owners of Aran from the twelfth to the twentieth century. Her approach is similar to that adopted by J.W. O'Connell (in Waddell *et al.*, 1994) and Robinson (1986) in that she lists and considers the various

8   "The 'ordnance' of the Ordnance Survey's title is of course a word from the realm of military practice of using ordnance, i.e. shell fire, to make long distance measures. Hence it was members of the British Army who engaged in this final element of taming the country, by the process of toponymics. The practice of mapping remains within the control of the military in most countries" (Seosamh Mac Muirí, personal correspondence, May 2008).

9   Thomas Davis (1814–1845) was a leading member of the Young Ireland movement, a writer and poet and was also heavily involved in the nationalist newspaper the *Nation*; see F.S.L. Lyons, *Ireland Since the Famine*, London: 1963, pp. 104–107.

possessors of the Islands and then examines the associated strategic and historical implications. Both Mould and O'Connell begin by examining the Islands' twelfth-century owners, the O'Brien family of County Clare, with Mould noting that "the islands seem to have been more oriented toward County Clare than County Galway in the Middle Ages" (1972: 75). However, Robinson also writes that given the Islands' position stretched between the two provinces of Munster and Connacht, it is unsurprising that they were also claimed by the "Ferocious O'Flahertys" of Connacht, who eventually ousted the O'Briens (1986: 5). Robinson continues with a succinct account of what occurred next:

> The merchants of Galway city, who regarded the O'Flahertys as mere pirates and smugglers against whom the Aran O'Briens had given a measure of naval protection, sought to advance the claims of the latter by referring the dispute to Queen Elizabeth. But the even-handed finding of her commission was that, as monastic lands, and the monasteries having been declared dissolved, the islands belonged to neither O'Flahertys nor O'Briens but to the Crown itself. In 1587 the Queen then granted them to an Englishman on condition that he keep a force of twenty English foot-soldiers there, and a castle was built at Cill Éinne [in Inis Mór]. Aran, guarding the approaches to the rich port of Galway, was henceforth a pawn in a European strategy (1986: 5).

Land rights and title claims passed more or less between the English Crown and its loyal landlords and agents based in Ireland for much of the sixteenth and seventeenth century. Paramount in the minds of all owners of the Islands, however, was the strategic position of Aran and the role the Islands played in guarding the access points to Galway and, thus, to Ireland. Oliver St John, who was on board the MSS Carew in 1614, provided a contemporary estimate of the Islands' value in maritime and military terms:

> The road in the Isles of Aran called Gregory's Sound wherein a hundred ships of good burthen may ride at any one time. An enemy possessing this sound may be master of all the isles of Aran (which are well inhabited) and command all the bay (of Galway). It may be saved by building a fort in the Great Island and be of great use and importance. It was therefore projected and the late Queen gave a liberal allowance of land etc. for the building of it, but according to the usual fate of this kingdom, it was not looked after, and so cast away. The English, Britons and Portugalles (in

times past) had a great trade of fishing here for cod, ling, hake and conger, which would continue still if it were undertaken (in Pochin Mould, 1972: 78).

Both Mould and Robinson comment on The Earl of Clanrickarde's[10] letter of 1641 to the Earl of Thomond, which notes the importance of the Islands: "Amongst all, I find none more necessary to be preserved than the isles of Aran" (in Pochin Mould, 1972: 78). Though garrisons were established in Aran from the 1500s onwards and battalions of soldiers were stationed there until late in the seventeenth century, the eighteenth century's relative peacefulness is reflected in the paucity of references to the Islands found in the State papers (O'Connell, in Waddell *et al.*, 1994: 74).

The Aran Islands in the Nineteenth and Twentieth Centuries

The time-frame which most concerns this study begins in the 1890s, a period of much destitution and of social and economic change on the Aran Islands, as well as in the West of Ireland in general. Though the Famine did comparatively little damage to the Islands' population as compared with areas of Connemara, for example, the greatest suffering which the islanders faced in the mid-nineteenth century was "the tyranny of the absentee landlord" (O'Connell, in Waddell *et al.*, 1994: 74).[11] In his essay "Changing Fortunes on the Aran Islands in the 1890s", Brian Harvey notes that:

> [b]y the turn of the twentieth century the West of Ireland had become a geographical expression synonymous with poverty and destitution. [...] Hardship on the islands off Mayo and Galway was so severe [...] that London philanthropists set up a committee to launch a large-scale relief programme (Harvey, 1991: 237).

10   Clanrickarde had ownership of the Islands for a time in the 1640s.

11   Population of the Aran Islands in 1841 was 3,529 as compared with the population of 1851 when population fell to 3,333. The population fell by only 9.5 percent during this period (Ó Gráda, 1999: 205).

The Congested Districts Board [CDB], which had been established in
1891, sought to aid areas such as Aran which were in financial and social
difficulty; a sub-committee of the CDB sought to establish a telegraph
communication link with the Islands and also to improve fishing and farming infrastructure.[12] The impetus to advance communication links with
the Islands was an important departure, even though it was viewed by
contemporary observers as a fairly innocuous move on the government's
part. However, this was not a purely benevolent development on the government's behalf; they also had more utilitarian motives for the enterprise.
Establishing lines of communication with the Aran Islands would, essentially, allow not just the islanders to have contact with the mainland, and
thus with medical support, but would also allow the mainland to have a
level of communicative control over the Islands and the islanders themselves. Another central facet of the creation of this telegraph service lies in
the more covert concept of still having a modicum of dominance over and
knowledge of the happenings on the Islands; there appears to have been
a fear of sorts about the potential strength of the Islands' people if their
needs were not met and so the authorities on the mainland and in London
decided to keep both an eye and an ear on proceedings there through this
new link. However, in debates from various meetings and letters presented
to CDB gatherings at the time, it is clear that, whilst many were sympathetic to the plight of the islanders, in the form of priests and missionaries
previously stationed on the Islands, there was a greater majority of people
who felt that the islanders were already in receipt of enough grants and aid
and that there were far worse-off people to be helped in other rural parts
of Connacht. Given that the Islands were relatively unknown entities, as
it were, with regard to their nationalist or republican tendencies, Harvey
notes that "for a population of only 3,163 there were three barracks and 18
policemen" (1991: 239). This is a noteworthy observation, not least because
it highlights the continual presence of armed forces on the Islands (over

12   The CDB also encouraged the West's fishing industry to modernise, and paid boats
      from Arklow to work out of Aran. The harbours were also improved around this
      time. See Robinson (1992: xv), and Breathnach (2005).

150 years of garrison presence in total) and also shows the tactical regard in which the Islands were held – i.e. as places of potential uprising and also as places of strategic importance – up until the early 1900s.

The establishment of the telegraph on the Islands "was speedy and was clearly motivated by a desire to promote purposeful economic development" (Harvey, 1991: 249). However, the Aran Islands were not well regarded, aided or thought worthy of preservation at a time when they most needed it. This revelation foreshadows an almost complete change in attitude just a few short years later with the establishment of the Irish Literary Revival and the surge to de-anglicise the country and protect the areas of Ireland most culturally and geographically valuable to their cause. However, it is also essential to document that the realities of poverty and destitution were still prevalent concerns and did not dissipate with the arrival of curious anthropologists and authors, although from some accounts at the time, this may have seemed to be very much the case.

Aran: Language and Essentialism

In answering Davis's call to keep, use, govern and know Ireland, the Irish people, and in particular historians, decided to designate and commemorate certain aspects as "Irish". O'Callaghan (2004) documents the prevalence of the essentialist reading of Irish history in both national consciousness and in traditional historiography. O'Callaghan emphasises

> the tendency, particularly evident in the writing of national history, to assemble historical knowledge in the form of a narrative that leads to an ending or goal. The goal is either the current state of affairs or the one about to be achieved. [...] A teleological construal of history is fundamental to the essentialist view of nationality [...] this elucidation of history is particularly evident in the case of Ireland, not only in nationalist propaganda but also in much scholarly historiography. Closely related is the tendency to see modern nations predestined in ancient and medieval societies and cultures. Thus, in most conceptualisations of Ireland, popular and scholarly, there figures an ancient Gaelic world seen as the modern nation in embryo (2004: 1–2).

Another point which O'Callaghan makes relates to the fact that "[i]n all colonial societies, certain sections attempted to idealise the indigenous culture in order to provide an alternative to that disseminated by the colonial power" (2004: 4). Integral to Ireland's identity and culture was its language; the colonists understood its functional role as a locus of power and sought to destroy it and replace it with their own to allow for administrative ease, the passing of laws, the mapping of the country, for example, and for ideological control. It was not enough to regain Irish freedom from English colonisation; it was also vital to make the emerging Irish state Gaelic in every sense of the word. In "thinking ahead to the kind of Ireland that might emerge following the achievement of independence [...] Michael Collins argued that 'we can fill our minds with Gaelic ideas and our lives with Gaelic customs, until there is no room for any other'" (Farren, in O'Callaghan, 2004: 4). In 1917, the architects of the new state sought to make Ireland Gaelic as well as independent. In fact, the Sinn Féin constitution "stipulated that, in an independent Ireland, education would be made truly national by the compulsory teaching of the Irish language and Irish history. The system of education would be used to build an 'Irish Ireland'" (O'Callaghan, 2004: 7–8). Much of the new curriculum drew on stories of old, pre-colonial Ireland, and by placing Irish at its core, sought to capitalise upon "the language as the distinctive lifeline and the principal thread of Irish nationality" (MacNeill, *An Claidheamh Soluis*, 5 October 1907, in O'Callaghan, 2004: 9). This indicated that language and history would be closely aligned as twin forces in an effort to undo the cultural and linguistic incursions of colonialism. Concurrently, at least in the eyes of education policy makers, Irish would be revived as a spoken language. The future of the Irish language was inextricably linked with its past. Irish, then, was to be seen as "the language of ancestors: the language of the nation used to reflect the nation back in time" (Tymoczko and Ireland, 2003b: 3).

However, "the conception of history and history teaching as a method of restoring and renewing the Gaelic past did not consider those whose past was not a Gaelic one" (O'Callaghan, 2004: 9). For example, in 1924, the *Catholic Bulletin* declared that "the Irish nation is the Gaelic nation; its language and literature is the Gaelic language; its history is the history of the Gael. All other elements have no place [...]" (1924: 269). In linking nationalism and the cultural revival in this way, the Catholic Church inextricably related itself to both pursuits. Those of unionist or Protestant upbringing or background were thus effectively written out of the revival's hierarchy and were told that as they did not conform to either the linguistic or religious criteria laid out, that this ruled them out of involvement in the cause. Though Roy Foster sharply criticised the cultural revival movement, stating that "the emotions focused by cultural revivalism around the turn of the century were fundamentally sectarian and even racialist" (*Modern Ireland 1600–1972*, 1988: 453), Brian Murphy has gone on to question this assertion on the basis that the ideals of the Gaelic League were clearly non-sectarian (1994: 80–84). What is of interest here, however, is that it is clear despite the stated non-sectarian ethos of the League, that there was an element of suspicion evident amongst its membership with regard to religious background and nationalist and/or unionist outlook of other members. It is understandable, then, that many people had difficulty in comprehending how writers such as Synge and Lawless could come from Anglo-Irish Protestant backgrounds and yet harbour such strong nationally-based sentiments in their work. Of course, it had not become evident to most people at this stage that Ireland was turning over a new literary and cultural page in its history, a page which would be created in the main by those who did not exactly fit the description of their class or political or personal persuasion as outlined in the *Catholic Bulletin* or by the greater majority of Irish nationalists.

Folklore, Myth, Tradition and Modernity: Aran as Authentic?

The West of Ireland provided a stable and traditional self-image for the Irish nation. In *Locating Irish Folklore: Tradition, Modernity, Identity* (2000), Ó Giolláin traces Irish folkloric traditions and examines the Anglo-Irish obsession with gaining access to the authenticity-rich West of Ireland.

Folklore, an area of Irish cultural history which has a place in popular culture and is prominent but ill-defined, "developed partly as a 'nationalist' reaction to a metropolitan culture with universal pretensions". In Ireland "it was a key element of modern history and national identity" (Ó Giolláin, 2000: 4). Bound up in this nationalist enterprise was the keen interest of many cultural-nationalists in Ireland's past, and thus the emphasis on looking back to real and authentic Ireland was more highly regarded than attempting to compromise with the oncoming tide of present and future modernity. The evasion of this "unavoidable compromise" (2000: 4) isolated both the nationalist cause and its relationship with folklore within the very areas which they chose to glorify and preserve, "limiting the concept of folklore to the countryside, and viewing it as the basis for a national culture" (2000: 4). Writing that "[f]olklore [has] an immediate emotional resonance" (2000: 2), Ó Giolláin explains how such a phenomenon became intrinsically linked with notions of the past and with sentimental nostalgia for days of old.

> It seems to have to do with the past, or at least the residual. It has to do with the countryside, in Ireland particularly with the West and even more so with the Irish-speaking West. Perhaps most of all with places like the Aran Islands or the abandoned Blaskets. It has to do with old people rather than young people. [...] If it tells stories it is orally and in intimate settings. It belongs more under a thatched than a slated roof, by a turf fire rather than a radiator, in a humble kitchen as opposed to elegant drawing-room. If it travels on land it is by donkey, bicycle, or – perhaps – Morris Minor. If it travels by sea it is by *currach* rather than by yacht (2000: 2).

However, Ó Giolláin concludes this list of ideas surrounding the traditional by stating that "these apparent truisms are not valid any more – if they ever were" (2000: 2). Most definitions of Irishness, or explanations of the make-up of real and authentic Irish identity, will invariably include some or all of the elements of traditional, folkloric Ireland which Ó Giolláin cites. Though Ó Giolláin might find that these truisms no longer apply in the Irish context, the promotion of Ireland both at home and abroad relies almost exclusively on the allegedly real nature of these images. Added to this representational mine-field is the Irish people's allegiance to these images, real or not, as something quintessentially and uniquely Irish, and something which is available to them upon entering the pseudo-Edenic geographical location of the West of Ireland in particular. It would appear that authenticity is not the overriding factor here; there is much more emphasis placed on having symbols of and recognisable associations with these mythical parts of Ireland. The real is secondary, and often detrimental to popular conceptions of what the West of Ireland should be like. However, again for the vast majority of people, their images and bonds with the West are so well created and widespread as to appear real and thus no alternatives are sought or considered. However, could there be anywhere in modern Ireland where some of these images, mostly of the country's past, are still viable realities, and if so, are they traditional in the purest sense of the word, or have they had to make way for modernity? David Gross's *The Past in Ruins: Tradition and the Critiques of Modernity* (1992) outlines the criteria for authenticity in modernity: "the linking of a minimum of three generations, the carrying of spiritual or moral prestige and the communication of a sense of continuity between the past and present, this feeling of consecutiveness" (1992: 9). Ó Giolláin writes that "[t]radition is imagined as a thread linking us to our shared past as we move forward and at the same time it legitimates what we do in the present" (2000: 8–9).

The Creation of the Gaeltacht: A Response to The Galltacht?

Before analysing the literature of the Aran Islands, another aspect of the West of Ireland's unique character and composition must be discussed and examined. The West of Ireland's linguistic composition is an essential field of inquiry and also shows signs of isolation and marginalisation in common with the region's geographical and historical position. In her essay *Cruthú Constráide agus an Turas Siar: An Ghaeltacht i dtús an Fichiú hAois* (2000)[13]

---

13 "The Creation of a Construct and the Journey West: The Gaeltacht at the start of the Twentieth Century."

Caitríona Ó Torna presents and develops the concept of the Gaeltacht, or
Irish speaking area, with particular reference to the Connacht Gaeltacht:

> [i]s constráid í an Ghaeltacht, mar a thuigtear inniu í, a tháinig chun cinn i rith aimsir
> na hAthbheochana teanga in Éirinn ag deireadh an naoú haois déag agus ag tús an
> fichiú haois. [...] nuair a samhlaíodh an Ghaeltacht mar thearmann spioradálta agus
> cultúrtha do mhuintir na hÉireann i gcoitinne (2000: 51).[14]

Drawing heavily on Kiberd's concept of the creation or (re)invention of
the Irish nation during the late nineteenth century, Ó Torna remarks on a
similar (re)creation of a distinct and separate region of Ireland which was
viewed as having linguistic and spiritual properties akin to that of Ireland
prior to colonisation and the cultural encroachment which this entailed.
Noting that, in a manner similar to the relationship advanced by Kiberd
with regard to Ireland and England, the Irish people sought out a region
that was uniquely Irish in nature and language in order to define them in the
face of colonial adversity, Ó Torna draws attention to the development of
the construction of such a place in the West of Ireland and also the growth
in the interest in travelling to such a place which followed its creation. As
Kiberd explains in *Inventing Ireland*, English writers from Cambrensis'
time sought to portray Ireland and the Irish as markedly different to their
own culture and nation in a project of self-definition. Formulaically then,
Ireland was depicted as not-England and similarly, England as not-Ireland
(1996: 30). In much the same way, Ó Torna comments, the conscious and
deliberate creation of a haven of culture and tradition in the West of Ireland
Gaeltacht was an exercise in designating what was *real* Ireland as opposed
to what was colonially-saturated Ireland. To adopt Kiberd's rule, the West
was Irish-Ireland and the rest of the country was the complete antithesis
of the region – it was English-Ireland, or at the very least, it was not the
Ireland that cultural and militant nationalists wished it would or could be
again. A literary evocation of this counterpoint takes place in James Joyce's

14 "The Gaeltacht, as we understand it today, is a construction, which came to prominence
    during the time of the Revival of the language in Ireland at the end of the nineteenth
    century and at the beginning of the twentieth century. [...] when the Gaeltacht was
    imagined as a spiritual and cultural sanctuary for the people of Ireland in general".

"The Dead", where Miss Ivors implores Gabriel Conroy to embrace the West of Ireland. Inviting him to go on an excursion to the Aran Islands, where "it will be splendid out in the Atlantic" (*Dubliners*, 1914: 242), Miss Ivors is disgusted to find that Conroy is completely uninterested in his own country. When he mentions his desire to travel around Europe, Miss Ivors calls him a "West Briton" (1914: 243). Seán Ó Ríordáin's call for a return to the Gaeltacht so as to facilitate a return to the well of language itself was aimed at Irish-language writers (*"Fill Arís* / Return Again", 1964: 41). Fearing the English language's "halter" (Ó Tuama, 1978: 53) on fellow poets' Irish, he advised them to travel to the most westerly districts of the Munster Gaeltacht and to replenish their souls and their pens:

Téir faobhar na faille siar tráthnóna gréine	Go west by the cliff's edge to Corca Dhuibhne
[...]	
Is chífir thiar ag bun na spéire ag ráthaíocht ann	And you will see on the horizon flourishing there
An Uimhir Dhé, is an Modh Foshuiteach	The Dual Number, and the Subjunctive Mood,
Is an tuiseal gairmeach ar bhéalabh daoine:	The Vocative Case on people's lips:
[...]	
Buail is osclófar	Knock and find an opening
D'intinn féin is do chló ceart	For your own soul and true form.[15]

The Journey Back and the Journey West: Romanticism and the Romantic View

Clearly [...] traditional pre-colonial indigenous forms are especially important both in the syncretic practice which develops and as an expression of a renewed sense of identity and self-value in the independence period. [...] the artist must return to the traditional sources for inspiration itself (Ashcroft *et al.*, 1989: 178).

15   Collinge's translation (1985: 385).

A chief strand in the West's re-awakening was the *"turas siar"* (Ó Torna, 2000: 51), the journey back or West, whereby Conradh na Gaeilge members organised field and day-trips to the Gaeltacht for people who wished to escape urban centre such as Dublin for a short time. The inherent notion of the passage of time implied in the phraseology of posters and other propaganda material for these outings was key, not least for the correlation it made between the past and the West, as though both were phenomena which implied the same thing. In the Irish word *"siar"*, this linkage is intrinsically evident, and though the English speaking audience may have been aware of this, it is also likely that the depictions of the West of Ireland as a place and a culture beyond time, or in fact as behind or outside of the constraints of time, did much to promote the notion of the West as being in a state of cultural and linguistic stasis, thus enabling it to preserve, in museum-fashion, its people and their traditions without fear of colonial incursion.

Ó Torna also documents the growth of the vision of Ireland as a bifurcated country from the times of eighteenth- and nineteenth-century Romanticism. While Ireland was progressing in historical terms during this period, a considerable interest was given to stories of past glories and traditions which gave Ireland's character a Janus-faced view of itself, one facing forward and one very much facing back in time and cultural outlook. The importance of a simple, uncomplicated way of life, coupled with a fluency of native language led commentators such as J.G. Herder to conclude that an amalgam of culture, language and nation was all the Irish needed to unite in order to maintain the country's distinctive position and heritage (1986: 149). Within the Romantic tradition there was also a noticeable interest in (re)connecting with the people who lived in the most remote areas of Ireland; predictably many of these people lived in Gaeltacht areas, as those who spoke Irish were viewed as being the purest of citizens from a cultural perspective, as well as being in possession of knowledge on customs and traditions which were dying out in other parts of the country. The seeking out of these "natives" by revivalists was not dissimilar to the project which English writers had in mind when contrasting the Irish people with their own people; in providing a contradistinction between real, true Irish people with Irish people who were slowly turning their backs on tradition and language, Romanticists were showing how a turn back to what they saw as authentic Ireland was imperative if the nation was to continue to sustain its unique character. The emphasis on communication between city dwellers and their rural cousins was all-important, as John Rennie Short explains:

> In comparison to the "savages" of the classicists the romantics saw the noble savage as being closer to a purer, simpler way of life. The life of the primitive other became a poignant contrast with the spiritual impoverishment and crude materialism of the contemporary. Where the classicists saw men no different from beasts, the romantics perceived the people of the golden age and a vision of life before the fall (1991: 53).

This idealisation of the natives and their culture is a highly important process of contrast and identification, but, as Ó Torna points out, the name *gaeltacht* itself stemmed from another process of defining one culture against the other, this time the English-speaking region of Ireland (the *galltacht*) against the Irish-speaking region, which became known as the *gaeltacht*. In a very illuminating explanation, Ó Torna explores the designation of the *gaeltacht* from its earliest incarnation and finds that *"[n]í ceantar pobal-teanga a bhí i gceist leis an bhfocal seo ó thus"* (2000: 53).[16] In fact, great changes occurred in relation to how the word was used from the seventeenth century onwards, when *gaeltacht* referred to a group of Irish speakers or to Irish heritage (Ó Torna, 2000: 53), without any mention of a specific locale or district for this language usage which we have come to associate with it today. Ó Torna writes that it was not until cultural revival times that the added dimension of region or specific area became attached to the concept of *gaeltacht*. Angela Bourke also notes that the word *gaeltacht* did not initially suggest a particular geographical location, but "something much more 'virtual': Gaelic-speaking people as a language community and cultural polity, wherever they happened to be" (2006: 82).

A fascinating aspect of this debate focuses on the fact that the word *galltacht* was in use in excess of three hundred years before the word

---

16 "At the outset, the *gaeltacht* was not defined as a region of Irish language distinction".

gaeltacht came into being (Ó Torna, 2000: 53–54). This chronology may
seem to contradict the ancientness commonly associated with our understanding of the *Gaeltacht*. It is, nonetheless, critical to see that the process
of defining one region against the virtues of another in order to achieve an
identity contrapuntal to the other is reciprocated not just by nations but
by smaller regions within one nation. Drawing again on Kiberd's analysis
of the English-Irish definitional relationship, Ó Torna comments that it is
often the more foreign of the pair that asserts its own identity on the matter
first (in this case, the English speakers designated the *galltacht* for their
own group identity) and that the opposing group's identity is only formed
or named later, invariably termed in ways that suggest their inferiority:

> *Ní cóir neamhshuim a dhéanamh de gur sa Bhéarla a fheictear trácht ar an Ghaeltacht
> naoi mbliana níos luaithe ná sa Ghaeilge, [...]. Is féidir a áiteamh gur cruthúnas é seo
> ar choincheapú na Gaeltachta ón iasacht, is é sin, ón nGalltacht agus sa Bhéarla. Is mar
> chuid de phróiseas bunaithe agus buanaithe chonstráid na Gaeltachta a deineadh tréithe
> ar leith a shamhlú leis na ceantair sin agus le muintir na gceantar* (2000: 59).[17]

During the revival period two quite distinct groups of nationalists began to
emerge, as Philip O'Leary (1994) has demonstrated. In *The Prose Literature
of the Gaelic Revival 1881–1921: Ideology and Innovation*, O'Leary documents the differences between what he refers to as "progressive nationalists
and nativist nationalists" (1994: 14–15). O'Leary explains these classifications further:

> [...] with regard to the central question of the Revival, the nativist position was
> essentialist and (pre)determinist, asserting that the answer had already been found
> in Ireland and had only to be rediscovered and properly understood in the light of
> the existing Gaelic tradition. Their focus was thus inward, *siar* in the dual sense of
> the Irish word, back to a real, imagined, or invented past where that tradition was

17   "It is important that it was in English that the first mention of the *Gaeltacht* was
      made and that it appeared nine years before any mention of it was made in Irish.
      It could be said then that this is evidence of the conception of the Gaeltacht from
      without, that is, from the Galltacht and from English. As a part of the process of
      founding and of making permanent the construction of the Gaeltacht, special traits
      were attached to the areas and given to the people of these areas".

most vibrant, and to the West, where it had maintained itself most tenaciously. Gaelic progressivism, on the other hand, accepted the reality of cultural discontinuity and believed that the emergent Gaelic nation would have to literally move forward, advancing both toward the future and toward the wider world from which it had so long been artificially isolated by British colonialism (1994: 15–16).

It might be possible to neatly define both positions as either looking for answers already provided by the past or as looking for answers that only the future could supply. One important image which nativists called upon time and again was of a "protective wall" (O'Leary, 1994: 19) or rampart which would ensure, according to an tAthair Peadar Ua Laoghaire, that "[i]f Irish is inside, infidelity must remain outside" (in O'Leary, 1994: 20). For others of nativist persuasion, this wall was predominantly represented in the form of the native language: "[t]here is no stronger rampart behind which nationality can entrench itself than a native language. Erect, then, the defence around your nationality which your foreign enemy has so long striven to destroy" (Father Patrick F. Kavanagh, *Ireland's Defence – Her Language*, Gaelic League pamphlet, 1902: 10; quoted in O'Leary, 1994: 20). In a more extreme lecture, Father Peter Yorke, a close friend of Father Eoghan O'Growney,[18] declared that:

> if a wall of brass, as Dean Swift said, was built one thousand feet high around Ireland it would be for the benefit of her people [...] if they could tow Ireland out into the Atlantic and free it entirely from English and Continental influences that such a measure would not be too much to restore to Ireland her diminishing nationality ("The Turning of the Tide", Lecture by Father P.C. Cooke, 16 September 1899; quoted in O'Leary, 1994: 20).

Proponents of these extreme measures were later satirised for their stringent views and were too often seen as representative of the Gaelic movement overall (O'Leary, 1994: 20). United by what Terence Brown has termed "a vision of national fragility" (1985: 62), many of these nativists believed

---

18   Father Eoghan O'Growney, a leading Gaelic League figure, visited Inis Meáin in 1885 and stayed in what is now commonly known as Synge's Cottage (Robinson, 1986: 129).

that the primary function of the Irish language and "its embryonic modern literature was to nurture and protect" native Irish values against the threat posed by English (O'Leary, 1994: 20). As late as 1942, however, there is still mention made of the need to fortify the country against the battering of the English language, and it is of note that the term "embankment" is used in much the same manner as "wall" and "rampart" were used earlier. Thomas Derrig, Minister for Education from 1932 to 1948, continued the government's plan to have the Irish language as the central core of the education system; he claimed, in a similar fashion to Pearse and MacNeill, that "[w]e in this country are threatened to be engulfed by the seas of English speech [...] We are trying to set up these embankments of Irish [...] in order to keep out the tide of Anglicisation" (*Dáil Debates*, 2 June 1942: cols. 761–762).[19] Many of these calls to protect Ireland and the Irish language invoked the twin images of water and erosion. This allusion draws attention to Ireland's island identity and to its vulnerability, while also emphasising the relatively short distance between England and Ireland and their shared sea. Notions of connectedness, of isolation and of penetrability, or the lack thereof, are all to the fore here.

In all these debates, what appears as most threatened and as most valuable is the Irish language; while nativism sought to vehemently protect the Irish language, progressivism sought to align Ireland's unique linguistic, cultural and literary heritage with European, often criticised by the nativists as "cosmopolitan", literary traditions. Without abandoning Ireland's past and while still "returning to the folk" (Hutchinson, 1987: 33), progressivism pursued the goal of "catapult[ing] the nation from present backwardness and divisions to the most advanced state of social development" (Hutchinson, 1987: 33). English literature was seen by nativists as severely damaging to their project, and thus it is straightforward enough to see why they objected so strongly to writers such as Synge and Yeats, being Anglo-Irish, Protestant (though Synge was of no religion at this time) and writing in English for an English language audience. That the

19   Full speech available at: <http://historical-debates.oireachtas.ie/D/0087/D.0087. 194206020021.html>.

Irish language was so strongly defended by priests and religious academics is not surprising either, given that Latin, with which the Irish language
was aligned, was the language of the Catholic faith and provided a code to
the nation's psyche which the English coloniser could not decipher. Thus,
regarded as guardian and protector (Ó Torna, 2000: 60) of Ireland's religion and as the most effective weapon against the literature of the Literary
Revival, which nativism viewed as being immoral (Ó Torna, 2000: 60), it
was, in Ó Torna's words

> *furasta a thuiscint conas ar glacadh leis gurbh iad ceantair dhúchais na Gaeilge gabhdán*
> *an traidisiúin, an Ghaelachais agus na sáruaisleachta* – a zone of pristine nativism,
> *mar a thugann Declan Kiberd (1996, 336) orthu* (2000: 60).[20]

Newspapers which were proponents of the cultural revolution and of
Conradh na Gaeilge such as *Fáinne an Lae* and *An Claidheamh Soluis*
regularly advocated the benefits of sojourns in the West of Ireland; reports
of the London branch of Conradh na Gaeilge visiting the West were noted
as was the growth in numbers of Irish League members holidaying in the
Gaeltacht region (Ó Torna, 2000: 61). However, some members, affili-
ated with progressivism, were wary of the value of such excursions, and of
the level of realism involved in representations given afterwards by those
who had visited the region. Pádraic Pearse was one such person; in *An
Claidheamh Solais* in 1902, he wrote that

> [i]t is worse than useless for a stray holiday-making Gaelic Leaguer to lecture grey-
> haired men and women, old enough to be his grandfather or grandmother, on the
> error of their ways (in Ó Torna, 2000: 62).

Much of Pearse's disapproval of such Leaguers' attitudes to the native
people of the West of Ireland reflects a concern for respect for the proponents of tradition but also a desire not to destabilise the authenticity and
the cultural power of these places and people. Pearse was hyper-critical

---

20   "... easy to understand why it was accepted that areas where Irish was spoken were
      receptacles of tradition, or Irishness and of super-nobility – a zone of pristine nativ-
      ism, as Declan Kiberd calls them".

of the influences of many of his own compatriots and believed that they were doing more damage to the West and the Irish language than colonialism and the English had done previous to this time. The sanctity with which the West was regarded was of paramount importance during the late nineteenth and early twentieth century, and though many disagreed on how best to protect the character of the West of Ireland during these years, most agreed that its cultural and spiritual value was incalculable. Synge's observations on the League's work are insightful, and suggest a mix of attitudes amongst the islanders regarding the learning of written Irish. He notes that the older generation on Inis Meáin displayed little interest in the language movement and that they placed more emphasis on the learning of English: "they speak English to their children, to render them more capable of making their way in life" (1992: 68). However, the island women, under the auspices of *Craobh na mBan*, or the Women's League, enthusiastically engaged with the efforts to promote the language. Úna Ní Fhaircheallaigh (Agnes O'Farrelly), a young Irish scholar staying at the same cottage just vacated by Synge, recorded the activities of the League in her diary and also helped with the League's work while there. Later published under the title *Smaointe ar Árainn* (Thoughts on Aran), Ní Fhaircheallaigh's diary is an invaluable source-book for this period of change on the Islands.[21] Tomás Bán Ó Coincheanainn, a native of Inis Meáin, was also heavily involved in Conradh na Gaeilge's work on the Irish mainland. He is credited with being one of the League's finest teachers and promoters (Sisson, 2004: 208).[22]

Caoilfhionn Nic Pháidín's *Fáinne an Lae agus an Athbheochan 1898–1900* (1998) provides a significant insight into the power of the English-speaking upper and middle classes during this signal period of cultural

21   See O'Farelly (2010 [1902]), *Smaointe ar Árainn / Thoughts on Aran* (translated and edited by Ríona Nic Congáil) and Nic Congáil, R. (2010) *Úna Ní Fhaircheallaigh agus an Fhís Útóipeach Ghaelach*.

22   Inis Meáin poet Dara Beag Ó Fátharta commemorates Tomás's work in the lines: "*Nuair a bhí Conradh na Gaeilge ag neartú a chuid fréamh / Bhí Coincheanainn go héifeachtach bláfar /* When Conradh na Gaeilge was strengthening its roots / Coincheanainn was blossoming" ("*Aimsir Synge*", 1990: 4).

change in Ireland. Though not frequently acknowledged, it was vital to the Irish language cause to get the support of these classes behind it. Joep Leerssen summarises the importance of this support:

> [t]he Gaelic language survived, not so much because the community of its native speakers survived and maintained the language, but because an English-speaking urban middle class in Ireland became sensitized to a Gaelic cultural heritage and adopted a Gaelic cultural identity of their own (1996: 133).

The central influence of Church and cultural nationalist groups is widely acknowledged, but perhaps the most important group of all is also the least considered in this debate: the people of the Gaeltacht themselves. Leerssen's analysis of the Gaeltacht individual's crucial position illuminates the almost impossible weight of authenticity he/she was expected to represent:

> The peasant is to provide symbolical goods [...] he is asked to furnish a native knowledge of the language [...] he is asked to provide that authenticity and that unbroken link with past traditions, which the revivalists by definition do not have, and cannot do without [...]. Occasionally his poems are written down and published, and he can win medals and diplomas by dancing at Oireachtas or Feis; but that is all he gets out of the bargain [...] the rural peasant is held to embody authentic, Gaelic Ireland, but his role in national developments and politics is a passive submissive one; the urban bourgeoisie holds an active leading position in the socio-economic and political sphere but at the same time lacks cultural authenticity. It is in these terms that a pattern of cultural trade-off (some might say exploitation) emerges (1996: 143).

Nic Pháidín remarks upon a similar basic construction of the native in the eyes of the revivalists; however, she is also keen to stress that the dignity and honour of the people of the Gaeltacht was very much at the heart of Gaelic Leagues' efforts to reinvigorate the region (1998: 66). What is integral to Leerssen's observation, however, is that, as Nic Pháidín also emphasises, *"ba iad 'an dream sin thuas i mBaile Átha Claith', mar a thugtaí orthu, a leag síos na rialacha ó thus"* (1998: 66).[23] Even with the best of intentions, it appears that a *them and us* relationship developed between

23   "It was 'that crowd up in Dublin', as they were called, who laid down the rules from the start".

the members of the Gaelic League and the very people they held in such esteem. The people of the Gaeltacht were objectified and categorised in neat and quantifiable order; Nic Pháidín notes that this outlook was held mostly by the leaders of the League, located for the most part in Dublin, rather than by the organisers or the teachers who spent considerably longer periods of time amongst Gaeltacht people (1998: 66). This bureaucratic mentality was for the most part ignored by members and did not signify anything more sinister, yet it does indicate the variously divergent ways in which those in the East of the country decided those in the West should be protected without consulting the very people involved.

Language as Power:
"Come to the West of Ireland and Save Your Soul"

Language is both a cultural and a colonial tool. In Ireland's case in par-ticular, the Irish language was held in national, psychological and religious regard as the living link with the nation's past. In *Inventing Ireland*, Declan Kiberd pays considerable attention to the theme of language and its power and subversive applications within the colonial and postcolonial situation. Perhaps no other area in Postcolonialism is as strongly contested, hotly debated or fervently written about as is the area of language. Its func-tion as a locus of power in the colonial arena, and its subversive nature in the "writing back" phase of postcolonial literature are important to note. Ireland's dual tradition brings to the fore the importance of language as a preservatory tool in that it can encapsulate and thus protect a language, saving it from the erosion brought about by colonisation and linguistic subjugation. Both Kiberd and Deane point to the colonial enterprise of naming, re-naming and to the dominatory power of the colonists' lan-guage over the people whom they colonise. With particular allusion to *Translations*, Seamus Deane treats of the influence that names have in the imperial context; "naming is a kind of owning and a kind of knowing.

Name a place and you have a reference, name a number of places and you have a system of relational references that can be organised on a map. The map itself can then be given a name – say, Ireland" (Deane in Peacock, 1992: 103). Declan Kiberd continues this "naming and owning" metaphor in the very title of his work "Inventing Ireland", as though it was a linguistic experiment instead of a geographical entity. However, for Kiberd, Ireland is a laboratory of sorts; "[t]hrough many centuries, Ireland was pressed into service as a foil to set off English virtues, as a laboratory in which to conduct experiments, and as a fantasy-land in which to meet fairies and monsters" (*Inventing Ireland*, 1996: 1). Thus Ireland became England's colonial, linguistic and cultural experiment; one based crucially around the power of language to subjugate, "civilise" and indoctrinate a colony to ensure its compliance with the rules and rubric of imperialism. The ensuing results of this experiment then, led to a deep-seated suspicion about language among the colonised people with regard to languages' power to adequately and realistically represent the people.

In Gearóid Denvir's essay, "Decolonizing the Mind: Language and Literature in Ireland", he analyses the success which the coloniser achieved once it had seized control of the colonised's national language and thus its cultural practices. He cites Ngugi Wa Thiong'o's book, *Decolonizing the Mind*, with regard to "the most effective weapon of imperialism [...] the cultural bomb" (1997: 44). Wa Thiong'o writes:

> The effect of the cultural bomb is to annihilate a people's belief in their names, in their language [...] in their heritage of struggle, in their unity, in their capacities and ultimately in themselves [...] It makes them want to identify with that which is furthest removed from themselves; for instance with other people's languages, rather than with their own (in Denvir, 1997: 45).

This is precisely what occurred in Ireland and in particular in Irish literature, whereby the Irish language went into serious decline and became even more marginalised. The divide between the advances in the East of the country and the stoically traditionalistic "backwardness" of the West grew even greater. As Kiberd explains:

The struggle for self-definition is conducted within language; and the English, coming from the stronger society, knew that they would be the lords of language. Few of their writers considered, even for a passing moment, that the Irish might have a case for their resistance. Henceforth, Ireland would be a sort of absence in English texts, a utopian "no-place" into which the deepest fears and the fondest ideals might be read (1996: 11–12).

The relationship between the Irish language, Irish language literature and postcolonial theory has been examined most recently by Máirín Nic Eoin (2005). Though Nic Eoin concurs with Titley's assertion that the postcolonial stage is the most important moment in the settlement and everyday life of the Irish language and of Ireland itself (1998: 91), Nic Eoin is aware that this has not been mirrored in the critical output of Irish language scholars and academics. Declan Kiberd's *Idir Dhá Chultúr* (1993), *Inventing Ireland* (1996) and Gearóid Denvir's "Decolonizing the Mind" (1997) have addressed how the vital role of the Irish language helped the Irish nation to re-fashion itself and its image of itself from the moment of colonisation onwards. However, as Nic Eoin observes, the paucity of Irish language critical investigation of the Irish colonial experience has led to the language and its history becoming a marginalised and under-examined discourse within the wider arena of the postcolonial (2005: 18–21). One area in particular which has been virtually ignored by English language postcolonial critics is that of contemporary Irish language writing. Writers such as Ó Direáin, Ó Flaithearta, and more latterly Nuala Ní Dhomhnaill and Ó Searcaigh are often briefly and brusquely treated of in English language criticism, often discussed in chapters titled "'The Gaelic Background' [...] The End of Tradition" (see Nic Eoin, 2005: 27). Of course, Irish language scholars were also guilty of seeing eighteenth- and nineteenth-century texts as representing the end of tradition, and a death of sorts was tangible in the way in which these texts and their authors were lamented. In what Denvir has called the "palimpsestization, and also the peasantization, of the Irish language" (1997: 51), the Irish language and its literary history was written over and virtually written out by the colonial language, making it almost impossible to see the traces of the original inscription on the palimpsest of the Irish nation. The eradication of any visible signs of the continuation of the Irish tradition has led to the creation of separate spheres in the Irish psyche as to how to treat of middle and contemporary Irish literature, as though it has stopped somewhere in the interim, conveniently around the time of colonial subjugation, and began again only after the English had left (see Ó Ciosáin on *Field Day*, 2005). The marginalisation of the Irish language had begun prior to the colonisation of Ireland, but, as Nic Eoin has commented, this was consciously forgotten and in its stead a story of the English language's dominance was recounted and took precedence in the Irish psyche (2005: 28–29). However, seeking to deny either language is a wasteful and unnecessary enterprise; the interweave of Irish and English is a central part of Irish identity. What is essential, however, is that an awareness of both traditions, separately and in unison, can lead to a fuller and richer story than any Irish versus English one ever could. Colm Breathnach's poem "*Trén bhFearann Breac* / Through the Speckled Land", from which Nic Eoin's study takes its name, gives a powerful insight into the interwoven linguistic countryside through which he travels (1992: 62–63). Although Breathnach is clearly upset and unsettled by the dominance of the English bold lettering on the signs he passes, and the italic, smaller font, which the Irish placenames receive, he concludes the poem by recognising that, rather than being one or the other, he must be between two cultures, as that is the current Irish situation:

Idir dhá dhath	Between two colours
idir dhá fhocal	between two words
idir dhá ainm	between two names
idir dhá aigne	between two minds
idir dhá áit	between two places
idir dhá theanga	between two tongues
a chaithim mo shaol	that I spend my life
idir dhá shaol	between two lives.

Nic Eoin comments that the Irish-speaking community is caught between two languages rather than being content with their bilingual status (2005: 280). Though this may have a large measure of truth to it, some writers have embraced this dual-linguistic reality and have begun to recognise that, rather than being caught between two opposing sides, the Irish speaker today should revel in the space between the two tongues and between the two cultures. Cathal Ó Searcaigh's poem "*Trasnú* / Intersection" (2000: 277–279) reflects this linguistic in-betweeness, and is illustrative of why many people are returning with renewed interest to the language today.

Ó tá muid ag fí ár dtodhchaí as ár ndúchas;	Oh, we are weaving our future from our past;
[...]	
Tá muid leath-réamhstairiúil	we are half-prehistoric
Agus leath-postmodern intertextual.	and half-postmodern-intertexual
[...]	
Tá muid teach ceanntuíach	we are thatched cottaging
Agus bungaló mod conach;	and mod-con bungalowing
[...]	
Tá muid rince seiteach	we are set dancing
Agus hócaí pócaí cairíócaíach	and hokey pokey karaokeing
Tá muid ag fí ár dtodhchaí as ár ndúchas;	We are weaving our future from our past.
[...].	

Though this is indicative of the contemporary situation, and though it appeals to a younger Irish speaking and Irish learning population (see also McCoy, "Ros na Rún: Alternative Gaelic Universe", 2003: 155–164), it is not the ideal situation. Nuala Ní Dhomhnaill's work on the silencing of female Irish language poets presents us with the most powerfully evocative argument for a distinctive Irish language medium. Her poem "*Ceist na Teangan* / The Language Question" (1990: 154) presents the native language as a child in a wicker basket, much like Moses in the biblical telling. Floating precariously among the reeds, the poet hopes that child/language can survive and make it safely to shore. Ní Dhomhnaill does, nonetheless, see the importance of translation. Biddy Jenkinson, on the other hand, is the only Irish language poet who refuses to have her work translated into English. However, though the influence of English is lamented by some writers and academics, others, such as Lillis Ó Laoire note that "[t]he world we live in today is a speckled world and we must realise that we are all *breacdhaoine*, 'speckled people'. We can only gain from embracing such a concept" (2004: 61). It was a central tenet of Ireland's postcolonial mindset to separate out what was truly Irish from what was obstinately English; the preservation of areas of Gaelic purity and linguistic wholesomeness went some way towards saving them from becoming assimilated into the larger product of modernising Ireland. However, a study of Conamara and the Aran Islands recognises that these sequestered places realised much earlier than the rest of Ireland that, historically and culturally, there could never be a full return to one secure and untainted past, not should there be. As Stuart Hall writes:

> [w]e cannot speak for very long, with any exactness, about "one experience, one identity", without acknowledging its other side – the ruptures and discontinuities which constitute, precisely, [...] "uniqueness". Cultural identity, in this second sense, is a matter of "becoming" as well as of "being" (1996: 394).

Though today, the West of Ireland and the Aran Islands are talked about in relation to what was, community efforts are focussing both on what was and what is now happening on the Islands. This marriage between tradition and modernity is proving successful, though vigilance and dedicated structures must be in place so as to safe-guard against the Islands becoming static representations of the past, or heavily modernised, a-cultural laboratories. Without question, the in-betweeness experienced by people, most often being represented as pure and uncontaminated, provides them with greater understanding of their place in the world and an insight into other cultural contacts which mono-cultural society sees as detrimental and unnecessary. Micheál Ó Conghaile, in the introduction to a collection of contemporary West of Ireland songs has this much to say about what Conamara represents today, and indeed it could be extended to the Aran Islands:

Is Conamara de chineál eile ar fad atá againn anois. Conamara an disco, an rock an' roll, an chountry and western, an walkman agus an chairiócaí. Conamara na night clubs, na bpotholes, agus na mobile homes. Conamara na videos. Conamara Chablelink, Conamara Sky agus na satailítí. [...] Seo é ár gConamara, an Conamara atá á shú isteach agus á análú againn chuile lá. An Conamara atá fórsaí móra an tsaoil ag brú orainn uaireanta, agus uaireanta eile an Conamara a bhfuil go leor againn féin ag glacadh leis go fonnmhar, an Conamara nua atá muid a chruthú dúinn féin. Seo é ár gcultúr anois, nach cultúr amháin é ach cultúir. Uaireanta is ar éigean a aithníonn muid muid féin sa tranglam (1993: 33).[24]

This study posits that, in their geographical, linguistic and cultural liminality, the Aran Islands, and their literature, present the possibility of examining preconceived notions of Irish identity from the position of the in-between. It is important to note that the predominant figures whom we associate with the Islands, Synge, Ó Flaithearta, Pearse, and more recently Ó hEithir, Robinson, and writers such as Dara Beag Ó Fátharta and Dara Ó Conaola represent individuals who were or are themselves in-between codes of one kind or another. The Aran Islands figured as a crossroads between Ireland and the imagination and between the past and present that was unparalleled in its magnetic pull upon intelligentsia, tourists, seekers and wanderers, from the eighteenth century in particular. Far from being a two-dimensional fragmented piece of the main, the Islands were uni-dimensional, and allowed each visitor to find, re-discover or lose themselves in the various layers of island identity. As Homi Bhabha observes:

> The borderline work of culture demands an encounter with "newness" that is not part of the continuum of past and present. It creates a sense of the new as an insurgent act of cultural translation. Such art does not merely recall the past as social cause or aesthetic precedent; it renews the past, refiguring it as a contingent "in-between" space, that innovates and interrupts the performance of the present. The "past-present" becomes part of the necessity, not the nostalgia, of living (1994: 7).

24   "We have a completely different Connemara now. Connemara of the disco, of the rock and roll, the country and western, the walkman and the karaoke. Connemara of the nightclubs, the potholes, and the mobile homes. Connemara of the videos. Connemara of the Cablelink, Connemara Sky and the satellites. [...] This is our Connemara, the one we absorb and inhale each day. The Connemara which is forced on us at times, and other times, the Connemara that many of us are gladly in acceptance of, the new Connemara that we are creating for ourselves. This is now our culture, not one culture, but cultures. Sometimes, we can barely recognise ourselves in the confusion".

Leerssen, Chronotope and the West: Standing Still on the Edge of Ireland

Joep Leerssen has carried out fascinating work on the association in Irish culture between time and place, especially the relationship between isolated or coastal areas and the past. This link has contributed to the further isolation of these areas but also to their being held in higher cultural and national regard for having withstood the onslaught of time and overarching modernism. The metropole or centre (in Ireland's case, Dublin) sees that

> "time stands still" at the periphery, in the backwaters, in the lost corners. Life is caught up in old-fashioned benightedness or (alternatively) still harbours ancient traditions. [...] History as a process is of the centre. The periphery is lost in a cyclical, natural or static time-warp, forgotten by history, bypassed by history (1996: 4).

Another important point which Leerssen makes concerns the East-West axis and the tensions and contradistinctions which this geo-cultural relationship creates. Leerssen's theory that "a region is centred on, dependent upon, a metropolis elsewhere, to which it is subordinate and which it cannot claim for its own" (1996: 187) shows the pseudo-symbiotic relationship which exists between the powerful East and the marginalised West. However, what Leerssen's observation fails to take into account is, with specific regard to the West of Ireland, the possibility of "either regional identity or reciprocal constructions of the 'metropolis' by the regions themselves" (Belanger, in Hooper and Litvack, 2000: 96). The construction of a regional identity based solely on its own merits was very much at the heart of the West of Ireland's character. This does not account for the entire story, however, and so an exploration of the ties and linkages between the West of the country with the East is necessary in order to evaluate the unique social, political and cultural formation of the West as region.

Another observation of Leerssen's which is central here relates to the importance of the concept of the chronotope. Barbara O'Connor's essay "Myths and Mirrors: Tourism and Cultural Identity" (in O'Connor and

Cronin (eds), *Tourism in Ireland: A Critical Analysis*, 1993), refers to the essential element of contemporary Irish tourist discourse, seeing representations of life in Ireland as being akin to that of a "pre-modern society" (1993: 70). What is effectively being described here is Leerssen's chronotope; "a place with an uneven distribution of time-passage, where time is apt to slow down and come to a standstill at the periphery [...]" (Leerssen, 1996: 226). The perpetuation of this chronotopical image of the West of Ireland persists to this day and it is this quality of timelessness and geographical separation which dominates discourse on the region in tourist brochures, literature and visual representations. Gerry Smyth's *Space and the Irish Cultural Imagination* (2001) concurs with much of O'Connor's theories on the West's touristic appeal and finds that

> [m]odern Irish tourist discourse [...] employs a kind of "spatial grammar" – inherited from earlier travel accounts and from certain developments in nineteenth-century cultural nationalist discourse – in which the movement westwards in space figures simultaneously as a movement backwards in time (2001: 36–37).

However, much of the movement inherent in such (re)discovery of the West has led to the destabilisation of what were, until now, assumed ideas centering on the myth, reality and authenticity of Ireland's Western periphery. In a re-reading of Leerssen's work on the matter, Smyth reflects that "[t]he chronotope is thus the basis of a peculiar mythology surrounding 'the West' in modern Irish culture, a belief that somehow a particular spatial location affords a qualitative difference in knowledge and experience" (2001: 37). In introducing the spatial aspect of the West of Ireland, Smyth allows for a greater scope of meaning with regard to the mythical representations of the region in that place is more definite and concrete, whereas space can allow for a multiplicity of views given its own inherent refusal to conform to a definable, cartographical, locatable *place.*

Being Inside and Being Outside: Introducing the Interspace

The usefulness of the interspace as a conceptual tool has rarely been examined in any great depth, especially with regard to exploring the binary oppositional pairing of insider and outsider as commonly employed by postcolonial literary theory. In the literature under review here, it is clear that the authors and their characters appear to exist in or at least pass in and out of an interspace of some form or other throughout their careers or throughout the course of the poetry and stories. Though the interspace also crosses over into the domain of utopian studies and to some extent island studies, it is its relationship with self and other, with insider and outsider, and also with writer and subject that is being scrutinised at this juncture. Before delving into this analysis, however, a short introduction to the interspace and its related subsets is vital. The interspace has connections with utopia itself, as well as with notions of binaries and liminality or in-betweeness.

> Like parallel space [...] the term "interspace" can be used as an interpretative tool and an enabling concept. It expresses indefiniteness and contradiction, negotiation and complexity, and it can be extended to refer to Lawless's place as an Anglo-Irish author, to her situation as a woman writer in nineteenth-century society and to the dialogic mode of writing resulting from these positions (Hansson, 2007: 7–8).

Hansson makes it clear that the interspace has at least two distinct functions: firstly, the interspace can symbolise a particular discourse of fracture and confusion, especially in a post-colony. Secondly, and perhaps most importantly, the interspace can perform as a personal statement of individual complexity or incongruity of self or situation. In the case of all four authors considered in this study, the interspatial identity which each assumes in order to overcome linguistic, social, gender-specific or personal obstacles is vital to an understanding of *Grania, The Aran Islands, Dúil* and *Dánta 1939–1979*. This is not to suggest that any of the authors, with perhaps the notable exception of Lawless, who created the concept, was consciously aware of their own interspatial identity, or their creation of an interspace for their characters and their work. What is important here, however, is to illustrate the concept of interspace as providing an artistically liberating arena for each of the four authors to exist within; given that Lawless, Synge, Ó Flaithearta and Ó Direáin sought to express lives of difficult, different and diverse existences, it is clear that a concept which allows for dissonance, fracture and hybridity would be welcomed.

In her biography of Lawless, Hansson's main focus is on Lawless's refusal to conform to both literary and societal norms, which results in the creation of an *interspace* in her writing, a space which allows for diversity, multiple voices and perspectives, as well as the scope to enter into the male-dominated arena of Irish literature. Though Lawless was quite happy to write about Ireland as a country, she stopped short of entering into any kind of nation-based debate and was thus regarded with suspicion; in fact "[m]ost of Lawless's writings are characterised by the double voice of a writer reluctant to provide an easy solution or a final answer. Such a feature may be regarded as unconstructive in a country's nation-building phase, but it has a lot to offer for a culture attempting to move beyond polarisation" (Hansson, 2007: 1). The duality inherent in much of Lawless's work both complicates and enriches her writing. Richard Kearney notes that "the double voice may even be an expression of the Irish mind itself [which] does not reveal itself as a single, fixed, homogenous identity but as double or dialogic" (1985: 9). To this end, Lawless's creation and use of the *interspace* gives the reader a vital insight into her own duality of mind and her complicated relationship with her own place in society and literary circles. Lawless created the term "interspace" while on holiday in County Clare. Lawless's geographical location at the time of creating her neologism is highly significant. Positioned in the heartland of the West of Ireland, overlooking the wild Atlantic and with a barren landscape surrounding her, Lawless was quite literally on the edge of Ireland and of Europe; from here she could be free of much of the trappings of her aristocratic background while also being free of the male-dominated world of politically-biased literature. The region is "an interspace between land and water" and does not "strictly belong either to the one or to the other" (1899: 604). [...] In such a landscape, ordinary tools are inadequate: "the measuring tape is all very well in its own place, but its place, somehow or other, does not seem to be here!" (1899: 607). However, in this interspace Lawless could still be Irish, could still be a female author and could still have a voice in her country's literary canon. The interspace, then, as Lawless views it, allows her to have access to a place outside of the stifling situation she found herself in from a gender and professional point of view, as well as allowing her, and providing her with much material, to remain a member of Ireland's literary tradition.

> Although in some ways the notion of the interspace harks back to Romantic ideas about landscape, the concept can also be seen as a very modern idea in its rejection of geographical borders. By re-imagining landscape as a conceptual rather than a geographical entity, Lawless responds to the needs of a modern society where land rights are much less crucial than in the agrarian society that went before it, and [...] questioning the very possibility of defining space [...] (2003: 123).

The interspace has also been compared with "paradoxical space", a feminist concept developed by Gillian Rose (1993: 140) which focuses on the fluidity and multi-vocality of both central and peripheral space. Another link is with Foucault's concept of *heterotopia* which also deals with the fragmentary nature of "spaces whose functions are different or even the opposites of others" (1982, in Hayes, 2000: 437). Though Foucault's heterotopia may sound like a utopia, it differs from it in that heterotopias are "incoherent and uncomfortable, and can certainly not function as uniting images for a group or nation. However, as a disorganised environment, a heterotopia is closer to the unpredictability of the natural world, and its fluid form involves the positive elements of tolerance, freedom, ambiguity and difference" (Hansson, 2007: 7–8). In offering to act as an in-between space, one capable of providing the necessary flexibility and lack of restrictions to completely immerse oneself in writing, the interspace was the perfect place for Lawless, an Ireland that was not-Ireland while simultaneously being her-Ireland.

Centre and Periphery:
Peripheries of the Periphery, The Difficulties of Neat Binaries

> Post-colonialism is quite distinct from anti-colonialism. Reactions against colonialism have manifested themselves in a variety of ways, but always posited on the premise of a binary opposition. Where post-colonialism differs, is that although challenging the hegemony of colonizing cultures, it recognizes the plurality of contacts between the colonizing and colonized (Bassnett, *Comparative Literature: A Critical Introduction*, 1993: 78).

In Jacqueline Belanger's "The Desire of the West: The Aran Islands and Irish Identity in *Grania*" (in Litvack and Hooper, 2000) the binary opposites of self and other and of centre and periphery are critiqued and contrasted through the vehicle of Lawless's *Grania*. Belanger suggests that "*Grania* can be read as pointing to and problematizing certain issues involved in the construction of the West by the Literary and Gaelic Revivals" (2000: 95). Lawless's means of doing so, according to Belanger, is by "represent[ing] the West as fractured into a number of spatial, temporal, social and linguistic areas" (2000: 95). Pointing to Leerssen's neat region versus metropole binary, Belanger finds that "the very fact that they are seen as peripheries of a periphery allows for a critique of such binary oppositions as those between centre and periphery, region and nation" (2000: 95). Belanger's difficulty with binaries mirrors the difficulty which many other critics (Graham, 1994; McLeod, 2000) have experienced in employing them. While it is clear that binary opposites do exist, it is rare, especially when taking into consideration complications and exceptions, to find perfectly definable and quantifiable entities that can be categorised in binary oppositional form. When taking a nation into consideration, on the other hand, it is almost impossible to suggest binary opposites, as even within these alleged opposites one often finds exceptions. "East" and "West" function correctly as geographical binaries, but they do not tell the full story.

For Lawless, "the characterization of a non-unitary West opens up the possibility of resistance to late nineteenth-century nationalist and revivalist discourse" (Belanger, 2000: 96). Given that Lawless's background and personal beliefs did not fit, strictly speaking, within either the East or the West's assumed character, she was forced to re-imagine her country as layered and fractured so as to assert herself within the smaller fissures between both established binaries. While *Grania* is considered as a novel which embodies many of the characteristics of the West, Belanger notes that the novel "can be read against the representations of the West deployed by both Anglo-Irish and Irish-Irish discourses" (2000: 96). Therefore, *Grania*, according to Belanger's reading, situates itself between both dominant discourses, in an interspace where identity is more fluid and thus more open to interpretation. All commentators on Lawless, and specifically on *Grania*, agree that the novel attempts to convey issues regarding outsider and insider sensibilities. However, up until very recently *Grania* was usually read as a classic example of this binary and very little else.

Bridget Matthews-Kane's "Emily Lawless's *Grania*: Making for the Open" (1997) provides an example of this type of analysis, whereby the author examines the use of the landscape and the sea as either symbols of protection for the quintessential insider or freedom for the devout outsider. Although Matthew-Kane's essay does suggest that the landscape works on a variety of levels (1997: 224), the author seems to fall into the trap laid before her by concentrating on the binary of insider reality and outsider metaphor. Though these factors are an essential component of *Grania*'s dramatic composition, Lawless draws more attention to the liminal condition of the protagonist's existence than to the actual categorisation of who is "insider" and who is "outsider" in the story. Perhaps it is simply because this disruption of the binary order which the story suggests does not suit the classic format of West as good and East as corrupted that many have chosen to focus on the more comfortable and/ or common images presented in the novel. Or perhaps, as Belanger has suggested and as Cahalan (1991a; 1999) and Hansson (2003; 2007) have also considered, it was problematic and controversial to an extent, to examine a novel set in the heart of the West of Ireland that did not conform strictly to the standard structure of novelistic representation of the region. Furthermore, it would have been quite complex to interpret Lawless's appropriation of the West as an area where she could play out her own personal understanding of centre and periphery, an understanding that upturned and destabilised the more commonly used binary of "them and us" or "centre and periphery". Belanger explains:

> While *Grania* does represent the West as archaic and timeless, the narrative action is also set in a concrete temporal moment. [...] Despite the depiction of the Aran islands (sic.) as remote from the rest of Ireland in time and space, there exists a certain reversal of centre/periphery distinctions made through the setting up of the rest of Ireland as foreign to the islanders themselves. This reversal is accomplished primarily through an inversion of perspective, in that the islanders see Inishmaan not as the West or the margin, but as their centre. Galway and the rest of Ireland are constructed as liminal and "foreign" to the islanders (2000: 98–99).

Cleverly, though ultimately to her professional detriment, Lawless inverted the binary opposite in order to give precedence to the centre and to show that the binary of centre and margin is often more personal and fluid than concrete and fixed. Lawless also shows that in undermining the static order of powerful centre and powerless periphery, her characters and their setting transcend this binary and instead transfer power and control to their own place and their own situations. In assigning authority to the periphery, and in transforming this periphery into the centre, Lawless achieves a transference of binary order and a mastery of collective regional power.

As Belanger highlights, the "linking of the native with the natural environment and landscape has a long history in colonial discourses, where the native 'barbarity' is linked to the wildness or impenetrability of the natural environment" (2000: 102). Thus, in most portrayals of the West in late nineteenth- and early twentieth-century novels, representations of the West's inhabitants and their landscape are mirrored in each other, in some way legitimising the more cultured and orderly interventions of those from the East. The inherent wildness of those presented to the reader in some way countenances the need to see them as insiders of a similarly wild and unknowable periphery. *Grania*, then, is a radical departure for two main reasons then: firstly, it is the first novel to position itself on the inside of the West's culture but which sees this culture not as other and peripheral but as self and centre. Secondly, *Grania* aligns wildness to the elements and to the outside world, but not to the inner, more personal world of the protagonist. Inishmaan is instead the ordered and known world, while everything outside of the island's boundaries is the unknown, the wild and the imperceptible. Though this reading may not seem revolutionary to a modern-day audience, for Lawless and for writers who were to follow in her literary wake, such a stylistic move was ground-breaking. Adding to the significance of this departure was Lawless's position as a female writer in a male-dominated arena. In this light, *Grania* could also be read as a feminist attempt to shift power from male to female hands, as Grania herself triumphs over all the male figures in her life, though ultimately suffers for her headstrong nature when she refuses Murdough's advice not to sail to Inishmore for a priest to bless her dying sister Honor. Even in this final act of defiance, Lawless is perhaps hinting at her own foolhardiness in entering a male-dominated domain, and finds in Grania's death an adequate symbol for the author's own predicament. Postcolonial theory shares many interconnections with Feminist theory, and has been known to follow what Ashcroft *et al.* call "a path of convergent evolution" (*The Postcolonial Studies Reader*, 1995: 249). Both bodies of thought have concerned themselves with the study and defence of the marginalised "Others" within repressive structures of domination and, in so doing, both have followed a remarkably similar theoretical trajectory. Feminist and postcolonial theory alike began with an attempt to simply invert prevailing hierarchies of gender/culture/race, and they have each progressively welcomed the poststructuralist invitation to refuse the binary oppositions upon which patriarchal/colonial authority constructs itself (Gandhi, 1998: 83).

Another fascinating aspect of Lawless's novel concerns the relationship between landscape and individual consciousness, particularly in colonial discourse, an idea advanced by Declan Kiberd (1996: 287). Belanger finds in this idea a useful way of studying *Grania*; "the landscape functions as a reflection not only of the consciousness of the native but also of the Anglo-Irish writer who, perhaps as Synge and Lawless did in relation to the Islands, saw in the isolation of place an external reflection of their own isolated state within the islands and within Ireland in general" (2000: 102). A more detailed examination of isolation and the individual as represented in Synge and Lawless's work is provided in Chapter 5, but at this point it is vital to consider at least one aspect of this theme which has relevance for both the insider and the outsider alike. While Ó Direáin and Ó Flaithearta

seem to fit the profile of insiders who wrote from the outside, both Lawless
and Synge are difficult to accurately define in this regard.

Synge, The Aran Islands and *The Aran Islands*

John Millington Synge's *The Aran Islands* provides the reader with glimpses
of Aran life from 1898 to 1902. One of the most widely-discussed aspects
of the work, however, does not directly pertain to the content of the book
itself, but rather to the more obliquely evident relationship which Synge
shared with the islanders and the island itself. Ann Saddlemyer, however,
is critical of the book's style: "[f]ar from being a contemporary travel
narrative, Synge's *The Aran Islands* is as artificial as his later plays" (2007:
120). Saddlemyer's greatest difficulty with the book seems to rest with
Synge's immaturity, and in turn the immaturity of his writing style; "there
is something raw and unprepared about his responses to life" (2007: 120).
Saddlemyer is also extremely critical of Synge's omission of certain aspects
of island life, which she regards as being "yet so far from his comprehen-
sion" (2007: 121). The essay continues with a litany of alleged examples of
Synge's "clumsy civilized form" (2007: 121) which is matched by his feelings of awkwardness in both social and linguistic endeavours. However,
while Saddlemyer regards these feelings as juvenile and unsophisticated,
it is hardly surprising that Synge should feel this way, given that he had
just arrived from Paris and now found himself at a great remove from the
life to which he had been accustomed. Although Saddlemyer feels that
Synge's social failings are representative of a lack of understanding of his
situation and company, it could be argued that in wishing to remain at a
distance from the people and their routines, Synge was showing more social
awareness than carelessness. At intervals during the book, Synge is at pains
to demonstrate his respect and reverence for the people, and suggests that
although he was welcome to join in their company and their customs, he
stayed on the outside of many of these occasions so as not to "jar upon

[the islanders' traditions]" (*The Aran Islands*, 1992: 30) and also to retain a level of perspective necessary for the writer.

It is strange to find Saddlemyer rebuke Synge's detached stance, and stranger still to find that she regards him as "[a]lways the traveler, never part of the circle" (2007: 121) as though this were a further indictment of Synge's failure in the book rather than a successful outcome of his time there. Synge never sought the comforts of the insider's way of life and never placed himself within that tradition, though he was gracious in slipping in and out of musical sessions and story-telling evenings. In Synge's relationship with the islanders Kiberd identifies not a desire to be accepted so much as a complete insider but rather a wish to seek "moments of communal solidarity among a people whose poverty is exceeded only by their richness of language" (Kiberd, in Grene (ed.), 2000: 84). Unlike Lawless's *Grania*, Synge is an outsider who knows that his place will always be outside. This awareness is Synge's own and his unwillingness should not seem strange, but a natural consequence of his own contentment with his identity as an Anglo-Irish writer (David Greene, in *Mosaic*, 1971: 2–3). Although Synge's commitment to Aran, in both personal and artistic terms, was immense, and although some might find it difficult to reconcile, Synge clearly saw no incongruity in his twin passions of the Islands and English-language literature.

It is evident in his descriptions of his initial impression of island life, and hinted at by his reading of Loti and Rousseau, that the island terrain was amenable to his solitary nature. However, in regarding the islands' inhabitants as a secondary concern, or in some way inconsequential to Synge's time on the Islands, Saddlemyer mistakes Synge's obvious regard for landscape and nature as paramount to his interest in the people he meets. As Kiberd has noted "[w]hen J.M. Synge set foot on Aran in 1898, he came [...] to learn Irish and to take instruction from the people on their cultural codes" (2000: 84). Saddlemyer finds that Synge's melancholia is "influenced primarily by the inconstant weather [...]" (2007: 122) but fails to consider that the islanders are themselves affected by these conditions, suggesting instead that their apparent separateness from their surrounding environment causes another level of separateness from Synge also. Synge's use of the landscape, and particularly the sea to symbolise his own vagaries of emotion does not cut him off from the people but rather heightens his respect for them in that he finds their resolve and their reverence for their natural world a common bond between them. Saddlemyer finds that while Synge "does not attempt to analyze or question the Islanders' thoughts and reasoning" (2007: 122) he still devotes large passages of the book to describing how the weather and the sea's many changes and moods affect his own mood. However, it seems again here that Saddlemyer has missed an essential point. There is not a separation between Synge and the islanders in regard to how the weather and the environs affect them, it is simply just a case of familiarity and being accustomed to their surroundings that makes the islanders seem oblivious to these elements. Synge is new to these conditions and so has more time to consider them and how they influence him personally. If we consider that in *Grania* references to the sea symbolise both the chance of freedom and also the dangers of isolation and containment, it makes sense that for a non-islander like Synge the sea should fascinate more for its dramatic changes rather than for its more symbolic value. The sea is more a backdrop and an indication of mood in *The Aran Islands* whereas in *Grania* the sea is symbolically-charged.

Saddlemyer finds the influence of music, particularly counterpoint (2007: 122) prevalent in Synge's arrangement of *The Aran Islands*. Aligned with this, Saddlemyer considers that the "separateness between himself and the world he enters is stressed by the circular structure" (2007: 122). However, Kiberd (1996: 2000), Gerstenberger (1964) and Gillen (2007) find that *The Aran Islands* is more episodic in nature, which would seem to suggest a more closed, resolved nature to the separate visits by Synge to the Islands rather than the open-ended and somehow unsettled cyclical structure advocated by Saddlemyer. The circular pattern that Saddlemyer presents also cements her belief in the dividedness of the relationship between Synge and the islanders. In music, however, Synge found a way into the lives and homes of many people on the Islands, and this would seem to contradict Saddlemyer's hypothesis. Synge explained that he "played for a large crowd, which had come together for another purpose from all parts of the island" (1992: 104) and was sensitive enough to play tunes which were familiar to the islanders themselves. However, as Synge notes in the introduction to the work, the "direct account" (*The Aran Islands*, 1992: 3) which he gives shows his respect and his regard for the people whom he meets throughout his time there. It would be difficult to deduce from his sincerely written account anything other than having been made to feel welcome and at home on the Islands.

> I have had nothing to say about them that was not wholly in their favour, but I have made this disguise [changing names and disguising identities in places] to keep them from ever feeling that a too direct use had been made of their kindness, and friendship, for which I am more grateful than it is easy to say (*The Aran Islands*, 1992: 3).

Recent writing on *The Aran Islands*, however, depicts the insider and outsider relationship as being central to the book's structure. One aspect which has been largely understudied in this dialogue is Synge's almost harmonious (though unconscious) stance in both camps, rather than his struggle to marry *either/or* positions. Perhaps Synge saw little use for such neat polarisations of character or identity, or perhaps he did not wish to court either position. Jacqueline Belanger finds that in both Lawless's and Synge's works dealing with the Aran Islands, "the projection of an increasingly isolated Ascendancy consciousness onto the people and landscape of the Western isles [is done] in such a way that the peasantry becomes literally both self and other" (2000: 106). This is an important point; it highlights the point made by Roy Foster (1988: 453) relating to the lack of status that was ascribed to the Ascendancy in the revival movement. One should also consider the more obvious threat to Ascendancy identity, though it is rarely stated explicitly: the process of regenerating Ireland's pre-colonial, native identity sought, in essence, to deny and eradicate the identity of the already-declining Ascendancy themselves. Belanger also shows how the "Ascendancy consciousness" found its mirror-image in the isolated inhabitants of the Aran Islands; the islanders functioned then as likenesses of the alienated self of the Anglo-Irish and also as the necessary other with which the writers could still find some level of contrast. Terry Eagleton's *Heathcliff and the Great Hunger* (1995) situates the Ascendancy's relationship with the West "within a continuous process of identification and alienation" (Belanger, 2000: 106). Eagleton writes that

[t]he peasant is "other" to the upper-class intellectual, who must therefore transform his own language to capture this difference, yet the peasant is also, as natural aristocrat, a kind of mirror image of himself. The loneliness of the disinherited intellectual finds its echo in the collective isolation of peasant life, but discovers there too a community which might compensate for it. It is not for nothing that Synge felt wonderfully at home on the Aran Islands, and a complete outsider (1995: 312).

Eagleton encapsulates the dilemma for both the Ascendancy and the peasant in this dualistic identity crisis. Both sets of individuals were to initially rely heavily on the other if for little else than to help define themselves against the other. This is a more internal, national example of what Declan Kiberd describes in relation to Irish and English affairs as "[e]ach nation badly need[ing] the other, for the purposes of defining itself" (1996: 2). Belanger suggests a possible reading of *Grania*, "as both the placement of the 'native' Irish within certain colonial essentialist relationships with their environment, and as a projection onto the native of the anxieties of the Protestant minority in Ireland" (2000: 107). The charge of essentialism is one levied against many of the representations offered by writers like Synge and Lawless. However, any essentialism associated with the West of Ireland must not be viewed as overtly damaging, artistically artificial or misleading. Ashcroft *et al.* note that a postcolonial country and the country that colonises it "realize their identity in difference rather than in essence. They are constituted by their difference from the metropolitan and it is in this relationship that identity both as a distancing from the centre and as a means of self-assertion comes into being" (1989: 167). The reality of the situation was that a level of fundamental and unchanging "essence" was attributed to the West, and the Islands in particular, so as to add to its perceived quality of timelessness and thus its function as a preservatory region. Given the pace of change in the rest of the country during the early part of the twentieth century, the West of Ireland was in fact a world away and a world apart from the rest of Ireland. The notion inherent within the timelessness of stasis also encouraged writers and artists to travel to the West, seeing in this static time-zone a perfect opportunity to "use the West to examine the self" (Belanger, 2000: 107).

In the case of island authors, however, the situation is very different, and especially so for Liam Ó Flaithearta and Máirtín Ó Direáin. Both authors' relationship with, and understanding of, notions of insider and outsider was far keener than that of Lawless and Synge. Although, as already stated, Lawless and Synge both acknowledged a sense of being outsiders in their own social backgrounds, an islander's sense of place is sharper than that of a non-islander, an aspect considered at greater length in Chapter 5 of this book. For the present, however, it is sufficient to state that this awareness of the nature of insider and outsider is more apparent to someone from a small, usually insular, region. Nonetheless, both Ó Flaithearta and Ó Direáin are exceptions to another rule: both were exiles, and forced outsiders writing from an insider's viewpoint. That this viewpoint changed significantly over the years since their departure from the island is only realised by both authors upon returning years later. So, one could hypothesise that a skewed vision of their insiders' awareness is what most permeates their work, written while on the outside of that chosen inside. What is evident, however, in both Ó Direáin and Ó Flaithearta, is a change in dynamic from youth to old age with regard to the disruption of both insider and outsider positions.

Conclusion

The Aran Islands occupied an interspatial linguistic and cultural position in the early nineteenth century that enticed and attracted many to their shores. The shock for many on arriving there related to the Islands' progress or its poverty, their pure Irish character or their interwoven Gaelic and English reality, or The Islands' capacity to reflect Ireland's past or its past-present. From some of the earliest commentaries on the Islands' lure, it is clear that a range of appealing characteristics enticed visitors to Aran. Geographically, the Islands were distinguishable from the Galway coastline, while also being geologically-linked with Co. Clare. Their visible nearness belied their actual distance from the mainland, a fact often adding to the experience of travelling to the Islands in the first instance.

From a military and colonial perspective, the Aran Islands were ideal locations for garrisons and coast-guard barracks; the port of Galway City was a vital entry point and the Islands, being at the mouth of the bay, were geographical custodians of that port. From an Irish Literary Revival standpoint, the Islands provided the most perfect focus and locus of literary, cultural and linguistic imagination. The Islands' size, shape and location provided a wealth of creative suggestion. Archaeological, geological and cartographical investigations provided not only empirical information, but simultaneously added to the mystique surrounding the people and place of Aran itself.

Liam Ó Flaithearta and Máirtín Ó Direáin's prose and poetic works represent the Aran Islands as inter-places, caught between the writers' own pasts and the present which they are forced or encouraged to realise upon returning to their homes in their later years. Often, however, as is also the case with both Lawless and Synge, Ó Flaithearta and Ó Direáin see Ireland as Other, and Aran as most central to their concerns and themes. The constant placement and simultaneous displacement of the Islands and, indeed, the island theme in their works, represents a struggle to identify a single or definable Aran identity. However, this adds greatly to the juxtapositional relationship which Aran and Ireland have enjoyed for centuries, carried through in literature, cultural understanding and in discussions about peripheries and centres of power and influence.

CHAPTER 4

The Mirror of Desire
Scáthán an Dúil

> They say (and the appearance of the place confirms this) that their land
> was not always an island. But Utopus, who conquered the country and
> gave it its name (it had previously been called Abraxa), brought its rude
> and uncouth inhabitants to such a high level of culture and human-
> ity that they now excel in that regard almost every other people. After
> subduing them at his first landing, he cut a channel fifteen miles wide
> where their land had joined the continent, and caused the sea to flow
> around the country.
> — SIR THOMAS MORE, *Utopia* (1975 [1516]: 35)

Introduction

This chapter will consider the potential benefits of adapting and applying
the methodologies advocated by utopian scholars like Sargent, Levitas,
Moylan, Pordzik and Wegner to the study of Aran Island literature.
Caitríona Ó Torna (2005) established a preliminary template for projects
of this genre in her investigation on the possible relevance of utopian theory
to the West of Ireland Gaeltacht. Ó Torna's very significant departure provides a route-map from which this work can proceed and expand. Her work
is not treated as definitive, however, and this book adopts a fluid approach
in respect to existing scholarship on the issues under review here. It builds
upon approaches presented in the above works, and while there are clearly
areas of overlapping thematic concerns, it does not apply any single framework to Aran Island literature. The themes of desire, expectation, and the

real and imaginary, as well as the essential value of the utopia(s) created or imagined will be examined. The idealisation and myth which surrounds the West of Ireland and Aran in particular, will also be investigated, as will questions relating to authenticity and the imaginative creation of the Gaeltacht in both Irish and English.

Proceeding from the contention that the Aran Islands literature considered here can be included in the utopian genre, it is necessary to identify the definition of utopia to be used in this chapter and the method of analysis to be extrapolated from this definition. Ó Flaitheartaʼs *Dúil* and Ó Direáinʼs *Dánta 1939–1979*, however, may not be readily identifiable as utopian literature. However, given the dearth of research dealing with Irish-language prose and poetry from a utopian studies perspective, it is unsurprising that these texts have received scant treatment in this field of enquiry. Nic Dhiarmada (2007) and Fennell (2007) have added greatly to this dialogue, and this book seeks to further it. The lack of a correlation between utopia and the active remembrances of Aran Islands authors presents its own difficulties. I suggest that the relationship between utopia and the real is not a divisive one, and that within Irish language writing in particular, a sphere which may be considered as utopian in nature does exist.

Aspects of Syngeʼs *The Aran Islands* and of Lawlessʼ *Grania*, on the other hand, sit more comfortably within the utopian tradition. Both texts treat of Inis Meáin, its inhabitants, customs, and geographical distinctiveness in the context of an other-worldly charm. Parts of both texts present the Aran Islands as having qualities that the larger island of Ireland could do well to aspire to, and are portrayed, at least initially, as desirable alternatives to the realities of life on mainland Ireland. However, both *The Aran Islands* and *Grania* are based on real, physical, locatable islands, and this would seem to jar with the common understanding that a utopia is constituent upon the unreal, the intangible, the metaphysical, the unreachable, the "nowhere" and the "not there". How then to reconcile any study of literature which, predominantly at least, represents real geographical areas with the study of utopia?

How Do You Define Nowhere?: Definitions of Utopia

Levitas (1990, 2007a, 2007b), Sargent (1994, 2007), Wegner (2002) and Moylan (1986, 2007a, 2008 [Lecture]) have all drawn attention to the importance, the essential need, of having a definition of utopia which can then be used to frame the method of analysis which a scholar may employ. However, as with most inter-disciplinary areas of study, there are countless contending definitions of utopia. It is rare to find anything amounting to consensus on what, or whom or where is *properly* utopian; it is even more uncommon to find complete agreement on what utopia means for a modern audience. Sargent's definition is perhaps the most widely known: "a non-existent society described in considerable detail and normally located in time and space" (1994: 9). However, a eutopia, which is similar to a utopia, is one which "the author intended a [...] reader to view as considerably better than the society in which that reader lived" (1994: 9). Thus, the key distinction between utopia and eutopia is that of the positive nature of the latter. Dystopia relates to a non-existent society which is, to follow from eutopia, worse than the society in which the reader lives (1994: 9). The anti-utopia reflects a critical attitude towards utopianism, calling it "social dreaming" (1994: 9). The critical utopia, coined by Moylan in *Demand the Impossible* (1986), is an important definition within the utopian taxonomy. It is aware of the constraints of the utopian tradition, whereby texts "reject utopia as a blueprint while preserving it as a dream" (1986: 10). What all these definitions have in common, nonetheless, is that they recognise some aspect or other of the utopian tradition; their competing visions of an impossible goal, a dream or a reflection of a better society is what differentiates the various classifications. Sargisson (2003) notes that while utopia does not have to be located in the future and that "it can be part of the transformation in the now" (2003: 17), she does not agree that utopia is realisable. She suggests, instead, that utopia is "just around the corner, always on the other side of the horizon, utopia is 'not yet', elusive, glimpsed but never grasped" (2003: 20). The horizon is a vital borderline, and from a utopian studies perspective, it represents a liminal zone where the "impossible and desired" (Sargisson, 2003: 20) just might be realised. Louis Marin's "Frontiers of Utopia" (1993) discusses the horizon and its zone of possibility:

> The use of the term *horizon* is in evidence from the second half of the thirteenth century onward. But at the early stages, it signified "limit", the limit of the gaze, the limit of sky and earth. By metonymy in the seventeenth century, it was used to designate the part of the landscape close to this line, and in the eighteenth century and the romantic epoch, *horizon* meant the opening of vision to the "extreme" of the gaze, the mystery of a remote space concealed from view, and, finally, the infinity of space. Oddly enough, *horizon*, which originally meant a limit, the power of circumscribing a place, connotes at the end, immensity, infinity: such is the limitless horizon of the ocean (1993: 406).

Tom Moylan's recent lecture "Making the Present Impossible: On the Vocation of Utopian Science Fiction" described the necessity of keeping utopia at the horizon, and, with particular reference to science fiction narrative, the importance of distance in the discourse.[1] The attempt to reach utopia is seen by Moylan, and indeed by Sargisson and Levitas, as the important exercise; though the utopia may not always be arrived at, the alternative journeys to get there constitute an important genre of their own. It is the anticipatory quality of utopian expression, according to Moylan, that allows a reader to continue with the narrative, and which impacts upon the reader's emotions with regard to the various plot and narrative twists along the way. Synge and Lawless can be thought of as explorers trying to reach and arrive at the horizon of the West coast of Ireland, discoverers and narrators of a journey to places far away, though, importantly, just within view from the mainland:

> Utopia is "nowhere": it is outside reality; a wish-world, in discontinuity with the real world, whose attractive features [...] are perfectional symbols of a harmonious cosmos strikingly and defiantly dissimilar not to any given set of social spaces and times but to that which is unchanging in the structure of human reality. It is transcendent to "this world": a "kingdom of heaven" [...]. But it is also "of" this world – nay, more of

---

1   Presented at the fifth Ralahine Utopian Studies Workshop, University of Limerick, 18 April 2008.

this world than any ordinary reality in that it is meant to represent a self-contained, self-sufficient and definitively "valid", "fulfilled", terrestrial human world envisioned by the human mind and embodying a race of men whose only mode of existence is to live out their humanity fully and uninhibited (Kolnai, [Dunlop, ed.]1995: 94).

In Aurel Kolnai's definition of utopia, we find resonances of what Leerssen described between the centre and the periphery, as though they were two separate entities. Kolnai also sees that utopia presents us with two separate possibilities: an indefinable nowhere and a particular, recognisable somewhere, or, in other words, a no-place and a someplace, or a "here". Though these two elements may seem dissonant, there is within them the germ of a very useful way of orienting utopia. A utopia by its very nature is outside current reality, but that is not to suggest that it is ethereal or imaginary, though this can often be the case. For the purposes of this chapter, the West of Ireland, and more particularly, the Aran Islands, will be considered using utopian theory. There is an important difference between the colloquial and "specialist academic use" (Levitas, 1990: 2) of the concept of utopia. Levitas' *The Concept of Utopia* (1990) makes a very useful, and often ignored, analogy between utopia in its colloquial form and utopia in its academic form. She comments on the fact that difficulties about definition arise predominantly as a result of the colloquial forms' dominance – a dominance which inevitably weakens the validity of the study of the academic (and in turn the political, religious, social) utopia (1990: 2). There is implicit in this analogy a much wider problem which is rarely discussed to any great extent. This focuses on the anti-utopian position with specific regard to the criticisms which utopians and academics must constantly withstand in relation to the "worthiness" of the utopian endeavour as a whole. This might explain the frustrations expressed by many scholars in achieving a definition for their subject area, but it may also account for the linking of all things utopian with all things fanciful, escapist, idealistic, and ultimately unrealistic.

For instance, to dismiss a place or a society as being "intrinsically impractical" would suggest that the more colloquial understanding of the term was in use; to question or explore the possibility of society's betterment through imagining it to be so would suggest a greater, more conceptual or

academic appreciation of the term. The lowercase "u" is often employed
for the more colloquial use of the term and an uppercase "U" is used for
the concept which explains the "desire for a better being" (Levitas, 1990:
199).[2] This book argues that aspects of the Aran Islands, and aspects of
the literature examined here, embody both uses of the term. Cultural
nationalists regularly imbued The West of Ireland, and specifically Aran,
with characteristics of being both of this world and also of being outside
of this world, in a space which we might nowadays designate as being
otherworldly. In examining the West of Ireland and Aran using utopian
theory it will become clear that the importance of place and space is to
the forefront of my work here and that each of these labels supports either
the more colloquial meaning of utopia, or the academically-oriented study
of utopia itself. Place, the seemingly more stable of the two terms, would
appear to encapsulate identity and place-based knowledge, whereas space,
the more fluid and largely indefinable of the pair, would seem to house
more vague and multitudinous levels of existence.

Aran, Myth and Utopia

Ireland's utopian tradition registers much of its success in its use of the past
as the more illuminating temporal location. Sargent's recent development
of his concept of *"utopian energy"* (2007: 310) may help to explain Ireland's
utopian situation.

> The general idea of utopian energies is that the will/willingness/ability to create new
> forms can be channeled in a number of different directions, that there may be only
> a limited amount of such energy at any given time [...]. This may help explain why
> certain countries, like Ireland, appear to have strong utopian traditions while having
> an erratic tradition of actual utopias. Utopia can be repressed, suppressed – includ-
> ing by poverty – or displaced. [...] Specifically, utopian energy is often displaced

2   The colloquial is more often than not used to signify a negative aspect or attribute.

into other projects that have a tinge of utopianism but are not normally considered utopian, like nation building, reform, and social movements advancing the status of a sub-group in society. All of these are, I want to argue, projects into which utopian energies can be displaced (2007: 310).

Such utopian energies emerged in the national movement to preserve and revere the West of Ireland, eventually leading to a new phase of utopian thinking about that region in late eighteenth- and early nineteenth-century depictions and characterisations of the landscape, population and environment of the West. In the writing of Lawless, Synge, Ó Flaithearta and Ó Direáin, these utopian energies are also tangible, particularly in the splits, and inter-spaces which class difference, insider and outsider, exile and linguistic separation caused the writers to suffer and to challenge. The geographical split between the Aran Islands and the larger region of the West of Ireland is another example of the way in which utopian energies emerged, creating a siphon-like effect whereby the magic, wonder and potentiality of the West of Ireland was even more distilled in the Islands; a purer, clearer, truer version was encapsulated there. If there was a utopian energy flowing through the de-Anglicisation and Literary Revival phase of Ireland's emerging postcolonial identity in the late 1800s and early 1900s, this energy was given its most powerful outlet in the creation of the Aran Islands as the ultimate utopian fulcrum.

The Aran Islands offered the writer, artist and social dreamer a variety of possible energies to capture and employ in their work. Above all, however, the Islands' substantial links with the past and the continuation of that past in the present was undoubtedly their strongest attraction. The society on the Islands was developing not in the aggressive way which we associate with modern development but rather "within the confines of the old" (Marx, in Sargent, 2007: 311). For these writers, Lawless and Synge in particular, there was the task of seeing beyond the more fanciful notions of the West of Ireland as some kind of *Tír na nÓg*. However, to imply that there was a utopian quality to both their work and to the world they found themselves immersed in is both to complicate and illuminate a very important strand in utopian theory; the hermeneutic power of utopia. Employing utopia as an "interpretive schema" (Wegner, in Moylan and

Baccolini, 2007: 113) with which to examine the West of Ireland and the
Aran Islands' literature and cultural power is a fascinating methodology
and one which Sargent and Moylan have both advocated in recent years
(Sargent, 1994, 2001; Moylan, 2005; 2007a). Ireland has become an area of
utopian enquiry only of late; Pordzik (2001b), Sargent (2007) and Moylan
(2007) have outlined and initiated the project of examining Irish literature from a utopian studies angle. These critics have commented that in
using the past as a zone of potentiality and as a springboard for the future,
Ireland's literature speaks to colonial literatures, historical literatures and,
of course, the utopian enterprise. Sargent writes, "[m]y contention is that
most utopias are inevitably recreations of the past placed in the future.
Much utopianism looks back at some improved version of the past to find
inspiration for the future" (2007: 311). In a footnote to "Choosing Utopia",
Sargent also finds that

> Ireland is a particularly interesting case of the use of the past. The more I look at Irish
> literature, the more it seems to me that the quintessential Irish utopia is an Irish past
> that never existed. I have begun to wonder if the Irish students of utopianism should
> be reading historical novels rather than looking for more works written explicitly
> as utopias (2007: n, 312).

Ireland's utopian tradition, then, may not extend to "works written explicitly as utopias" (Sargent, 2007: n, 312). However, it does exist, albeit in less
obvious guises. It may appear incongruous to align a nation's history and a
nation's utopian traditions, seeing as the former charts temporal and actual
occurrences, and the latter often deals with juxtapositions of past and future,
and also with desired-for happenings, though not always realisable ones.
The difficulty here is how an individual views time and space, and whether
or not that individual can see flexibility in time and space as possible or
preferential to linear, clearly stated events. Another obstacle in addressing
history and utopia as concurrent or at least cooperative experiences lies in
how we imagine utopia, what it represents and its relationship with reality.
Utopia may not be a useful evaluative cultural phenomenon for a majority of
people. Instead it may designate a fantasy land, one which offers only delu-
sion and distraction. And, in some instances, this is precisely what utopia
does. It offers itself as a positive alternative to the negativity of the world in

which the individual lives. However, the core issue remains this: what is the use of dreaming or imagining or writing about a place that does not exist? The two most succinct and straightforward answers are: because "Utopia [...] is absolutely essential" (Sargent, 2007: 303) and because imagining a place to be such that it is better brings about a change for the better in the individual's life and society; "[i]t is easier to get somewhere [...] if you have a clear idea of where you want to go" (Sargent, 2007: 305).

The gap, however, between where you are and where you want to go to or be is ever-present and must be negotiated if this gap is to be traversed. This space between the "here" of the present and the "there" of utopia is portrayed in the language and imagery of desire, enchantment, hunger, yearning, struggle, fear and inexhaustible hope. These elements can manifest themselves as "body utopias [...] [which] express the most fundamental needs and desires of the human being, such as food, shelter, and safety" (Sargent, 2007: 301–302), or as aspirational utopias, whereby the dreamer or writer hopes to depict the better society in order to instigate a national move towards that better place.

This book proposes a new utopian layer, that of the liminal utopia. The liminal utopia represents an in-betweeness, or an interspatial relationship with both the better and the "other" society; the protagonist in this case having a foot in both camps. The liminal utopia also represents the relationship between the zones of contact of island and mainland whereby the utopia and the dystopia are brought into and out of contact with each other in order to delineate their positions and also to test one against the other for signs of improvement or disimprovement. These liminal utopias reflect, at their most basic level, a microcosmic view of the world, a world that is most often an island or an island within a larger island tradition. They could also be termed mini utopias; however the diminutive implied here belies the variety of contact between the dreamer and the dream, and between the utopia and the dystopia. The liminal utopia also addresses the important gap between utopia as imagined reality and the utopia as cultural reality. This latter utopia may seem a paradox; if we are to adhere to definitions then a utopia, judging by Sargent's taxonomy, is "a non-existent society described in considerable detail and normally located in time and space" ("Three Faces", 1994: 9). If, then, a utopia portrays a non-existent society, how can utopia also represent a cultural, or any other type for that matter, reality? The real here posits the main difficulty.

Place and Space in Utopian Studies

Within utopian studies, space plays a vital role. Henri Lefebvre's proposition that utopia acted as "a counter-space that began to insert itself into spatial reality" (quoted in Moylan, 2000: 69) points to utopia's position as a unique space in its own right. The notion too that utopia should, according to Sargent, "describe in a variety of aspects and with some consistency an imaginary state or society" would seem to suggest the idea of the creation of a space which stands separately from a more specifically *mappable* place. It is also interesting to note that "the negotiation of that gap between needs and wants – the space "that utopia offers to fill" (Levitas, 1990: 189) – constitutes the most fundamental activity of what can be named as utopia: the utopian "education of desire [which] nourishes the sense that 'something's missing', and is a necessary inspiration to social transformation" (Levitas, 1990: 111). This gap or missing component could be interpreted as a space in itself, one which provides an area where the desires and hopes for a better society could be played out and understood. Space in utopian studies could also represent the gap between the more dystopian elements of a particular society and the contrasting utopian desires for that society's betterment.

Máirtín Ó Direáin creates a poetic and imaginative interspace which symbolises the geographical and emotional gap between the island and the city, and between the actual island and the created island of his poetry. Isobel Ryan also highlights the interplay between place and space within a vernacular and cultural tradition in her discussion of Ó Direáin's work. Drawing largely on the work of the noted social geographer Yi-Fu Tuan, Ryan investigates the relationships which Ó Direáin had with his island home, and how this relationship changed with distance and time. Ryan also looks at the emotional connection which Ó Direáin had with both the actual and the real versions of Inis Mór which he created, noting that while there is a security in connection with a particular place, there is a broad sense of artistic freedom in the qualities which space provides the artist. The relationship with both space and place, however, has much to do with levels of attachment and longing, stability and freedom.

Tuan observes that "[p]lace is security, space is freedom: we are attached to the one and long for the other" (1977: 3). Ryan is interested in investigating the attachments which people seem to have with "geographical features such as rivers, mountains, and islands [so as to] have a touchstone on which to base their emotions" (2002: 267). However, Ryan is well aware that "[t]he concrete thing gives them food for imagination which may never be called for if they stay at home all their lives" (2002: 267). Such geographical connectedness, then, inevitably manifests itself in some way or other in the immigrant's subsequent endeavours. In *Carraig agus Cathair*, Ní Riain also draws our attention to issues of permanency and temporariness, as well as to issues of narrowness and broadness. Ní Riain writes:

> *Is cúis bhróin agus míshástachta don fhile saol na cathrach. Samhlaíonn sé suarachas agus neamhdhaonnacht léi agus fiú amháin cúinge. Is é an cur síos a thugann an Direánach ar na fir agus ar na mná san fhilíocht is fearr a léiríonn an chontrárthacht idir saol na cathrach agus saol an oileáin* (Ní Riain, 2002: 5).[3]

Though his characterisations of individuals in both the city and on the island are usually general in nature, as Ní Riain notes, their lives differ in that the city dwellers' lives reflect dystopian narrowness and a pettiness or inhumanity while the islanders' lives offer a picture of broad possibility and happiness.

Inextricably linked with this debate is how the West of Ireland became a literary, linguistic and cultural utopia in the early part of the nineteenth

---

3   "City life is a source of sadness and dissatisfaction for the poet. He associates the city with miserliness and inhumanity, and even narrowness. The depictions which Ó Direáin gives of the men and women in his poetry best portray the contrast between city life and life on the island".

century. The special qualities ascribed to the West can be examined using utopian theory, in that concerns with place, space and interspace are common to both postcolonial and utopian theory. However, it is the manner in which these places, spaces and interspaces are used, manipulated and conceived of that offers the most striking difference with regard to both theoretical viewpoints. With postcolonial theory the areas and regions discussed are usually physical, real places. However, within utopian theory, though often based in reality, spaces used and described here are far less tangible and thus more difficult to locate or express in writing. It is in the imaginary or personal realm that most of the areas and places which will be examined, find their greatest articulation possible.

In the interspace's relationship with liminality, in particular, there is much substance and cause for inquiry. Colin Graham's essay ("Liminal Spaces: Post-Colonial Theories and Irish Culture", 1994) highlights the power of the liminal, or the transitional, in Irish culture in relation to notions of representation and the manner in which the Irish nation makes room for more than the binary opposites of Irish and/or non-Irish. Graham emphasises the "fractured range of complex cross-colonial affiliations which have existed within the British-Irish cultural axis" (1994: 41), refuting the linear progression of colonialism advanced by Fanon in *The Wretched of the Earth* (1961) which appears in the form of "colonisation > resurgence > nationalism > liberation > the nation" (1994: 30). In presenting this format, which until recently was taken as the nation's narrative, Graham cleverly shows that such neat, almost clinical, progression cannot encapsulate the entire reality of what occurred. Indeed, in categorising these stages in such a manner, Graham's portrait foregrounds the "liminal spaces" (1994: 33) of a typical postcolonial nation's narrative. Graham's liminal spaces are concerned with where "coloniser and colonised meet directly" (1994: 33). However, this book suggests an expansion of this coloniser/colonised meeting to include areas where the nation meets with itself, in a form of self-examination, most often represented using the figure of a mirror. The imperceptibility of the West of Ireland's cultural power, for example, provides us with an excellent example of a liminal space; where one culture comes into contact with another with the result that "hybridity, liminality and ambivalence [are prioritised] result[ing] from a shift within Irish

Studies to theoretical structures which refuse binary categorisations [...]" (Patten, 1999: 285).

As Ó Torna points out, *"ba chuid de shamhlú agus d'fhorbairt nóisean an náisiúin é cruthú chonstráid na Gaeltachta"* (*Cruthú na Gaeltachta 1893–1922,* 2005: 153).[4] Inherent in this observation are the twin forces of imagination and development, factors which are central to creation, both of actual reality and more imaginatively-based concepts. Ó Torna notes that:

> *Útóipe an chultúir dhúchasaigh a bhí sna ceantair Ghaeltachta mar a shainigh go leor de scríbhneoirí na hAthbheochana í, ceantair a raibh an seansaol Gaelach fós i réim iontu agus sliocht na nGael ag maireachtáil iontu go dílis de réir an traidisiúin. Is léir [...] go mbíodh blas na samhlaíochta agus na cruthaitheachta go minic le sonrú ar an gcur síos a thugtaí ar na ceantair Ghaeltachta agus ar phobal na Gaeltachta agus gur mhó a bhain an íomhá sin le hÚtóipe ná le saol iarbhír na gceantar cúng. Áitím gur scríbhneoireacht Útóipeach a tháinig ó pheann roinnt scríbhneoirí na hAthbheochana, ar scríbhneoireacht í ina raibh constráid na Gaeltachta idéalaithe á cruthú agus á múnlú* (2005: 153).[5]

The Gaeltacht of the West of Ireland was created in response to what many authors and artists regarded as the dystopian quality of modern(ising) Ireland. Just as the Gaeltacht was seen as having a preservatory function, it was also envisaged as being outside of normal time constraints and was thus in chronological "discontinuity with the real world", as suggested by Kolnai (1995) and Leerssen (1996). Thus the creation of the Gaeltacht and the West itself fitted neatly into what Sargent has described as "a radically different society than the one in which the dreamers [writers] live" (1994:

---

4   "The creation of the construct of the Gaeltacht was a part of the imagination and the development of the notion of the nation".

5   "Gaeltacht regions were utopias of native culture as defined by many Revivalist writers, areas where the old way of life of the Gaels still held sway and with families of Irish still living there, loyal to their traditions. It is clear that there was often an element of imagination and creativeness to be found in the descriptions given of these Gaeltacht areas and of their people and that these images had more to do with utopia than with the actual life of these confined areas. I argue that some Revivalist authors were clearly writing utopias, with the construct of the idealised Gaeltacht being created and fashioned by them".

3). Though Ó Torna is not advocating the position that all writing from Revivalist authors should be considered as utopian in nature, she does, nonetheless, see the benefit of examining some writers' work using utopian theory so as to come to a more rounded appraisal of the work itself.

However, though "social dreaming" (Sargent, 1994) and "a vision to be pursued" (Levitas, 1990) are commonly associated concepts of utopian thinking, when applied to West of Ireland and Aran literature, it becomes apparent that these ideas also get tied up in the romanticism and myth-based dialogue which forms a central, if complex, part of the make up of the West as both a real and an imaginary socio-cultural entity. The essential point or demarcation here relates to idealisation; the West of Ireland was, for all its positive cultural offerings, "to prove exclusive rather than inclusive [...]"; the "West became an idealised landscape, populated by an idealised people" (Brian Graham, 1997: 7). Writers such as Pearse were accused of further idealising the region in the writings which emanated from their journeys to the West of Ireland. For those of divergent faith, political or linguistic leanings, many cultural nationalists could only imagine, and idealise what lay beyond the boundaries. Thus we are left with two sets of people, two sets of ideals and two interpretations of the same place. The most powerful and influential of these groups were those who were excluded from the West's traditions. Anglo-Irish writing clearly foregrounds the production of a utopia in the West of Ireland, one which allowed them artistic and personal, though largely imaginary, access to the area.

Philip O'Leary views Pádraic Pearse's writing as having a significant utopian character, writing that Pearse's project was "a conscious attempt to create a Gaelic utopia against which to measure the contemporary Ireland with which he was so utterly disillusioned" (1994: 127). Though Pearse was often criticised for such attempts, it is clear to O'Leary and to Ó Torna (2005) that his conscious creation of a world that would run counter to the one in which he lived was a form of creative escapism and a demonstration of the possibility of a better future for his compatriots. The inspirational, though ultimately unrealised, Revivalists' writings were not, however, empty artistic vessels, but were instead efforts to instigate and encourage a move by the people of Ireland back and West towards the country's cultural and linguistic repositories. As Ó Torna eloquently writes, *"[t]heastaigh uathu todhchaí a chruthú ar pháipéar mar sprioc don náisiún"* (2005: 158).[6] The notion of the paper utopia described here is not a new phenomenon; one could argue that More's 1516 *Utopia* was just that. However, Ó Torna's emphasis on utopia's provision of a purpose or objective is important to consider.

Intentional Community as Alternative Space: Aisling Árann

Aisling Árann[7]: The Aran Project, was established on Inis Mór by the Celtic priest Dara Molloy in 1985.[8] Its mission statement explains that *"Aisling Árann* is a vision or dream. It is the vision or dream that brought people together on Inis Mór, to live a life rooted in the Celtic, in right relationship, and working for transformation".[9] Sargisson and Sargent suggest that intentional communities come together in order to create, or recreate, a world which will benefit the imagination, the community and the environment. Intentional communities also "explore utopian phenomena that are not constrained to the world of fiction and that exist in the world here and now" (2004: xiii). The *Aisling Árainn* community grow their own food, run an eco-friendly hostel, conduct spiritual classes and produce the *Aisling* magazine, which is also available online. They are, in effect, a community within another small community, and function on the ideals common to most intentional communities. No research has been carried out on this community to date, though it provides a fascinating way in which to examine the impact of the Aran Islands' attributed utopian

6   "... they wanted to create on paper a future as an objective for the nation".
7   Translates as "Aran's Dream".
8   See also <http://www.iona.org.uk> for details of Iona's intentional community, one similar in design and outlook to the *Aisling* project on Inis Mór.
9   <http://www.aislingarann.ie/fourways.html>

function upon people's imaginations and their lives, not least the people
who have come to join in the *Aisling* project since its inception.

Fantasy, Myth and the Real in Utopian Studies

I am, of course, aware of the difficulties associated with using utopian theory
to examine a place or region which is already highly mythologised, and I am
also conscious of the fact that, as Levitas has stated, "the very term utopia
suggests to most people that this dream of the good life is an impossible
dream – an escapist fantasy, at best a pleasant but pointless entertainment"
(Levitas, 1990: 1). However, Ó Torna suggests that the writing of some
Revivalist authors was far removed from being mere "pleasant but pointless entertainment", and insists that this writing was instead *"dlúthchuid de
phróiseas samhlaithe na hÉireann [...] á cruthú ag fiontraithe intleachtúla an
ama"* (2005: 155).[10] By positioning utopian writing alongside the significant
attempts to apportion valuable cultural and traditional attributes to the
West of Ireland, Ó Torna designates a zone of inquiry for utopian writing
and theory, one which shares much in common with notions of creation,
idealisation, literary production and national self-fashioning. Not alone
was the West of Ireland created as the actual antithesis of the East/rest of
Ireland, it was also an imaginary or possible antithesis of all of Ireland, and
offered a possible solution for the confused identity of much of the Irish
population who did not fit the mould or who in some way, did not come
under the criteria of Irish traditional nationalism.

   Solidifying Ó Torna's claim that Revivalist writing embodies much
of the utopian tradition is the fact that, although much of the work has
its origins in the imaginative and dream-like realm, there was a *"bunús ag*

---

10   "A central process in the imagining of Ireland [...] being created by enterprising
     intellectuals of the time".

an mbrionglóideacht chéanna i bpobal iarbhír na Gaeltachta" (2005: 155).[11] Although Ó Torna (2005: 156) is also aware that *"Útóipe na Gaeltachta"* does not sit comfortably into the designations of literary utopia, intentional utopian community or utopian social theory (Sargent, 1994: 4), she finds that the Gaeltacht utopia would seem to embrace aspects of all three taxonomical referents. Ó Torna's main difficulty with situating the West of Ireland's Gaeltacht into the category of literary utopia relates to it being based on an actual place. However, as Moylan and Sargent have both recently highlighted, reality is not an enemy of utopia, although this may have appeared to have been the case given the term's etymological meaning as a *no place* or as a *not place*.[12] Thus, Ó Torna does not continue her analysis of the Gaeltacht as utopia as perhaps she sees the difficulty of reality as an insurmountable obstacle; she does however, suggest that because the Gaeltacht utopia does not fit the exact profile of the three main strands of the utopian tradition, this makes it an area where substantial and important research could be carried out (2005: 155). This work proceeds upon this projected trajectory and identifies further potentially enlightening avenues of investigation and research.

From a linguistic and etymological stance, Seosamh Mac Muirí has examined the link between "the negation or 'non-ness' of place associated with the word [utopia]" and has found that this element is a "secondary development". He writes:

> Utopia represents the Indo-European [pronounced] *aiw- (i.e. vital force, life, long life, eternity) > [written] ou, plus –topos. The development of "vital force" to mean "not" is dealt with by Watkins in his *Indo-European Roots* (2000: 103). This Indo-European *aiw-, through its derivative *yeu-, "vital force", "youthful vigour", has given the initial part of *"óg"* to Irish as in the title *Tír na hÓige*, latterly, *Tír na nÓg* [the land of eternal youth], and Irish equivalent of Utopia (personal correspondence, May 2008).

---

11   "... a basis of this dreaming in the actual community of the Gaeltacht".
12   Sargent's comments came following my presentation on Máirtín Ó Direáin's Utopian Imagination at the second Ralahine Centre workshop, University of Limerick, 1 December 2006. Moylan has also commented on the importance of reality in the utopian project during discussions on this work.

It is, then, not at all surprising that the Aran Islands in particular are mar-
keted and imagined in popular consciousness in terms of such a never-
never land.

Place and Memory: Remembering, Authenticity and Myth

Graham's *In Search of Ireland: A Cultural Geography* (1997) takes a fascinating look at the importance of landscape and its associated cultural
and ideological underpinnings. Graham suggests that the conscious
creation of the West of Ireland as a potential utopian project was heavily concerned with cultural practices, and with the preservation and
consolidation of these within the sphere of geographical and imaginative place. Graham contends that creation is at the heart of any cultural
endeavour; "[culture] involves the conscious and unconscious processes
through which people live in – and make – places, while giving meaning
to their lives [...]" (1997: 2). This creative effect, the making of places,
suggests a futuristic element, one which is generally taken as central to
the utopian process. However, Levitas has recently argued that "utopia
is not always located in the future" ("The Archive of the Feet: Memory,
Place and Utopia", 2007c: 19). She offers some very thought provok-
ing ideas on the present state of "utopian longing" (2007c: 19) and on
the essential correlation between utopia and place, and the associated
memories which both share.

      The concept of memory as a link to the past, and as a link between the
past and the present is central to the literature under review here. Máirtín
Ó Direáin and Liam Ó Flaithearta, for example, employ their island memories when writing about their home as exiles from that home. With particular regard for the *pastness* inherent in memory, as well as for the myths and
levels of authenticity which memory carries with it, Levitas's essay provides
much food for thought and examination:

The relationship between memory and Utopia is a complex one. At first glance they are antithetical: memory refers to the past, Utopia to the future; memory is what has been, Utopia is what is to come, the novum, the Not Yet. Yet reflection reveals this apparent antithesis as illusory. First, Utopia is not always located in the future. Images of lost paradises and golden ages are placed in the past, accompanied by versions of the Fall. Usually these are beyond the memory of any living individual, inscribed in the collective memory as myth or history, as something that must not be forgotten. The recent past may be the repository of utopian longing [...]. Second, a remembered utopia is always a reconstruction of the past [...] representations of future utopias are always simultaneously dependent on existing cultural resources. Indeed, the intelligibility of all cultural production rests on shared memory [...]. Third, utopian representations of the future – claims that the future may be qualitatively different from the present – involve a process of transcending the past. This is never a simple forgetting. It always involves *managing* the past, both individually and collectively. Thus, memory and forgetting, and their management, are necessary component parts of the utopian project. Forgetting may be more typically associated with dystopias (2007c: 19–20).

This passage from Levitas provides essential ways of thinking about the past, utopia's role within the past, and ways in which to reinvigorate the past so as to bring it into the future. Memory's role in this passage-of-time formulation is central, though its link with nostalgia is something which Levitas is keen to highlight as detrimental. Levitas writes that the idea of nostalgia is difficult, "implying as it does an outsider's critical assessment of longing for the past. The definition of memory and desire as nostalgic is almost always a political and delegitimizing act, similar to the rejection of radical alterity as 'pejoratively' utopian" (2007c: 21). Thus it is clear to see the links which nostalgia and the more negative connotations regularly applied to utopia share. Raffaella Baccolini's essay "Finding Utopia in Dystopia: Feminism, Memory, Nostalgia, and Hope" (in Moylan and Baccolini, 2007) provides an insight into nostalgia's relationship with both memory and utopia. Baccolini's interest in dystopian fiction and literature informs her views on utopia, and Baccolini notes that "a constant awareness of a 'slight suffering' is the necessary condition of Utopia" (2007: 162). Baccolini argues that "we need to keep remembering and that one of the things that makes memory and possibly nostalgia relevant for Utopia is that we must keep feeling uncomfortable" (2007: 162).

However, Baccolini proposes that "[m]emory, then, to be of use to Utopia, needs to disassociate itself from its traditional link to the metaphor of storage and identify itself as a process [...] not fixed, or reachable, but in progress" (2007: 172). This interpretation is crucial to understanding the differences between memory and nostalgia, which has "traditionally been viewed as a type of conservative or regressive memory" (2007: 172). Nostalgia, considering its links with *algos*, or pain and *nostos*, or return "stands for the painful desire to return home" (2007: 172); critics have seen nostalgia as the poor cousin of memory, "characterized by loss, lack, and inauthenticity" (2007: 174). However, reappraisals of nostalgia, beginning with Jameson (1974) have led to a reinvestigation of nostalgia's role in memory and also in utopian studies. Jameson's remarks on the matter are important:

> [...] there is no reason why a nostalgia conscious of itself, a lucid and remorseless dissatisfaction with the present on grounds of some remembered plenitude, cannot furnish as adequate a revolutionary stimulus as any other (1974: 82).

Though nostalgia remains largely regressive, if used correctly it can function to support the memory of the writer and can help to recognise the irretrievable past of moments remembered. Indeed, as Baccolini suggests:

> [n]ostalgia [...] shares with Utopia some important features. Both are informed by desire [...] nostalgia and utopian tradition are connected through displacement [...]. Nostalgia, then, can be seen as the refusal to let go of the past in its attempt to recover the irretrievable and to open a space for the possible (2007: 175).

In examining memory, Levitas aims to reinvigorate the relationship which it shares with utopia and also to emphasise the more positive connotations of this relationship. Levitas employs Paul Connerton's work on collective memory and suggests that "the mental spaces within which memories are mapped always refer back to the material spaces that groups occupy" (Levitas, 2007c: 22). For the island authors considered in this book, there is strong evidence to suggest that memory and space and knowledge of this space are integral parts of the remembering strategies which both Ó Direáin and Ó Flaithearta use within their work.

Embodiment and Utopian Spaces

Connerton (1989) provides a very useful explanation of social spaces which both collective groups and individuals need and make use of throughout their lives:

> Our images of social spaces, because of their relative stability, give us the illusion of not changing and of rediscovering the past in the present. We conserve our recollections by referring them to the material milieu that surrounds us. It is to our social spaces – those which we occupy, which we frequently retrace with our steps, where we always have access, which at each moment we are capable of mentally reconstructing – that we must turn our attention, if our memories are to reappear (1989: 37).

In reconstituting memory, in retracing and remembering one's past, there is a substantial amount of re-creation involved, in giving life to a time, place and memory. In stressing the importance of embodiment, the less demanding role which recognition plays is appropriately downplayed; recognition does not, according to both Levitas and Connerton, carry as much imaginary potential or as much significance for re-memory as pseudo-embodiment does. Connerton sees that "memory also operates through incorporation and performance" (1989: 72), pointing to the considerable weight of individual and collective performativity of memory. Connerton's illumination of the critical importance of memory's "spatial and embodied character" (Levitas, 2007c: 23) rather than on its more personal, visual or nostalgic character is crucial to understanding the processes of re-memory and re-creation of the island in both Ó Direáin and Ó Flaithearta, and this spatial and embodied character is also in evidence in Synge's work.

Levitas develops upon Simon Schama's work *Landscape and Memory* (1995) in "The Archive of the Feet" (2007c). Echoing much of Connerton's work on the subject, Levitas writes that Schama "has remarked that our embodied sense of physical place, the way in which our body knows where to go, which way to turn, is laid down very early. When street layouts [...] change, what is generated is a dream-like sense of dislocation and an *embodied* sense that something is wrong. If the social spaces wherein we retrace our steps [...] are effectively obliterated [...] they are literally no

longer *recognizable*" (2007c: 25). Levitas builds on Schama's "archive of the
feet" metaphor (1995: 24), to capture the stages which one passes through
in order to re-embody or remember a particular period of time. The idea
of travel or journey inherent in the archive of the feet, however, is a very
useful way to contemplate the active ways in which the individual moves
backwards and forwards through time and through personal remembrances
in order to portray or convey certain emotions and memories. Nonetheless,
as Levitas goes on to explain, as landscapes and social spaces change, more
often than not in the period between the individual's first and last visit
to a particular setting or place, then the feet, or here the imagination,
cannot travel back. The obstacles of change or progression and of erasure
of certain elements of place do not allow for accurate or straightforward
remembrance, and so, as in Levitas's suggestion, the past becomes something
which must be renegotiated, transcended and managed if it is to be of any
use to the individual who wishes to remember and re-embody it.

Visual Memory and the West of Ireland

With regard to utopia, however, Levitas notes that, for Schama, "[q]ues-
tions of memory and place are [...] significant in the visual and fictional
representation of place – and thus in the representation of no-place, or
Utopia" (2007c: 25). Thus textual and photographic accounts would seem
to have a large part to play within a variety of "cultural manifestations of
utopianism" (2007c: 25). Levitas concludes with a cogent explanation of
the significance of both memory and utopia:

> Thus, individual and collective memory, in both inscribed and embodied forms,
> operate not only within the text. They affect, in ways we may forget, the generation
> of the text itself. They affect how we read particular texts. And our embodied and
> spatially embedded memories govern which utopias survive and which disappear,
> apparently without trace from memory, as they are lost from the archive of the feet
> (2007c: 40–41).

The West of Ireland's landscape, particularly during the Revival period, could have been seen as "a collage encapsulating a people's image of itself" (Duncan, 1990, in Graham, 1997: 3). The people referred to here, of course, are not the inhabitants of the West of Ireland, but rather those Revivalists and cultural nationalists who used the West of Ireland as a symbol for all that was good and pure in their country. That this image was presented as an accurate reflection of all that the West encapsulated suggests not just inauthenticity but indulgent fantasy. Utopia allows for a dialogue between both the past and the future. Nonetheless, it would seem that looking backwards in order to see how to move forwards implies a dangerous side-stepping of the here and now of the present. The present, with its attendant realities and the problematical relationship which it shares with both the past and the future, would appear to be less appealing than either of the other two timescales. Bloch's comments on this subject are concise and salient:

> Thinking means venturing beyond. [...] Real venturing beyond knows and activates the tendency which is inherent in history and which proceeds dialectically. Primarily, everyone lives in the future, because they strive, past things only come later, and as yet genuine present is almost never there at all (Bloch, 1995: 4).

However, if Revivalist authors such as Pearse were in fact projecting utopian ideals onto the West of Ireland, and hoping that this could point a way forward, i.e. *this is what we would like Ireland to be like*, then it is clear that this was a doomed project from the start, based on idealised visions of place and time.

Myth, National Identity and Utopia: Past(s), Present(s) and Future(s)

Sargent's recent "Choosing Utopia: Utopianism as an Essential Element in Political Thought and Action" (in Moylan and Baccolini (eds) 2007) also emphasises the relationship between national identity and utopianism. Drawing on the colonial model, Sargent "hypothesised that colonies produce utopias, often with a concomitant dystopian experience for the colonized" (2007: 309). In an earlier essay, "Utopianism and National Identity" (in Goodwin, ed., 2001), Sargent explains that the "utopianism of a country both reflects and helps create that country's national identity" (2001: 87). The author's hypotheses collate around Benedict Anderson's work on "imagined communities" (Anderson, 1991; Ch. 1). It is both the imagined nature and the imaginative potential of these communities, and the subsequent identity(ies) of the inhabitants of these communities that are most essential here; Sargent argues that "at least part of what we imagine is a utopian national community" (2001: 88) and that "the imagined communities and the utopian expectations regarding that community change over time in relationship with each other" (2001: 88). At the heart of this relationship between utopianism and community identity is national myth (Sargent, 2001: 88):

> Every country teaches its children stories about its past that are either demonstrably false or simply shaded to put the nation or its founders or leaders in a particularly good light. These myths are part of the creation of national identity and frequently have a distinctly utopian tinge to them if they are not explicitly utopias themselves. These myths are part of a collective national memory or subgroup memories that include many eutopian and dystopian stories and experiences. Utopian literature frequently uses these memories to build either the justification for overcoming the past or support for the future eutopia (2001: 88).

Myth is a central, if problematic, element of of national identity. In problematising myth's role within national and utopian consciousness, Sargent highlights the contribution of myth to the creation of a national identity, a role which should not be underestimated. Stephen Sayers' essay "Irish Myth and Irish National Consciousness" notes that "all [the] definitions stress the fanciful and fallacious nature of myth" (2004: 272) and yet, etymologically and archaically, the word was associated with "revealed truth" (2004: 272). Implied in this, it appears, is an element of authenticity of the ancient; that is to say, myth is ancient, or at the very least old, and must have some grain or constituent of truth in it, i.e. the story must have started somewhere. In Ireland's case, "[e]ven in its most elementary forms, [myth] represents an incipient rejection of the modern world, [...] and it indicates a desire to find a more agreeable way of life" (2004: 273).[13] Nonetheless, critics suggest that myth is obsolete. "They will simply promote the claim that myth is the product of a different age and a different people, [...] totally out of place in the modern world" (2004: 274). However, Sayers identifies a possible reason for the strength of the pejorative cast in which Irish myth is often viewed. The associations made between myth and "stereotypes of Irishness [such as] blarney and superstition" (2004: 275) have caused many critics of Irish myth to react "to what might be seen as the ruthless marketing in recent years of what has come to be defined as Irish culture" (2004: 275).

In a lecture on modernity and contemporary Ireland (Mary Immaculate College, Limerick, 22 February 2005), Seamus Deane commented on the marketability of Irishness and of Irish culture as a commodity, and in so doing, addressed the roles of myth and authenticity in relation to the Aran Islands. Indeed, in much the same vein, Sayers writes that "Irish [culture] [...] affirms itself only in sentimentality and in an [...] indiscriminate, but lucrative 'Disneyfication' of folktales for the global market" (2004: 275). As myth and folklore share common threads, it is understandable, though lamentable, that both are usually mentioned together and discredited on the basis that they refer to fantasy and are clearly out-of-date. However, myth, like folklore (see Ó Giolláin) "can inform a distinctive kind of consciousness that defines, binds and gives courage to a community. It grounds people in their lands, links one generation with another and inspires action" (Sayers, 2004: 278). Crucially, as Ernst Cassirer suggests, "myth lays the basis for nationhood. It is behind the feeling of nationality, and gives it its force" (1946: 280). It is this aspect of myth, the laying down of a narrative and generational understanding of tradition and place, that most reveals the true nature of myth as a liberating and historical constituent of nationality. Myth stretches from a country's past, through its present and often informs its future. In this way, it can be seen to have a relationship, albeit an underdeveloped one in Ireland's case, with utopia. Myth's temporality,

13   Sayers earlier notes that "the study of Irish myth is often seen as an opportunity to reclaim the wisdom of some golden age" (2004: 273).

then, also has implications for a country's postcolonial history, given that it is embedded in the pre- and post-contact language, and represents and thus legitimates the colonised culture's "pastness".

In his lecture on modernity, Deane briefly examined Synge's *The Aran Islands* and, though not explicitly, suggested that Synge had looked for a eutopia in Aran. However, this author would argue that what Synge was in fact looking for in Aran was not a more positive society from that of his own, but a different, perhaps more possible, society. He did not shy away from the more negative aspects of island life, nor did he present Aran as a counter-cultural pedestal from which to look down on Irish society; instead, he saw is as other, as potential and possible, and yet somewhat outside of his grasp. Kiberd writes that "*The Aran Islands* might be read as a document in the history of 1890s anarchism, with the community on Inis Meáin presented as a version of the commune, a utopian zone where most of the discontents of civilization seem to be annulled" (2000: 94). However, the qualification of "might" here is telling. *The Aran Islands* has often been read in this fashion, and, as stated, there are aspects of the text that could suggest Synge's capacity for social dreaming. Nonetheless, the Islands are much more complex that this reading, and Synge's interpretation of them is closer to an alternative to utopia.

The Irish Context: Myth and Utopia

Richard Kearney's *Transitions: Narratives in Modern Irish Culture*, addresses the relationship between myth and utopia. Kearney writes: "[a] major question arising from our studies of the transitional tension between tradition and modernity is that of the role of *myth* (1988: 269). Though many equate myth with "the fetishization of false consciousness" (1988: 273), Kearney stresses the "more liberating dimension of myth – the genuinely *utopian* – behind its negative *ideological* dimension" (1988: 274). Though many dismiss the colloquial and often negative aspects of both utopianism and myth as mere fantasy, both utopia and myth offer liberation for the individual consciousness and the national character. Myth highlights the histories and glories of the past, suggesting "that better worlds can be achieved", while "utopias suggest that still better can yet come" (Sargent, 2007: 308). It would also appear that national myth and utopian thinking often converge at times of internal national crisis; for example, Sargent shows how colonial domination in Ireland produced utopian texts. He writes that "[e]ach country will have a unique way in which national identity is created by and reflected in utopian literature. And that way will be derived from a version of the past [...] suitably revised" (2007: 309).

The temporal relationship between utopia and the past is highly significant, although utopia is predominantly associated with futurity. It is perhaps because utopia aims for the future betterment of society rather than the reversal of past events that critics have chosen to focus on the future; yet, utopia sprang from a past, was inevitably influenced by it, and thus dreamed of a future with which to improve upon the past. However, there was an inherent distrust of the past in much utopian criticism during the 1970s, 1980s and early 1990s as the political traumas with which countries struggled created an uncomfortable dialogue with the past. This was also the case in Ireland, where the emphasis on concerted forgetting was ushered in by successive governments, and efforts towards creating a lasting peace in Northern Ireland and a stable Irish economy were made paramount.[14] It is understandable that a post-colony such as Ireland, which still negotiates territorial and/or dominion issues with its former coloniser, would want to focus its attentions on present and future matters, given that overcoming the difficult histories of their relationship was still a reality for many living in the North of Ireland. However, the past informs the present and future, and painful though it may be, the Irish past has just as much to teach us presently as our dreams of the future.

14   See the process of "active forgetting" in Kundera's *The Book of Laughter and Forgetting* (1978).

Postcolonial and Utopian Studies:
Ireland's Emerging Inter-Disciplines

It is in its synergistic capacity that utopian studies has found its strongest claims to legitimacy, and it has in turn functioned as a highly constructive element in current debates on postcolonialism in particular. Ralph Pordzik's *The Quest for Postcolonial Utopia* (2001b) illustrates the inter-relations between the two disciplines. Pordzik's work looks at the inter-section between utopian and postcolonial literatures in order to achieve what he calls a "cross-cultural comparison", in much the same way as this book does. The juxtaposition of postcolonial and utopian studies thus provides Pordzik with an opportunity to access the influence which spatial, geographical and cultural implications have on both literature and wider society. The theoretical framework which both postcolonial and utopian studies provides Pordzik with is enormous, while also highlighting the scope which such a framework could have if integrated with other disciplines such as postmodernism and poststructuralism. In any event, the linking of postcolonial literature and theory with utopian literature and theory has allowed Pordzik to analyse and broaden the literary classification which Sargent began in the 1970s, bringing to light new and diverse fiction from former colonies which add to our understanding of utopian and postco-lonial debates. It is important to note here that one element in particular unites postcolonial and utopian theory – that of definition. The question of who or what is properly postcolonial has plagued postcolonial theory and criticism for decades and utopian studies finds itself burdened with the same difficulty. This, of course, has implications for the consideration of Aran as properly postcolonial or properly utopian.

Ralph Pordzik's article "A Postcolonial View of Ireland and the Irish Conflict in Anglo-Irish Utopian Literature since the Nineteenth Century" (2001a), examines Ireland and Britain's political relationship and how this impacted upon and influenced the texts produced at that time. It also offers a fascinating reading of these texts, written by British and Irish authors, and investigates the creation and subsequent disavowal of identity and national ideals in these texts. Of importance also is the manner in which British authors created dystopian texts which portrayed Ireland as a nation of ill-bred, reckless and anti-British layabouts. This is an interesting binary if one considers the earlier representations of the British and Irish in Kiberd's examination of both nations in *Inventing Ireland* (1996).

One possible way of examining the relationship between, and understanding of, Ireland and Britain's post/colonial associations is through an investigation of the "large body of utopian and dystopian fiction produced in Ireland over the last 120 years" (2001a: 333). Pordzik sees that the writers of these utopian fictions

> [n]ever ceased to engage the complex power relations that helped shape the cultural consciousness of Ireland and the Irish. Their culturally and politically diverse tales, sketches and novels are especially revealing with regard to the projection of colonial and postcolonial issues onto the level of utopian narrative that emerges as their most significant feature (2001a: 333).

The Irish, as depicted in the texts which Pordzik has chosen to examine, embodied carelessness and seemed to show that Ireland was a nation in need of control from a stronger and more civilised country such as Britain. Pordzik highlights how these stereotypical characteristics of Irishness encapsulate much of the debate which both revisionists and anti-postcolonial critics have used to invalidate Ireland's claims to postcoloniality. Rather unjustifiably, the situation has been viewed as less aggressive than a colonial encounter would be, and more an exercise of neighbourly intervention. Pordzik also shows that the development of the Irish utopian novel came about as a result of Ireland's long drawn out struggle with Britain over the issue of Home Rule and self-government. The themes of these early texts "projected a better future under a national Irish government" (2001a: 334) and envisioned a unified, struggle-free nation, a veritable dream land. Titles from the time allude to these desires: *Ireland's Dream: A Romance of the Future* (1888) and *Hibernia's House: The Irish Commons Assembled* (1881). Most of these texts were published under pseudonyms to protect both the author's identity and therefore saving him/her from police attention and, one might hypothesise, to save him/her from ridicule for writing of something which seemed quite fanciful, and ultimately unattainable.

An important text of this kind, L. McManus' *The Professor in Erin* (1918), depicts an ardent cultural nationalist professor (based almost entirely on Douglas Hyde) who decries the Irish situation and suggests that, "if it were to retain a distinct and recognisable identity, [Ireland] needed to de-anglicise itself, in language, customs, and habits of mind" (2001: 336). In the years following this, however, novels portraying an alarmingly dystopian vision of Ireland began to emerge: authors of these texts were seen as counter-Revivalist in orientation. The most famous of these is Eimar O'Duffy's fantasy *King Goshawk and the Birds* (1926). These texts "started demythologising some of the ideals of the earlier Revivalists [...] and turned increasingly to anti-utopian or dystopian fiction" (2001: 337). Another important example from this time is Joseph O'Neill's *Land Under England* (1935) which offers a dystopian vision of a country dominated and constitutionally tied with England, ultimately suffering for its proximity to the larger power, though inextricably bound to it. Looking at texts from the 1970s and 1980s, Pordzik's work highlights the growing preoccupation once again with the utopian form in Irish fiction. From this period, Frank Herbert's *The White Plague* (1982) places traditional visions of Ireland against the more modern symbols of Irish advancement and economic wellbeing, creating "a contested site of cultural codes each designed to preserve (or efface) a particular version of cultural and national identity" (2001a: 341).

In her book *Utopian Imagination and Eighteenth Century Fiction* (1996), Christine Rees discusses the fact that the "idea of utopia, in any period, has to begin somewhere. One way of tackling its origins is to look at what writers are responding to, or reacting against, in their own society [...] each writer interprets cultural signs in relation to what is familiar" (1996: 4–5). Rees illustrates the impact which social and/or political occurrences may have on literature and in turn that literature gives clues to what society was experiencing at any given time. Thus, utopia is often referred to as a mirror which is "tilted by the author to catch new angles on familiar aspects of his or her society" (1996: 2). However, a mirror can also alter our perception of reality and can often provide a very different picture to the one which we would expect it to reflect. To relate this to a utopian text, "the imagining of fictional alternatives – whether entire social structures, or different modes of living – which are deliberately designed to contrast with, or comment on, dominant cultural forms" (1996: 3) can serve to underline the value of an alternative perspective, but should always be in order to improve or enlighten citizens on how to better the society in which they actually live as opposed to the utopia which they imagine.

Utopia and Language

Postcolonial and utopian theory both share a concern with language. Language has the ability to appropriate and to deligitimise, to create and to destroy. From a utopian perspective, languages can encapsulate specific utopian desires. Anderson (*Imagined Communities*, 1991) has spoken of the utopian possibility of the mother tongue, and the role which a first language can play in forming an individual's view of the world, and his/her relationship with time and memory. Nic Dhiarmada (2007) has identified how the *aisling* tradition of eighteenth-century Irish-language poetry exemplified the poet's desire for political and social change.[15] The utopian vision of the *aisling* was "predicated on remembrance, on nostalgia" (2007: 367). Though nostalgic reminiscences can often prove whimsical, considering nostalgia "not only [as] a mode of memory but also a mode of history [...] as a response to social conditions" can be a very helpful critical and cultural tool (Dames, in Nic Dhiarmada, 2007: 367). Regarding nostalgia as an enabling mechanism in both literature and society, however, presents its own difficulties. Our understanding of the Gaeltacht as

---

15   Aisling, meaning vision or dream, was a literary genre primarily associated with the political poetry of eighteenth-century Ireland. It would "combine the messianic prophecy that better times were ahead with another important motif: the personification of the country as a (supernatural) woman. This latter motif is linked inextricably to the non-rational [...]; it links Ireland furthermore with liminal settings [...] and she invariably appears when the poet is isolated from human company and in a troubled frame of mind" (Leerssen, 1986: 249).

both a linguistic and cultural enclave is heavily influenced by nostalgia, and with looking back. However, if we take nostalgia to be a force for realistic, historical and memorial analysis, then its relationship with the past would seem to inform the present. In taking inspiration from the past as a springboard for a better future, nostalgia liberates the static historical and cultural underpinnings of the nation and "creat[es] [...] an Irish radical memory [which] deploy[s] the past and challenge[s] the present, to restore into possibility historical moments that had been blocked or unfulfilled earlier" (Whelan, 2002: 60). The West of Ireland provided the ultimate utopian destination, and symbolised a rejection of all things dystopian and modernist. The Gaeltacht, at a significant remove linguistically, was an idealised blueprint for the nation, becoming a "fossilized [...] embodiment of what had been lost, imagined through a haze of romantic nostalgia" (Nic Dhiarmada, 2007: 369). However, Gaeltacht writers were among the first to reject the romanticised utopian smokescreen of the West, and began to express their own difficulties with such overarching perceptions. From Pádraic Ó Conaire's short stories to Brian Ó Nualláin's *An Béal Bocht* and Bob Quinn's cinematic work on Connemara, Irish language writers began to rupture the nostalgic veil around the nation's ideas of its own past and its traditional present through the very medium that was supposed to preserve these idealised people and their culture. Ironically and tragically, however, while the "State ideology paid lip service to the Irish language and idealized the Gaeltacht as a nostalgic utopia" (Nic Dhiarmada, 2007: 371), it simultaneously paid only scant heed to the actual, living Gaeltacht which was haemorrhaging its best writers from the start of the 1900s. Ó Conaire's depiction of emigration in *Deoraíocht* (1910)[16] portrayed a harsh and hostile life away from the comforts of home, and many of his short stories were equally unrelenting in their depictions of exile. In Ó Conaire's "Nóra Mharchis Bhig", for example, the return of Nóra from England signals controversy and highlights the tension caused by her expectations of homecoming and her emotional difficulty in settling back into her former community. Her father's rejection of her at the

16   "Exile".

end of the story mirrors the rejection of many Irish people of their own realities in favour of a more suitable Irish identity, situated in the romantic utopian of the West of Ireland. Though Nóra had no choice but to leave her rural life, her father sees what he regards as the taint of modernity in her behaviour and refuses her requests to stay. Máirtín Ó Direáin, much like the character of Nóra, wishes to escape the confines of city life and reimmerse himself in the solitude of island life. However, unlike Nóra, he understands that his reengagement can only last *"seal beag gairid"*, cognisant of the reality of life as an exiled-islander.[17] Nic Dhiarmada regards Ó Direáin's desire to return home in order to alleviate his dislike of the city's noises and distractions as "a form of original nostalgia" (2007: 373). Indeed, Ó Direáin's earliest poetry does see the island as the cure for all ills, and there is, without question, a realisation on the part of the poet that he is far removed both physically and psychologically from his home from the moment he leaves. The island of his childhood and of his poetry is on the horizon of his vision, and he continuously strives to reach out and write it. In his later poetry, however, the utopian longing of his earlier work gives way to the realistion that changes have occurred and that his words and his creations are no longer sufficient defences.

> Aran as a physical space, therefore, can no longer act as "home", can no longer act as balm for the poet's growing alienation from modernity [...]. Aran now becomes an Aran of memory, an idealized space. The poet tells us in one poem, *"thosaigh na clocha glasa / ag dul i gcruth brionglóide i m'aigne"* ("the grey stones began / to turn to dreams in my mind"). Aran, synonymous with the "grey stones", now becomes an unattainable past utopia, which is contrasted with an increasingly dystopian version of the present categorised as *Ár Ré Dhearóil* (Our Wretched Era). In Ó Direáin's work, nostalgia becomes, therefore, a refusal of the present and of the future combined, a reactionary and bitter insistence on the superiority of the past, a mode of memory as intimation of death with no future imaginings possible (Nic Dhiarmada, 2007: 374).

---

17   "... for a short time", from *"Faoiseamh a Gheobhadsa* / I Will Find Solace" (1980: 19).

Place and Promise: Utopian *Dúil*, Desire and Tension

> One must preserve the tension between tradition and utopia. The problem is to
> reanimate tradition and bring utopia closer (Paul Ricoeur, in Kearney, 1988: 269).

There is a tangible tension in almost each story in Ó Flaithearta's *Dúil*.
Similarly, in Lawless's *Grania*, there are signs of the fraught relationships
which exist between Grania and her family and also between Grania
and her environment (see Baccolini on "feeling uncomfortable", 2007:
162). Máirtín Ó Direáin's thematic and personal difficulties lie substan-
tially in the imaginative realm, and are teased out and examined especially in his later poetry. For Synge there is also an awareness of being
caught between two systems of thought, of action and of landscape, of
tension and of satisfaction of desire. Synge, Lawless, Ó Flaithearta and
Ó Direáin all thirst in creative and personal ways to achieve glimpses
of their desired-for hopes and dreams. To taste, however fleetingly, the
artistic and personal fulfilment which they seek, each writer, and each of
their characters and themes, must first negotiate the challenges and the
gaps lying between their work and their hopes for their work. The fulcrum around which the central desire inherent in their work revolves is
an island. Though this is quite apparent in each author's case, it is in how
and why they use, manipulate and give voice to this peripheral location
that speaks most clearly to both utopia and the utopian hermeneutic of
desire for a better being.

The utopian element that unites the four authors' works is desire. This
desire, however, is manifested in a variety of ways, and through multiple
textual and authorial techniques. Desire is a central utopian concern, and a
highly significant aspect of a utopian consciousness of being. Desire, however, is not confined to corporeal or spiritual longing; imaginative desire,
creative and artistic desire, linguistic desire and, perhaps most importantly,
the desire for a better way of being in the world and of knowing the world
are all essential constituents of the concept. Both Sargent and Levitas
emphasise the central importance of desire within the utopian tradition.
Though Levitas does not concur with Sargent's claim that "utopianism is a

universal phenomenon" (1994: 3), both recognise the value of desire within the phenomenon itself. Paula Murphy has recently stated that "[t]he existence of utopian ideals in theory and in literature can be regarded as an effect of human desire" (in Griffin and Moylan, 2007: 244). What this desire represents, however, is uncertain; most authors and scholars take it as a given element within the wider range of utopian engagements. Levitas (1990, 2007a) has come closest to suggesting what utopian desire might signify and suggest, and Moylan (2007a) also highlights the primacy of desire in the utopian project. Sargent and Wegner (in Moylan and Baccolini, 2007) also communicate the importance of desire. This noted, the desire which motivates an individual or a society to seek to better itself either through envisioning an imaginary place and using that as a focus of motivation or by imagining a potentially better version of an actual place is tantamount to any understanding of that utopia's foundation. Sargent writes that "[u]topias [...] are historical artifacts that are brought into being at particular times and places and usually by identifiable people whose reasons for doing so are in principle knowledge" (1994: 6).

The notion of being *brought into being* again invites a comparison with the createdness of the West of Ireland's landscape and constituted nature as well as the necessity felt by writers and cultural nationalists to bring about a place, both real and at some level imaginary that would lead to both artistic endeavour and to cultural betterment. Thus, by bringing into being – or at the very least, reawakening – the West of Ireland as a cradle for cultural, geographical and linguistic purity and preservation, a tangible feeling of desire is evident. However, one constituent element commonly associated with this desire for a better way of being in the world, though which is in fact antithetical to what utopian desire signifies, is that of perfection or the search for the perfect in the imagined or real society. Sargent is unequivocal on this issue:

> Some authors insist that the utopian society must be perfect and therefore realizable. [...] People do not live "happily ever after" even in More's *Utopia*. [...] perfection has never been a characteristic of utopian fiction, but the misuse of the word continues (1994: 6)

Perfect, perfection, and their variants are freely used by scholars in defining utopias. They should not be. [...] Perfection is the exception, not the rule. [...] opponents of utopianism use the label *perfect* as a political weapon to justify their opposition (1994: 9).

The reason for this brief discussion on the idea of the perfect, or of perfection and its inherent dangers within the utopian project relates to the associated danger of seeing everything outside of this anticipated *perfect world* as being in some way defective. The charge of perfectionism was levelled at both Synge and Lawless with regard to their representations of the Aran Islands. Ironically, however, Synge was castigated for showing the darker sides of island life (evictions, excessive drinking scenes), perhaps jarring with readers' perception, and for not integrating himself fully into the seeming perfection of the life on the Islands. Lawless, meanwhile, was critiqued for stepping outside of her boundaries as a female, for entering a male-dominated tradition, for seemingly misrepresenting island life, and also for presenting a less-than-perfect portrait of Grania's life and times. However, neither author sought perfection and, importantly, in both the introduction to *The Aran Islands* and *Grania: The Story of an Island*, Synge and Lawless state that they have presented, in order, a realistic and uncorrupted picture of life there (*The Aran Islands*) and a fictionalised story of one island woman's life, though one that is based on some observational concreteness (*Grania*).

The Mirror Image: Perfect though Fleeting

Desire, and perfection, might well be best examined using the metaphor of a mirror. As Rees has shown, utopia as a mirror is often positioned by authors in order to throw new light on his or her society (1996: 2). Sargent ("Choosing Utopia") writes that "[u]topias hold up a fun fair mirror to society that corrects the distortions in the present by showing a better alternative. Once seen, it becomes the responsibility of the viewer to work to achieve that or some other better world" (2007: 308). However, one must always remain cognisant of a mirror's potential to refract as well as to reflect; what one sees is not always what one expected to see.[18] Rees' and Sargent's hypotheses, then, are that a mirror captures previously unseen aspects and offers different, more pleasing, perspectives on what is already visible. It follows that a mirror can also simultaneously reflect and distort both the familiar and the unfamiliar, morphing the past and the present into one image.

The mirror itself might be thought of as a liminal object; it allows for the transfer of the image and the reflection of that image, but in some way stands between the image and the reflection, storing some of its qualities, hiding some and changing others. A mirror also makes visible aspects that we cannot see, while also magnifying aspects we might not wish to see. In much the same way as a camera captures an image and then later reveals that image to us in a framed and often stylised way, the mirror contains an image and, through the processes of reflection and refraction, sends that image back to the viewer to examine and contemplate. However, there is an immediacy to the images captured in mirrors, and they cannot contain or retain the fleeting image for longer than a moment or two. And yet, the human race desires images of moments, and of places and of individuals living in their unique environments. The snapshot quality of Synge's work in *The Aran Islands* captures and reflects this desire, as well as actual images of the islanders themselves. Anne Burke's PhD thesis (2008) on photographic representations of Irish culture and heritage reveals that Synge did not actually bring a camera to the Aran Islands, as documented on several occasions (Gerstenberger, 1964; Kiberd, 2000; Saddlemyer, 2007), with the intention of photographing the islanders. Instead, Synge, having met and purchased a camera from a travelling salesman in Inis Mór, proceeded to take his very first photographs with a camera on Inis Meáin, clearly realising that the written word alone could not express

---

18   I am most grateful to Dr Patricia Lynch for pointing this out during undergraduate lectures on contemporary Irish writing (2004).

and capture all that lay around him.[19] Synge's written and photographic relationship with Aran, however, is difficult to define, particularly from a utopian perspective. Helena Fernandez Pajares's MA thesis (1999) considers Synge's work as presenting "a utopian island in which he portrays himself outside [...] the forces of the modern world" and thus, making the island a "utopia by projecting onto it his own vision of the world beyond social, economic and political strictures" (1999: 5–6). However, while there are arguments for some aspects of this analysis, Synge's nexus with his work and his passion for the Islands does not lend itself to simple classification. Considering *The Aran Islands* as a utopian narrative, however, adds to this difficulty while also revealing salient observations about the Islands' cultural power and about Synge's understanding of temporal-spatial concerns. As Wegner (2002) suggests, "[n]arrative utopias are more akin to traveler's itineraries, or an architectural sketch, tracing an exploratory trajectory, a narrative line that, as it unfolds, quite literally engenders something new in the world" (2002: xix). The brevity inherent in sketches, itineraries, diary entries and photographs emphasise the multitudinous visions and versions of island life on offer to the author; there is so much to capture that a novel or a lengthier volume of work would not do justice to the motion of life there. I do not believe, however, that Synge projected his own vision onto the Islands. The very fact that he did not bring a camera with him highlights this; he did not come with a set agenda, he went to the Islands seeking possibility but not searching for concrete answers. There is an unconcluded sense to *The Aran Islands*, which mirrors the reality of Synge's own premature passing and thus, perhaps, his unfinished work on the Islands. Although Synge saw evidence of tradition and early traces of modernity on the Islands, there is a palpable sense that he did not want the

19   The visitor was a school teacher named Redmond, well acquainted with the Islands. Synge mentioned to Redmond his disappointment at not having brought a camera with him to the Islands and Redmond quickly offered to have his Lancaster hand camera sent out to the Islands and to sell it to Synge if he was happy with it (see Stephens, 1974: 117). I am most grateful to Dr Anne Burke for alerting me to this fact, and for pointing out that a note in Synge's diary on 17 May duly states that the camera arrived (TCD MS 4419, 17/5/1898).

Islands to function as alternatives to his own society, but as places apart in their own right, a world in opposition to that of the mainland while also influenced by that very place and its people. Though utopian fiction often offers its readers avenues of possibility, Synge problematises this and offers instead a picture of a place where "the cannot" is just as possible as "the can" of utopian dreaming.

In a similar fashion to Synge's work, Lawless's *Grania*, though in novel form, reads much like a documentary; indeed, Synge may owe an even greater debt to Lawless than he was happy to concede in that her memorable descriptions of the journey between the mainland of Galway and Inis Meáin would seem to foreground similar observations which he made in the opening pages of *The Aran Islands*. Lawless's *Grania* opens with the following *mise en scène*:

> Clouds over the whole expanse of sky, nowhere showing any immediate disposition to fall as rain, yet nowhere allowing the sky to appear decidedly, nowhere even becoming themselves decided, keeping everywhere a broad indefinable wash of greyness, a grey so dim, uniform, and all-pervasive, that it defied observation, floating and melting away into a dimly blotted horizon which, whether at any given point to call sea or sky, land or water, it was all but impossible to decide (1892: 1).

This is quite similar to Synge's descriptions in the first pages of *The Aran Islands*:

> [...] we left the quay of Galway in a dense shroud of mist. A low line of shore was visible at first on the right between the movement of the waves and fog, but when we came further it was lost sight of, and nothing could be seen but the mist curling in the rigging, and a small circle of foam. [...] A dreary rock appeared at first sloping up from the sea into the fog [...] (1992: 3).

While it is likely that the authors would have obviously been taken by the sudden appearances and disappearances of the Islands through the mist and fog of morning and rough weather, it is crucial to note that both Lawless and Synge immediately make reference to the difficulty of deciding upon the shape and location of the "dreary rock" before them. Louis Marin's work on travel and utopia provides an interesting method by which to read the opening pages of both *Grania* and *The Aran Islands*:

From the time of More's book and for centuries later, utopias tend to begin with a travel, a departure and a journey, most of the time by sea, most of the time interrupted by a storm, a catastrophe that is the sublime way to open a neutral space, one that is absolutely different: [...] the process of travel may be a way of displaying, just in the front, a utopian space (1993: 414–415).

Hy-Brasil, Aran and Otherworldly Voyages

"No angel who ever came to Ireland to help Gael or Gall returned to Heaven without first visiting Aran, and if people understood how greatly the Lord loves Aran they would all come there to partake of its blessings" (Cormac mac Cuilennáin, King-Bishop of Cashel, died AD 908)

The island of Hy-Brasil, thought by many to represent the lost lands found in Celtic mythology and folklore (Curran, 2007: 63), became aligned with Aran's Edenic, utopian imaginings from as early as 1684.[20] Between 1325 and 1865, Hy-Brasil, or at least a variation on the name, was marked on maps as being just southwest of Galway Bay.[21] Imagery of a phantom or lost island surrounds Hy-Brasil, as it fades in and out of cartographical and popular accounts from the time.[22] Significantly, towards the end of the nineteenth century, the island disappears off the maps for County Galway, reappearing off the north Antrim coast as "Green Island" (Curran, 65). Moylan suggests that "with the Celtic Otherworld and Christian Heaven" of early Irish literature, "the anticipation of an alternative space resonates

---

20   Roderic O'Flaherty's account of O'Brasil (1684) charts the appearances of the enchanted island, as viewed from the Aran Islands.

21   Hy-Brasil appears as Brazil, Brasil, Isle of the Blest, Green Island and O'Brasil on maps and in texts (Jeans, 2004: 39).

22   "The Islands of Aran [...] are still believed by many of the peasantry to be the nearest land of the far-famed island of O'Brazil or Hy Brasail, the blessed paradise of the pagan Irish. It is supposed even to be visible from the cliffs on particular and rare occasions" (Murray, J. (1866) quoted in Jeans, 2004: 38).

[...] through the centuries" (2007b: 299). In his study of St Brendan's Voyage, or the Navigatio Sancti Brendani, the sphere of the island comes into play as Moylan charts the spatial, imaginative and spiritual quests of early Irish pilgrim journeys.[23] Having previously sought out monastic islands such as Iona, and the Orkney and Shetland Islands, gaining him the title "Brendan the Voyager", and later, "Brendan the Navigator", St Brendan completed the journey from Ireland to Newfoundland between 565 and 573. As a literary creation, the Navigatio belongs to the early Irish genre of the *immram*, or the sea-adventure story.[24] The allegorical significance of the stories relates to the journey to Heaven, or the land of promise, but there is a considerable amount of literal emphasis placed on the travel itself, its attendant dangers and surprising discoveries. However,

> in the expanding and popular reception of the text across a changing medieval world, the text also begins to suggest to later readers the possibility of a fulfilling space in the *present* world, a promised land of peace and plenty that bespoke a fresh meaning in the overtly utopian mode in the centuries to follow (Moylan, 2007b: 305).

In a fashion similar to Cambrensis' description of the Aran Islands, the Navigatio details the Edenic, pastoral and plentiful vision of the various islands St Brendan and his crew stop at on their journey. Moylan puts forward the theory the text aligns itself with the "*proto* or *latently* utopian" narrative, which, in the sixteenth century formed the literary utopia (2007b: 312). The literary utopia, then, had both a linear narrative, which traced

---

23   St Enda, still associated with Inis Mór, established a monestary there in AD 485 and became known as the founder of Irish monasticism (O'Connell, 1994: 136). It is thought that his residence in Inis Mór enticed other saints to travel to the island, most notably St Columcille and St Ciarán of Clonmacnoise who sought out solitude and solemnity on their pilgrimages. St Enda's feast day, 21 March, is still marked on Inis Mór, and a village (Cille Éinne), ruins and crosses continue to record his name there. Áras Éinne, Inis Oírr's arts centre, also bears the saint's name.

24   "There is a recurrent motif of sea voyage in Irish legend [...] most powerfully evident in the *immram* chronicles of expeditions and adventure written mainly between the seventh and nineth centuries" (Kearney, 1997: 113). The most famous of the *immrama* is perhaps Immram Brain Mac Febuil (Voyage of Bran, son of Febul).

the "voyage, arrival at a strange new place; tour of the new, challenging, space led by a knowledgeable guide; and return home accompanied by a report on the efficact of that wonderful place", as well as the non-linear image of that space, "a space that is more plentiful, nourishing, and fulfilling than any previously known by the text's travelers and one that enables its discursive creators to think and to enact new social possiblities" (2007b: 312). It is Moylan's contention then, that the Navigatio continues to supply the modern (Irish) utopian tradition with much of its elemental features (2007b: 312), signifying as it does, the desire inherent in much Irish utopian fiction with what he terms "soul utopia[s]" (2007b: 313), or the yearning for a better way of being. Though religious utopian narratives expound upon the transitional movement from a state of sinfulness to a space of divine perfection, it is, perhaps, within this shift from sin to goodness, or from naivety to realisation that the most important journey takes place. The attempt at reaching the shores of the possible seems to have been a quest from the earliest time and reveals the personal, spiritual and societal underpinnings of much utopian narratives.

Hy-Brasil often appears as St Brendan's Isle, and myths abound as to his landing on the lost island during his travels, providing another link with the religious and pure quality associated with offshore islands and the heavens. Given that Hy-Brasil, St Brendan's Isle and Isle of the Blest are all inter-changeable names for the island further strengthens this point. Roderick O'Flaherty, whose study of Aran was the first of its kind, documents that from "the Isles of Aran and the west continent, often appears visible that inchanted island called O'Brasil, and in Irish Beg-ara or the Lesser Aran, set down in cards of navigation" ([1684] 1846, in Ó hEithir, 1991: 15–16). Though O'Flaherty considers that the mystical island could indeed be real rock-formations, he nonetheless records the testimony of islanders in relation to sighting of O'Brasil. He remains uncertain, however, towards the end of his account whether "it be reall and firm land, kept hidden by speciall ordinance of God, as the terrestiall paradise, or else some illusion of airy clouds appearing on the surface of the sea" (in Ó hEithir, 1991: 16). Hugo Hamilton's recent description of the Islands as "an illusion, out of reach" (2010: 174) would seem to echo O'Flaherty's account. Writing in relation to England's plans to use the port of Galway city rather than her own docks in case of war, James Joyce describes the city as "the mirage which blinded the poor fisherman of Aran, follower and emulator of St Brendan, appears in the distance" (from the Italian, *"Il Miraggio del Pescatore di Aran"*, in Ó hEithir, 1991: 109). It is fascinating to think of Aran as the centre rather than the periphery, and of Aran fishermen discovering the mirage of the urban hub of Galway. Máirtín Ó Direáin has described his peoples' imaginative capabilities in great detail, and also their realisation that Aran was, to them, the whole world.

In his poem, *"Buaile Bheag"* / "Little Field", Ó Direáin illustrates the importance of the small patch of land to which he escaped in need of inspiration. The little field, of course, is also symbolic of the small island, and of the artist as an isolated and isolating figure in the community. Describing it as *"fearann coimirce m'aislinge, / Mo dhomhan go léir"* (1980: 57)[25], the field and the island eventually fade from his view and the poet is left alone, bewildered by the disappearance of his vision, *"[c]á bhfuilir a bhuaile / A fuaireas dom féin?"*.[26] Pádraig Standún's recollections of arriving on Inis Meáin in 1970 register his sense of what he regarded as the otherworldly character of the island. Having "reached a new world [...] appear[ing] out of the mist", Standún was "not ready for the culture shock" of seeing men and women still wearing traditional clothes such as petticoats and homespun trousers (in Waddell *et al.*, 1994: 307). Describing himself as a "more realistic romantic" having lived on the Islands for many years, Standún writes that though "I'm around longer than any tourist, journalist or anthropologist [...] I'm still a blow-in, a stranger, an interloper" (1994: 307, 309). Passing as he does, through the veil of mist to the light acquired by insider knowledge, Standún's *immram* reveals much about the realities and romantics of island life. While travelling in a currach to Inis Oírr to say mass there, the priest found himself at the mercy of the Fowl Sound's waves and currents. However, the exhilaration upon safely landing on the island threw into focus the "adventure [that] had changed from the frightening to the romantic", with Standún comparing the shape of the currach

25   "... the secure land of my dream / my entire world".
26   "... where are you field / that I found for myself".

with "the shoe of Christ walking on the water" (1994: 308). Standún does, nonetheless, caution that island life is certainly not "some kind of heaven on earth" (310), veering away from the Edenic portrayals and instead advising that "isolation [...] can make you forget that there is a world out there beyond the sea" (310). The insular environment which island living both facilitates and forces upon individuals, finds its counterpart within the monastic tradition. Islands also function as fantastic stop-overs for voyagers wishing to re-charge their souls and replenish their stocks.

This liminal point between departure and arrival often marks the beginning of great stories. Ó Flaithearta's stories "His First Flight" and "Going into Exile" detail the pain and difficulty of leaving for a young seagull and for a sister and brother about to depart for America. All three protagonists balance on the literal and metaphorical edges of the island, and though their fates are sealed, they linger another while on their ledges. Mary and Michael Feeney are attending an American wake in honour of their going away but both siblings are anxious at the prospect of what awaits them over the horizon. Patrick, their father, comments that "it's a cruel world that takes you away from the land made for you", to which Michael retorts: "what did anybody ever get out of the land but poverty and hard work and potatoes and salt" (O'Flaherty, 1966: 100). Mary, the younger of the two, sees that she has no place at home any longer, being on the cusp of leaving, and begins to dream of fine clothes and opportunities but also of the detachment which such a change encurs; "in a few hours they would be homeless wanderers [...] cut adrift from [home]" (1966: 104). In "His First Flight", the young seagull sits frightened, wary of the approach of his first air-borne manoeuvre. The distance between himself, the sea beneath and his family on the opposite cliff-face seems unbridgeable and he fears he has neither the strength nor the skill to fly. When he eventually does summon the courage, he is surprised at the sensation of the air under his wings, and also of the water supporting his body when he lands. His courage for leaving his perch is rewarded, but also signals the end of his youthful innocence and his departure from his homeplace. The use of animals in Ó Flaithearta's stories is mirrored in Ó Direáin's use of the prisoner in his poetry.

Both Synge and Lawless's narrative sketches also illuminate the disori-
enting characteristic of sailing to the Islands in hazy weather, and watching
them "appear" from the mists. *Grania's* opening section depicts:

> that low line of islands which breaks the outermost curve of the bay of Galway, and
> beyond which is nothing, nothing, that is to say, but the Atlantic, a region which,
> despite the ploughing of innumerable keels, is still given up by the dwellers of those
> islands to a mystic condition of things unknown to geographers, but too deeply rooted
> in their consciousness to yield to any mere reports from without (1892: 2).

Many of Ó Flaitheartá's stories depict the mist-laden landscape of Aran
and, by contrast, the clarity of vision and purpose of his protagonists on
days of clear weather. Examples of this technique are found in "Milking
Time" and "The Wave" (in Kelly, ed., 1999: 170, 28), and, most poignantly,
in *"Daoine Bochta"* (1953: 85). The blurring of the lines between life, death
and the natural environment emphasises the connection between all three,
and proximity of each aspect as experienced in the lives of the characters.
In *"An Beo / Life"*, Ó Flaitheartá's positions life alongside imminent death,
set against a backdrop of emigration, a poor winter and economic difficulties for the family of newly-born baby. Perhaps Synge's *Riders to the Sea*,
presents us with the most poignant of all expositions of this veil between
life and death. Maura, the maternal protagonist, has lost sons and now a
husbad to the sea, and yet she busies herself with the concerns of living,
preparing their funerals and, in the closing scene, accepting the inevitabil-
ity of death and its proximity at all times.[27]
   In "Looking Eastward", a poem written in 1885 and collected in *With
the Wild Geese* (1902), Lawless describes a scene similar to that found in

---

27   Synge's depiction of the keening woman in *The Aran Islands*, and Ó Direáin's por-
     trayal of the dignified female mourners in *"Dínit an Bhróin /* The Dignity of Sorrow"
     (1980: 21) and in *"Brón mo Mháthar /* My Mother's Sorrow" (1980: 58) further
     emphasises the stoicism and understanding of island women in relation to death
     and fate. In Blasket Island writing, we find Sayers' account of losing her son Tomás
     through drowning (1936: 213–216), and Tomás Ó Criomhthain's description of the
     loss of his children (1937: 186–200).

Grania.[28] The poem's significance is two-fold: first, it was written prior to her visiting the Aran Islands and second, it pre-empts one of Lawless's most pertinent themes as displayed in *Grania*, the "restless and inert" (Grubgeld, 1983: 16) nature of land, sea and human. In the poem, Lawless "compares Ireland to the moaning and murmuring sea" (Grubgeld: 1983: 16) and the land blurs with the seas and skies surrounding it. In much the same way that *Grania*'s opening passages portray a bleak and unforgiving landscape, "Looking Eastward" compares the greyness of the sea with the lights of homes in the distance:

> Blurred is the arch of sky, mistily grey in the
>   zenith,
>   Lost and void in the distance, filled with the
>   haze of September.
> Few and low gleam the lights, seen through the
>   doors of the cabins,
>   Small red eyes of flame, set in brown time-
>   wrinkled faces.
> Overhead the clouds dart and scatter like sea-
>   birds;
> Underfoot, from its caverns, moans and mur-
>   murs atlantic,
>   Moans and murmurs now, as it murmured and
>   moaned at the dawning.
>   Eastward to-night I gaze, to where, like a wave
>   grown hard,
>   Rises a long green ridge, set in the swell of the
>   sea
>   (from *With the Wild Geese*, 1902: 48–49).

While Linn's contention that Lawless's verse "contain[s] a curious blend of stoicism and personal lament which gives them a whining, unappealing tone" and also that "her verse is uneven, and a striking image or line is often followed by bombastic and empty rhetoric" (1971: 201) may carry

---

28   Dr Heidi Hansson very kindly provided me with copies of *With the Wild Geese* (1902) and also *The Inalienable Heritage and other Poems* (1914).

some weight, using her poetry in conjunction with her novels is a valuable exercise. Grubgeld, however, unlike Linn, is happier to avoid reading too much of Lawless's ill-health and melancholic disposition into her analysis of her poetry and focuses instead on a somewhat less-biographically charged interpretation of the work. Grubgeld's PhD thesis, *Private Geographies: Land and Life in the Irish Literary Renaissance: Emily Lawless, George Moore and J.M. Synge* (1983), suggests that in Lawless's writing "the land becomes a rich, multifaceted repository for her thinking on personal consciousness, national affairs, and the scientific dilemmas of her age" (1982: 9). Grubgeld also notes that "*Grania: The Story of an Island* (1892), more graphically reveal (sic.) the dichotomy and paradox which characterizes the fabric of her profound relationship with the west of Ireland" (1983: 9).

Grubgeld's interpretation of the poem reveals that the "land takes on the character of an immobile sea, and both land and sea are simultaneously restless and inert. [...] she depicts the swift degeneration of a country which refuses to move of its own accord. [...] Ireland is beset with simultaneous immobility and insecurity" (1983: 16). As in Patrick Pearse's poem "The Mother", Lawless sees the island (both an Aran Island and a possible metaphor for Ireland) as female and reflects on the dangers and trials which the island and/or mother suffers as a result of the crashing waves and the changing times. The island and the generations whom she has raised now find themselves at the mercy of the elements. However, in "Looking Eastward" and in many of Lawless' other poems, the distance between the poet and her subject and also between the island and its corresponding mainland remains a constant; it is rarely bridged, either psychologically or in reality. There are of course innumerable reasons why Lawless focuses so directly on obfuscations of distances, on loss of place and on gaps and spaces between herself and what she desires. Grubgeld argues that "[w]hile her writing does not reflect contemporary interest in Celtic myths, current politics, or Gaelic folklore, it does thus reflect a new interest in [...] geography full of medieval and modern associations" (1983: 13). However, although it is correct to say that topography and geo-cultural significance were her main interests, Lawless does, at times, perhaps unconsciously engage with Ireland's Gaelic past and present. Grubgeld states that "[s]he was fascinated by the effect of geography on the Irish character" (1983: 13) and yet does not seem to see any incongruity between this and her suggestion that Lawless was not interested in Celtic myths, folklore or current politics. Surely geography, particularly Irish geography, would encapsulate all these elements, none more so than the geography of the West of Ireland. Lawless's interest in topography effectively grounds her in all elements of the West of Ireland, and her scientific background would have made her aware of the importance of recording and analysing all aspects of her surroundings.

Nonetheless, perhaps Grubgeld's point could also be interpreted as highlighting Lawless's fascination with chasms, gaps and anomalies. In "Isserclan: A Letter" from *A Point of View* (1904), Lawless describes the distance between herself and the landscape, and her frustrations at not being able to bridge that divide:

> How rarely now do we together stand
> Here where the clouds above us dreaming pass,
> [...]
> 'Twixt that old shore and this on which we stand –
> As twixt two headlands crowned each with a home –
> Spreads a wild waste of waves, a cold rough strand
> Whitened with drifting foam,
> [...]
> Across this space malign and black
> [...].

The ambiguous "we" of "Isserclan: A Letter" could represent Lawless's own in-betweeness, her divided self. The Aran Islands certainly provided Lawless with the appropriate topography in which to examine her own personal desires, and her own professional difficulties. Lawless looked to Aran to offer her a picture, and possibly even sets of images, with which to illustrate her own divided mind, her own duality of interests, and her own liminal nature. Lawless's desire for the West of Ireland, and her own desire for refuge both artistic and personal, allowed her to create liminal utopias whereby she could escape, recreate, embellish and distort societal and personal norms and gender-ascribed roles.

Ó Flaithearta: The Search For and The Satisfaction of Desire

Liam Ó Flaithearta's collection *Dúil* (1953) presents the reader with glimpses, akin to those of Synge's in *The Aran Islands*, of the everyday struggles and observations of island men and women. Louis de Paor suggests that Ó Flaithearta's experience of writing film scripts is reflected in his writing, wherby he presents predominantly external pictures of characters which must be interpreted by his readers without the assistance of more internal details (in Ní Annracháin and Nic Dhiarmada, 1998: 22). What makes *Dúil* even more fascinating, however, is how Ó Flaithearta uses the notion of desire in such varied ways and how this desire creates a bond – often fraught – between the individual and some aspect of his or her place identity. Apart from the repetition of the word *"dúil"* throughout the collection, each character suffers from and desires to satisfy a palpable hunger and/or thirst during the course of each story. Before delving into the individual tales, however, it is important to consider the importance of Ó Flaithearta's own personal desire to produce a collection of his short stories in his first language. Inherent in Ó Flaithearta's struggle for linguistic expression in Irish was a desire to capture some elements which he felt could not be adequately conveyed in English. The jacket notes from the 1953 edition of *Dúil* highlights the satisfaction of desire which Ó Flaithearta experienced upon completing the work:

> *Cé gur le Gaeilge a tógadh é, is é seo an chéad cheann dá leabhra líonmhara a chum sé sa teanga sin. Adhmhófar, dar linn, gur barr bisigh air filleadh ar theanga a shinsear. Sa chnuasach seo tá cuid de na gearrscéalta is fearr dá bhfuil scríofa aige* (Sáirséal agus Dill, 1953: jacket notes).[29]

---

29 "Although he was raised with Irish, this is the first of his numerous books that he wrote in that language. We believe that it is a healthy decision for him to return to the language of his ancestors. In this collection are some of the best short stories he has written".

Emphasising the psychological and emotional lift which Ó Flaithearta enjoyed upon finishing the collection, Sáirséal agus Dill stress the satisfaction of returning to the well of language for the author. *Dúil's* power rests largely on Ó Flaithearta's eye for minute detail, and it is in these minutiae that desire manifests itself for the characters in the stories. Cognisant of the scale, size and shape of his own island home, and the emphasis on the smaller rather than the bigger picture, Ó Flaithearta cleverly uses this diminutive scale to frame the larger, more esoteric, questions about life, struggle, death, longing and enchantment. The most mundane and routine elements of life are, in Ó Flaithearta's work, moments of realisation. In one of Ó Flaithearta's few poetic enterprises, *"Na Blátha Creige"* ("The Rock Flowers"), the poet asks the flowers why they have chosen such a wind-swept and bleak place to grow; the flowers respond by saying that it does not bother them that they flourish in a barren place, for they are enchanted by the sea's music. Indeed, Ó Flaithearta embues his stories with a similar, if not always quite so emotive, wonderment at the most ordinary of happenings. A brief scan of the titles of the short stories collected in *Dúil* illustrates this point: *"Bás na Bó"* / "The Cow's Death", *"An Chulaith Nua"* / "The New Suit", and *"Daoine Bochta"* are but three of the story-titles which highlight the ordinariness-as-backdrop which Ó Flaithearta employed throughout this work. To say that each story in *Dúil* contains a revelation would be over-stating the case; however, in their simplicity of form, content and action, each story focuses on the forward motion of each character from a moment of desire to a moment of some level of satisfaction, painful insight or mini-realisation. In some cases this realisation is mundane in the extreme, and in some other cases it is fleeting, such as in the title story *"Dúil"*. The young boy's joy at reaching the window in order to touch the sunbeam which he had noticed dancing on the floor suddenly dissipates when he realises he cannot hold onto the light. Nonetheless, he achieves another form of satisfaction at his mother's breast and this quells the desire he felt moments earlier at the window. However, until his mother comes to comfort him, the infant feels alone. His efforts to reach the source of light have taken much energy, as he is still crawling: *"[m]hothaigh sé na pianta a bhí ag crá a choirp. Thuig sé go*

raibh achar mór siúlta aige go dtí an áit ina raibh sé aonraic" (1953: 14).[30]
As he had been enchanted, *"faoi dhraíocht"* (1953: 12), by the light, upon
returning to his mother's arms he reconnects with his first understanding
of magic, his mother's womb: *"[a]nseo le taobh na bruinne ina bhfuair
sé an beo ní raibh aon bheann aige ar phian ná ar chontúirt an tsaoil.
Anois ba hé glór binn a mháthar a bhí á chur faoi dhraíocht [...]. Nuair a
dhún sé a shúile faoi dheireadh [...] bhí sé ag craitheadh le dúil in aistear
eile a thabhairt [...]"* (1953: 15).[31] Perhaps the most important aspect of
this story rests in this final sentence, the young infant's desire for a new
attempt at seeing the world is nurtured upon satisfying another desire.
Ó Flaithearta's focus on the child's journey represents the growth of his
imagination, and the much longer journey through life which the child
is beginning to contemplate at the end of the story. Seeing that there is
a much bigger world outside of the safety of his mother's arms and his
own comfort zone, Ó Flaithearta brings to life the epiphanic nature of
the everyday. Though the child does not catch the sunbeam in his small
hands, he graps the enormity of a much larger concept, that of the world
outside of his own. Ó Flaithearta gives voice to the utopian quest to
travel life's paths and the many attempts that people make to grasp at
life's mysteries.

Ó Flaithearta's stories based around animals also underscore feelings of
desire, and often the fear which the fulfilment of that desire might entail.
In *"An Seachac"*/ "The Hawk", and *"An Fiach"* / "The Hunt", both hawk
and dog respectively track down their prey, experiencing anticipation and
exhilaration as they kill the young lark and the agile rabbit. Ó Flaithearta's
describes with ferocious accuracy the mouth-watering desire experienced by
the animals. The hawk, *"éan álainn an bháis"* is depicted as having a deadly

---

30   "... he felt the pains that were tormenting his body. He understood that he had walked
a great distance to the place where he was alone".
31   "... here next to the womb in which he received life, he did not fear the pain or
danger of life. Now it was his mother's sweet voice that had him enthralled [...].
When he finally closed his eyes [...] he was shaking with the desire to make another
journey".

greed in his desire-swollen eyes (1953: 16–17).[32] The hound is similarly greedy, and Ó Flaithearta describes him as shaking with desire (1953: 131). In "Bás na Bó", however, Ó Flaithearta portrays a profound desire, that of a mother for her offspring. Having given birth to a stillborn calf, the cow goes in search of it, smelling the ground for traces of its presence. Her body, initially sore from the exertions of birth and confused by the absence of her calf, becomes immune to pain and instead, gives way to excitement, then fear and, upon seeing the body of the calf on the rocks below, horror. Her desire for her calf is so great that she lets out a loud bellow and leaps from the cliff to join her young (1953: 47–51).

"An Scáthán" presents a parallel between Lawless's Grania and the young girl of Ó Flaithearta's story. Both girls are headstrong, independent and daring: "[c]ailín ríbhreá dea-dhéanta! [...] Bhí sí caol, ard, gan smál gan easpa, gorm na mara ina súile agus áilleacht an róis ina leicne. [...] A Dhia Mhóir an Iontais!" (1953: 32).[33] Ó Flaithearta's girl, like Grania, longs for the freedom of the cool waters, and at the end of the story, swims naked in the rock pool. However, the young girl firstly considers thoughts of drowning, and the freedom which that would give her from her chores and worries. This is an unusual desire, the desire for death, but the girl has been working in heavy clothing, under the hot sun and begins to equate her desire for freedom with freedom from corporeal form. Ó Direáin's poem "An t-Earrach Thiar" / "Spring in the West" (1980: 33) offers a comparative image of the women of his childhood, gathering periwinkles, with their weighty skirts gathered under them so as not to get them wet.[34]

32 "... the beautiful bird of death".
33 "... a very fine, well made girl! She was slender, tall, perfect, with sea-blue eyes and the beauty of the rose in her cheeks. [...] God of Wonder!".
34 The strength (both physical and mental) and distinctiveness of the women of Aran is a shared thread between all four authors considered in this book. Grania "could use her muscles in every sort of outdoor labour as a man uses his" (1892: 111), Synge's women maintain the family-home and comfort the bereaved. Ó Direáin's women, as above, are tenacious and hard-working and Ó Flaithearta's women are predominantly strong-willed and emotionally stoic.

Mná i locháin	Women in the shallows
In íochtar díthrá,	At furthest ebb,
A gcótaí craptha,	With their skirts tucked up,
Scáilí thíos fúthu:	And reflections beneath them:
Támhradharc sítheach	A tranquil sight
San Earrach thiar.	During Spring in the West.[35]

Like the girl in *"An Scáthán"*, Lawless's Grania also longs for freedom, and though her skill at sailing gives her some of this liberty, she is confined to home and to land by Honor's illness and Murdough's inability to farm or tend to the crops. When Grania drowns at the close of the novel, she achieves, rather ironically, a measure of the freedom the sea offered her.[36] The young girl in *"An Scáthán"* quickly abandons the thoughts of death when the cold waters startle her into realisation. Having been mesmerised by the heat of the sun and the coolness of the tide washing against her ankles, she awakens to find herself scurrying further inshore from the swell. Another parallel between *"An Scáthán"* and *Grania* centres on both girls' desire to be as one with their surroundings. When the girl in Ó Flaithearta' story desires communion with both the cool water and the hard rock, she is, perhaps unconsciously, signalling her sexual awakening. In Lawless's novel, Grania's desire to understand her feelings and her body better lead her to embrace a familiar boulder on the edge of a cliff; "[She] put her head against the big boulder, invisible but still present, a familiar object sustaining and comforting" (1892: 254–255). In so doing, "Grania, and perhaps Lawless as well, believes these familiar stones and cliffs can reveal the thoughts and feelings she can not quite articulate by herself. The role of place in the production of this New Woman is therefore given a tangible appearance in Grania's interactions with her geography" (Edwards, 2008: 427).

---

35   Mac Síomóin and Sealy's translation (1984: 15).

36   Lawless' portrayal of drowning pre-empts that of Synge's in *Riders to the Sea* (1904), though the latter refers only to the drowning of men at sea. Synge's delicate fascination with the grief experienced by the women left behind is counterpointed by Grania's understanding of her own fate, and the helplessness of her situation once Murdough refuses to fetch a priest for Honor (1892: 352).

Ó Flaitheartaʼs use of the mirror in the title of this story is very relevant here, and also to the character of Grania in Lawlessʼs novel.[37] In using the rock-pool filled with sea-water and the sea itself as a mirror for their own introspective purposes, both Grania and the young girl emphasise their longing for the freedom to choose their own paths, and to escape their present lives. However, the seaʼs inherent flux and often dangerous nature cannot accurately reflect the girlsʼ decisions or choices and so, with each wave, new choices, new forms of escape and new challenges present themselves. Both Grania and the young girl in *"An Scáthán"* have tempestuous natures, and this is mirrored in the changing seas around them; in *Grania*, the seaʼs moods, storms and calms are all effectively used to foreground the turbulent character of Graniaʼs own peripatetic and often melancholic nature. What emerges from all the stories in *Dúil*, and indeed in cross-comparisons with Lawless, is that desire is at the core of an individualʼs power to motivate, change, and choose direction and satisfaction in life.

However, to associate the motivation for a better way of living or of being with perfection belies any attempt at reality, even if this reality is created or artistically manipulated. For the exile, nostalgia also carries within its structure a certain amount of desire for perfection, usually linked with the home place which is always in opposition with the exileʼs new home, but this remembered or sought perfection primarily reveals itself to be a heavily nostalgic enterprise rather than an accurate portrait of the reality of the situation. Of course, perfection guards and protects against the reality of distance and alienation from oneʼs past, but ultimately it only serves to create an inaccurate vision of what was once oneʼs reality, and this in turn further isolates the exile from both his/her past and also from any eventual return. Declan Collingeʼs thesis on Máirtín Ó Direáinʼs

37   In the novel itself, Lawless describes how, after a shower of rain, the limestone rocks "reflect every atom of light as upon a mirror" (1892: 178), and later, documents that, "owing to the wetness of the rocks and to their absolute horizontality, the whole drama of the sky was repeated twice over; the same shaft of light, seen first far off upon the most remote horizon, telling its story again and again with absolute faithfulness upon the luminous planes of rock as in a succession of enchanted mirrors" (1892: 202).

nostalgia for Inis Mór refers to the danger of seeking to re-connect with a past that is remembered as perfect but which was, in reality, far from that. Collinge refers to Ó Direáin's "Aran-tinted spectacles" (1985: 241), ones which Ó Direáin was forced to remove following his first journey back to his home place after an absence of almost eleven years. *"Árainn 1947"* reflects the poet's bitter disappointment upon realising that even the Aran of his poetry, the created version, no longer exists. In a second betrayal, however, Ó Direáin also realises that the real island is also changed beyond recognition. Thus a double sense of death overwhelms the poet and he vows never to visit again.

Ó Flaitheartas's characters are clearly searching for, longing for, and waiting on the edges of the island and in some cases their own sanity for the arrival or the reaching of some sort of essence to fulfil their lives. Ó Flaitheartas's personal quest for individual fulfilment as well as his desire to feel at ease in either or both linguistic codes, seems to be mirrored in these stories. Unlike Ó Direáin's however, Ó Flaitheartas's work does not seek or find any level of perfection; the characters portrayed in the stories, either human or animal, are never content or satisfied, nor do they find resolution. They are depicted bleakly; they get on with their lives, accept their lot, make the most of their situations and face the reality of their existences. In *"Daoine Bochta"*, for example, Pádraig Ó Dioráin struggles to find the energy to collect seaweed necessary to fertilise his potatoes as he is starving with the hunger, weak from illness and fearful for his family's poor health. He feels *"[m]aide mór an bhochtanais ag lascadh a dhroma"* (1953: 86), an ever-present symbol of the Ó Dioráin family's struggle.[38] With the death of his young son, the story concludes with Pádraig and his wife united in grief. Though many, including De Bhaldraithe (1968) and Daniels (1988), find these unromantic portraits disturbing and unnecessary, they may well result from Ó Flaitheartas's refusal to entertain the oft-cited nostalgia which exiled authors seem to gravitate towards. However, though many of his short-stories are cruelly realistic, and although Ó Flaitheartas could certainly not be accused of wearing "Aran-tinted spectacles" his work is not dystopian

---

38   "... the big stick of poverty lashing his back".

in nature. He does not present a society which is worse than his present one, instead he writes about mini-socities which reflect the liminality of existence, and of people caught between the good and bad, success and poverty, unity and separation. Nonetheless, given Ó Flaitheartaʼs notoriously cantankerous behaviour (Ó hEithir, 1977, Denvir, 1991, Cahalan, 1999), it is difficult to trace a utopian thread through his work. Denvir writes that certain stories reflect the divided character of Ó Flaitheartaʼs attachment to his home place and so can oscillate (1991: 56). It does seem to be the case they they vacillate between reverence and disdain. This oscillation between love and hate for homeland and home place is also mirrored in postcolonial studies and foregrounds the difficult, and often painful yet constant relationship which emigrants or exiles have with their home nations, town lands, and islands. There is reason to consider some of Ó Flaitheartaʼs work as exhibiting signs of anti-utopianism, which is "a society [...] that the author intended a contemporaneous reader to view as a criticism of utopianism" (Sargent, 1994: 9). Ó Flaithearta does not see Aran as utopia, but neither does he see it as a dystopia. Instead, Aran is in-between both these designations, in an interspace which has features of both utopia and dystopia, but which is ultimately its own place, in its own right.

Ó Direáin and the Desire for an Interspace Between Inis Mór and Dublin

A new point of departure from which to analyse and explore Máirtín Ó Direáinʼs poetry may lie in a broader and more inclusive understanding of the poetʼs treatment of the interspace between place and space, between island and city, and also between reality and metaphor. The concept or notion of the interspace is one which was first developed in literary geography; it would thus seem apposite to employ such a concept in any discussion of poetry in which geographical and literary understandings and interpretations are to the fore. Though the "notion of the interspace harks back to Romantic ideas about landscape, the concept can also be seen as a very modern idea in its rejection of geographical borders [and also in its] re-imagining [of the] landscape as a conceptual rather than a geographical entity" (Hansson in Boss and Maher, 2003: 123). Ó Direáin's poetry embraces such conceptual landscapes and frees the geographical island of his birth from its limited or *mappable* borders in order to transport and poetically mould a utopian island of his own creation.

Thus, it would appear worthwhile to consider, through an analysis of his poetry, the creation of an interspace – based on Aran and always for the benefit of Aran – which made it possible for Ó Direáin to maintain a relationship with his beloved homeplace, while also honing his poetic and linguistic imagination. In fact, it is clear that the island and the city are quite loosely defined geographical entities in Ó Direáin's eyes in the first instance, and are only very rarely depicted as tangible and actual realities. Árainn and Baile Átha Cliath are, in Ó Direáin's reality, quite unreal, and thus ripe for poetic interpretation and artistic amelioration. The interspace discussed relies heavily on Ó Direáin's poetic imagination; however, it should also be noted that the interspace which I discuss here can function as both a real *and* an imaginative poetic device.

In addition to this, however, it is relevant to consider the actual act of poetic creation itself as providing another (inter)space in which Ó Direáin's work functions. As Ní Riain notes, *"déanann an file ionad cónaithe den fhilíocht agus é díphréamhaithe sa chathair. Is caidreamh fileata ealaíonta atá aige leis an oileán mar sin, rud a bhíonn coinsiasach go maith san fhilíocht dhéanach aige. Ní cur síos tuairisciúil atá a dhéanamh aige ar Árainn; tá Árainn fhileata á cruthú (sic) aige"* (Ní Riain, 2002: 42–43).[39] Creating a poetry which acted as a space where the poet could, in essence, live out his new existence, is clearly one of Ó Direáin's strongest, and most personal, interspaces. Such an interspace allowed him to live in a city which

---

39 "... the poet makes a home for himself in poetry while he is uprooted in the city. He has, therefore, a poetic and artistic relationship with the island, something which is fairly apparent (and consciously done) in his later poetry. His portrayal of Árainn is not descriptive; he is creating a poetic Árainn".

he initially disliked, while simultaneously protecting him against the more nostalgia-filled remembrances of his home place. He could, in effect, be in and represent two places at the same time through his creation of a poetic interspace, chiefly carried out through his employment of generic and relatively vague descriptions of both island and city life and dwellers. Though not completely devoid of exact descriptions, by maintaining a relatively detached view of both city and island life, Ó Direáin was able to address both existences and ponder his own self between and in both urban and rural places.

It is clear that the rocks and stones which become the central themes of Ó Direáin's poetry are much more than physical geological entities and begin, after time, to take on roles which may often be attributed to individuals or community figures, in much the same way as John Montague treats of his childhood in his poem "Like Dolmens Round My Childhood, the Old People".[40] The rocks and stones of Ó Direáin's poetry also offer a stark contrast to the environment in which the poet finds himself whilst living and writing in Dublin. Here again we see that "we only become aware of how important it [the geography around us as children] is to us when we leave the home environment and suddenly start defining the 'new place' in terms of what is not present from the old familiar place" (Ryan, 2002: 267). Perhaps Ó Direáin might never have been able to write the poetry he did had it not been for his distance from the place. However, his use of symbols also allowed him to create a distance between himself and the city in such a way as to permit him to maintain his allegiance with the island and its way of life, while also negating the chances of becoming saturated in urban life.

Returning to the central concern of desire, however, it is apparent that for Synge, Lawless, Ó Direáin and Ó Flaithearta, the desire of creation, of belonging, of knowledge or of artistic freedom is paramount in their creative *oeuvres*. Ó Flaithearta's very title of his collection of short stories (1953), *Dúil*, or desire, circumscribes a space of central importance for the theme. In Irish, of course, *dúil* can also connote appetite or hunger for something either physical or imaginary, and a liking or longing for something either

40   From *Selected Poems* (1982: 26).

attainable or just out of reach. The notion that either a physical, spiritual or personal appetite must be satiated is important here. Each of the stories in *Dúil* is based on this need or desire for fulfilment, whether it is individual or collective. Gearóid Denvir's *An Dúil is Dual* (1991) draws on this theme of desire, and although Denvir does not incorporate any utopian theory into his work on Ó Flaithearta, he does suggest that there is more to the author's understanding of *dúil* than is usually interpreted (1991: 48).

Conclusion

The Aran Islands' colonial and postcolonial reality was more than some cultural nationalists and writers could tolerate. It was thought necessary to create a literary, cultural and liminal utopia there so as to overcome the realities of contamination and corruption which ensued from the garrisoning of the Islands. The Islands were moulded and re-branded to reflect personal and communal desires for the perpetuation of Gaelic Ireland and for the preservation of home from the position of exile.

However, it would be misleading to suggest that disillusionment was often the dominant emotion experienced by tourists and writers on the Islands upon discovering the Aran utopia's existence or lack thereof. The utopian elements that made the Aran Islands such attractive and enticing features on the Irish landscape and figures in the Irish mindscape were not lessened upon reaching Aran. In fact, the constant re-utopianisation of the Islands ensured that as they were discovered in one epoch, the Islands quickly became re-energised in the Irish imagination and this necessitated the various re-discoveries and re-engagements with Aran which continues to this day. That the Islands still find themselves described, in literary terms, in a fashion similar to Lawless' and Synge's time should not cause surprise. It is in the utopian energies which surround Aran up to contemporary times that readers, tourists and Island-based scholars find a continued wealth of ideas, images and magnetic pulls towards interpretations and investigation.

CHAPTER 5

You are an Island on the Sea
Is Oileán Tú ar Muir[1]

> Never has there been such a real possibility of studying different islands on their own terms, or of gathering islanders together. Nor has there ever been as much justification, so much urgency, for such a development. Locality has come within global reach. [...] [I]sland studies has never been more pressing, nor more possible.
> — BALDACCHINO, "The Coming of Age of Island Studies" (2004: 280)

Introduction

The place which islands occupy in debates on cultural, socio-historical and geographical specificity is central to an understanding of most island literature. This is particularly the case with Aran Island literature. Given an island's microcosmic association with the macrocosmic figure of the mainland, it is little wonder that individuals are often more concerned with comparison between the "here" of the mainland and the "there" of an offshore, insular and isolated island, than with any in-depth analysis of what the "there" might actually signify in its own right.

The centrality of the island metaphor, again from a distinctively Irish stance, has become of paramount importance within cultural and geo-

---

1 Professor Mícheál Mac Craith of NUI Galway kindly explained the nature of this saying. Its origins are found in an Old Irish morning prayer, emphasising the heavenliness of the Western islands of Ireland.

literary areas of interest. However, the island metaphor or symbol has often had more to say to and about the macrocosm of the larger island of Ireland that it has had to say about itself. Island studies, an area of academic enquiry since the early 1980s, has begun to re-direct and re-focus its scope of vision from thinking with islands, using the island as a mirror to hold up to the nation, for example, to thinking about islands themselves, and this will undoubtedly have far-reaching and important consequences for how island nations think about and think with islands.

This chapter examines the impact which the discipline of island studies has had on the re-emerging interest in Ireland's islands, and particularly the literature of the Aran Islands. Three aspects of theory from within the discipline will be employed throughout the chapter. Firstly, it will examine the metaphorical deployment of the island to indicate difference and the distance from the mainland, and the relationship which this shares with postcolonial considerations of insider and outsider, and also with the erosion and eradication of difference in order to create a sense of conformity and cultural and linguistic sameness. Secondly, the space which an island terrain provides a writer with will also be evaluated. Lastly, I will examine the internal and personal geography of the island terrain as experienced by Lawless, Synge, Ó Flaithearta and Ó Direáin, and as demonstrated throughout their work and through their various protagonists and narratives. The poetry of Dara Beag Ó Fátharta highlights the continuing Aran writing tradition, as well as some more recent examples from Dara Ó Conaola and Peadar Mór Ó Conghaile.

Some secondary island studies theories will also be utilised throughout the chapter to provide additional substance to arguments and to highlight the many relevant facets of the discipline and its value within the broader field of Irish studies. From an island studies perspective, the work of Baldacchino (2000; 2006; 2007), Royle (2001, 2003, 2007a, 2007b), Péron (2004) and Hay (2006) will be employed as interpretive and evaluative tools, complementing the examination of Lawless, Synge, Ó Flaithearta and Ó Direáin's work as outlined in previous chapters.

The Aran Islands and the Difficulties of Contemporary Islandness

For over four centuries, the Aran Islands have simultaneously basked in and suffered as a result of geo-literary and cultural influences. The Islands have been variously depicted as the last outposts of national culture, as bastions of language and heritage, as sequestered and special utopias where time and traditions stand still, or, especially in recent times, as little more than empty signifiers of an age long gone and long forgotten. The weight of cultural authenticity may well have taken a considerable toll on the Islands of late, none more so than on Inis Mór, where "[t]he island that is best known for exploitation of heritage, [...] has rendered [itself] into little more than a living, interactive museum of itself with islanders as actors [...]" (Royle, 2003: 27). However, Royle and others (Nutley and Cross, 1999 [article], Gibbons, 1996 [chapter 2 in particular]) also recognise that to enable the Islands to survive, a certain level of cultural "cashing in", or to use Royle's more loaded idiom, exploitation, is seen as a necessary evil if the Islands are to survive at all. Thus, the marketability of the Aran Islands presents the islanders and the Islands themselves with a dangerous proposition: be true to yourselves, your history, heritage and your island, or mould yourselves and your island around what the tourists go there to find, even if it is not there any longer. Another aspect of this difficulty, and one often disregarded in the debate, concerns the ways and means of accurately and realistically celebrating Aran heritage while also highlighting the real and the actual as it is on modern-day Aran. A marriage of this kind, between the past and the present, a union, if you will, of tradition and modernity, would undoubtedly present a more up-to-date and realistic portrait of the Aran Islands than positioning them in either the past or the immediate past would do. If one debunks, or, at the very least, detracts from the myth of Aran as a type of prelapsarian Eden of Gaelic purity and spirit, there is the very real danger that the Islands may suffer economic consequences and face further de-population.

A recent campaign (2005) initiated by Comharchumann Inis Meáin
which offered the chance to relocate to the island was, in effect, playing
heavily into the hands of similar Fáilte Ireland tourist campaigns which
focus on the tranquillity and natural beauty of the Islands, "the real heart
of Gaelic Ireland" (Fáilte Ireland's *Ireland's West*" Campaign, 2006–7).
Though the relocation brochure offered prospective families some preliminary information regarding the island, there were inaccuracies in the
literature. There was no mention whatsoever, rather unsurprisingly, of
the fact that Inis Meáin's population is in fact rapidly decreasing[2] or that
employment is at an all-time low. While this campaign sought to help
re-populate the island, which would in turn help to foster a greater base
for both employment and higher numbers attending the island's schools,
and that a poster or brochure which negatively portrays the island would
be of absolutely no use whatsoever, the fact remains that perpetuating the
myth that the Aran Islands can survive on their geographical merits alone
only serves to confound and confuse the challenge of successfully marrying tradition and modernity for the benefit of outsider and insider alike.
However, in all of this it is vital to consider the fact that were it not for the
careful preservation of culture and heritage which the islanders, deliberately
or incidentally, have carried out over successive centuries, there would be
little to attract tourists or returning emigrants back to the Islands in the
first place. To attempt to let the ebb of the past and the flow of the ever
fast-paced present coexist together is a task of the highest order and level
of difficulty. This difficulty reflects the importance of the challenge facing
the Islands today.

2   Census figures for 2002 put Inis Meáin's population at 187. According to the 2006
     Census, 154 people now reside on the island. Comparable figures for Inis Oírr are:
     262 in 2002 and 247 in 2006 (<http://www.cso.ie/census/documents/census2006_
     Table%208–11.pdf>).

Irish Island Studies: Royle's Contribution

The academic field of island studies has grown into a strong, multi-disciplinary and multi-faceted area of scholarship. However, Irish islands have not received sufficient critical attention within the discipline. Prof. Stephen Royle, however, has begun the dialogue and has set about examining Ireland's island identity (2003), its relationship with its offshore islands (2001, 2003) and also the way in which Irish islands market their isolationary and peripheral nature in both positive and negative ways (2003, 2007a).[3] Royle's signal contribution to the development of an Irish island studies approach is both welcomed and valuable, particularly with regard to Island literature and its contribution to how and why Irish islands exert such a continual literary presence in both our understanding of Ireland's own island identity and also the more metaphorical uses of that identity.

In a recent, thought-provoking essay (*Irish Geography*, 2003) Royle explores the culture of "heritage tourism" (2003: 23) in operation on many offshore Irish islands today. Royle writes that "Ireland has cashed in on its heritage [...] [this is] particularly the case in the traditionally less economically advanced Western regions, which have also been seen as somehow representing a truer, purer, certainly more rural form of Ireland than the East with its greater contacts with outside influences from Britain and Europe" (2003: 23). It is clear from Royle's own travels to many of Ireland's islands that some are more celebratory of their heritage and traditions, whereas other islands see their "islanded" nature as being a potentially fruitful economic enterprise to pursue. Though Royle is at pains to show that without heritage-based attractions and tourism, many of these islands would suffer economically, he is also clear on the dangers of over-marketing or of over-exploiting these unique places.

Royle observes how, in finally giving islands official government department status in the form of the Department of Arts, Heritage, Gaeltacht

---

3   Professor Royle is now Professor of Island Geography at Queen's University, Belfast: "a marker of the maturity [...] [of] island studies" (2010: 5).

and the Islands[4], "[t]his official association of islands with heritage and arts may imply that they are seen as museum pieces" (2003: 25). Of interest also is the placing of the designation "Islands" to the end of the Departments' nomenclature. However, as Royle shows, even with governmental backing and significant funding, depopulation of Ireland's islands continues apace. One factor of particular merit in this debate concerns Royle's point in relation to the museumification, to coin a phrase, of many islands off Ireland's coast. Where at one level this process may seem like a necessary cultural exercise, i.e. preserving and exhibiting a particular island's heritage to the public and to tourists, at another level there is the danger of being viewed as quaint, unsuitable for change or not requiring change in the first instance. This latter difficulty also leads to further problems in that the focus of the island's people inevitably shifts to preservation and stability rather than progressive change and modernisation which could equip the islanders for more sustainable economic and cultural futures. The double bind of celebration and exploitation is very much to the fore here, as is the issue of economics dominating island life.

While a number of islands are considered in Royle's piece, his interest in the Aran Islands is of primary importance to this study. In contrasting Inis Mór with Inis Meáin, Royle successfully highlights his own hypothesis on the dangers inherent in both the exploitation and celebration of island heritage. His obvious disdain for cultural performativity is counterbalanced perfectly by his experience of Inis Meáin. Here, the author finds "more of the Aran traditions are still actually practiced on this island" (2003: 28) as opposed to Inis Mór, where Royle finds little in the way of tradition. On Inis Meáin, Royle discovers that instead of abandoning heritage and culture, or worse still, acting it out for tourists, the islanders have found ways of marrying the island's past with its present in ways that celebrate rather than exploit. However, Inis Meáin's record as the least unspoilt and least visited of the Islands might not be in the island's best interest in the long

---

4   As of 2010, this is now the Department of Community, Equality and Gaeltacht
     Affairs. See <http://www.pobail.ie/en/Islands> for the Department's mission state-
     ment on islands.

run. Royle notes that "[t]his is a conundrum; unspoiled places are getting little money from tourism. [...] perhaps money from tourism might be necessary to keep any sort of traditional, living heritage on them, even a spoiled one" (2003: 30). The delicate balancing act is set to continue.[5]

Island Studies:
Some Important Theoretical and Critical Considerations

Islands, for the most part, are contrasted against a backdrop of mainland *sameness*, and thus become invested with properties of difference and of often unrealistic cultural perpetuation and preservation. An island is very rarely considered as a physical geographical entity in its own right; more often than not an island is not a mainland, does not have modernisation as its chief aim, and does not subject its inhabitants to a constant barrage of progress and merciless commercialisation. Thus it is clear to see that a link which seeks to join an island with its contrapuntal space, the mainland, would be viewed as a dangerous prospect, confusing the binary of island and mainland, of them and us, and also defying the boundaries of both areas in a way which confuses the island space even further. The mainland is ever-changing, fluid, whereas the island is imbued with constancy, un-changing and un-changed definition. In joining two such diverse elements and time-scapes together, a turbulent relationship is to be expected, if only in the initial period.

Françoise Péron's work on "The Contemporary Lure of the Island" (2004) finds that "the enhanced impact of islands on the human imagi-nation is not a passing fad: there is rather an essential contribution of,

---

5   *Comhdháil Oileáin na hÉireann* / The Irish Islands Federation, supports and encour-ages inter-island and island-based industry, development and community affairs. Royle sees them as highly successful "pressure group" (1986). See (<http://www.oileain.ie>).

and by, small islands and their inhabitants to the urban and globalised civilisation of our time" (2004: 326). Though Péron's work centres predominantly on islands off the north-west coast of France, she affirms that there appears to be a common understanding of the cultural importance of small islands and their associated geographical fascination. However, as Péron notes, "[w]e are encountering today something which is more than just curiosity about a specific geographic feature of space surrounded by water" (2004: 326). The *lure of the island*, as Péron refers to it, exerts a considerable force upon both islanders and non-islanders. Two maps accompany Péron's essay, one drawn by an islander, and one drawn by an outsider, both of the same island but with two very different outlooks on that island. The islander, a fourteen-year-old schoolgirl, emphasises on her map all the "key maritime and terrestrial features [...] she embellishes the terrain and surrounding sea with colour" (2004: 326). The girl does not illustrate any roads on the island, and focuses instead on the lighthouses and the ports and quays on the coast. Importantly, she points out the airstrip, perhaps "in anticipation of having to leave the island where she was born" (2004: 326). The sea, as depicted on this map, is a strong presence, and alive with fish and boats.

In stark contrast, in the second map, by the fifteen-year-old girl who has spent her holidays on the island since she was very young (2004: 326), Péron finds "a deliberate attempt at demonstrating familiarity on her mental map, riddled with topographical and infrastructural detail" (2004: 326). This second map shows each individual road on the island as well as townlands, houses, graveyards and inland lakes. The detail with which this non-islander represents her summer home is startlingly professional and precise, and yet there is little animation to the surrounding sea and the detail is a little too distracting. Péron notes that this attempt to show over-familiarity with the island terrain highlights the young girl's awareness that her link "with the island is not natural and somehow may have to be justified [...] this is a very different way of claiming the land as her own" (2004: 326). While the islander's map shows routes for getting on and off the island, the non-islander's map illustrates routes around the island interior and shows little concern with ways out of or off the island itself. Citing Meistersheim (2001), Péron avers that "[i]t is not by chance that ever since classical antiquity, the spatial representation of the island has been conveyed by the image of the labyrinth" (2004: 330). The second map, drawn by the non-islander, shows a likeness to a labyrinthine map; it is almost confusing in its detail and density of scale. It is clear, although not represented on the first map, that because the island girl is intimately aware of her island sphere, she sees no need for excessive detail, foregrounding the naturalness which comes from such intimate geographical knowledge. The second map's creator feels, conversely, that in order to justify her love for the island, she must present an overt geographical illustration of her relationship with the terrain. Synge and Lawless's work reveals a fascination with geography that is not necessary in Ó Flaithearta and Ó Direáin's writing, given the readers' understanding of the writers' intimacy with the Islands.

Identity and Islandness: I Know My Island, I Know Myself

Godfrey Baldacchino's "Islands – Objects of Representation" (2005) makes a valuable observation on how individuals represent islands and their own island identity. In an exercise similar to that of Péron's, Baldacchino asks three students to draw a rough sketch of an island on a blank sheet of paper. The results are significant.

> Ask anyone to take a sheet of paper and to draw an island as seen from the air. Most likely, that person would draw a stylized image of a piece of land, without much detail other than being surrounded by water. It would fit between the space confines of the sheet. It would also, uncannily, have an approximately circular shape (2005: 247).

Though this circular character is often attributed to islands, there is no island which is circular, nor is there any island whose dimensions would fit so neatly on a piece of paper (Baldacchino, 2005: 247). It is important to question, then, this fascination with the creation of a perfect(able) representation of an island. For Baldacchino the answer "lies in an obsession to control, to embrace an island as something that is finite, that may be

encapsulated by human strategy, design or desire" (2005: 247). Such neat-
ness, such compactness, suggests that "[b]eing geographically defined and
circular, an island is easier to hold, to own, to manage or to manipulate,
to embrace and to caress" (2005: 247). Images of possession, of affection,
almost human in nature, and of control, are to the forefront of this desire
to contain and know islands. Being circular, an island appears to have fixed
limits; one might feel confident of circumnavigating an island's terrain
without danger or difficulty based on its shape. Péron writes that, especially for a mainlander, an island is "not quite of this world [...] it remains
stubbornly different" (2004: 331). However, though going to an island is
"still an act of sensual disorientation" (2004: 331)

> [t]he island, with its hard, clear outline engraved on the hazy surface of the sea, seems
> to incarnate an isolated and self-sufficient world. It can thus appear as a form of the
> world that is complete in itself. There is consequently something reassuring about it.
> It permits the illusion that "reality" may be experienced in its entirety (2004: 331).

For outsiders, or mainlanders as Péron refers to them, having arrived on
the island, they begin the task of inventorying the terrain, thereby under-
going a "symbolic rite of ownership, measuring every contour, pacing out
the distances, discovering the length of the coastline for themselves and
getting to know it physically in all its twists and turns" (2004: 331). This
cartographical and personal exercise highlights the degree to which most
people will go in order to feel that they have gained control and intimate
knowledge of an area. Péron avers: "[i]t is as if, by measuring – and thus
mastering – this microcosmic island, they are engaging vicariously in the
control of the macrocosmic Earth" (2004: 331). This has resonances with
what Brian Friel has portrayed in *Translations* as the process of naming as
being in some way a process of geographical and cultural ownership. What
both have in common, i.e. Friel's and Péron's opinions on *getting to know* a
place, is that there is a pseudo-colonial or territorial element to the enterprises described. Ownership, possession, desire for intimate mastery of a
particular location; each of these implies a link with the colonial mentality
regarding land and acquisition. However, there is also a clear association
between these desired-for places and utopia. Though less rigorous and

aggressive, and though rarely analysed, the utopian project does aspire towards owning, or mastering, a particular location.

Microcosm and Macrocosm: Little and Large

In an article on Ireland's relationship with the European Union, Fintan O'Toole looks at Ireland's relationship with its offshore islands. O'Toole writes that as Ireland's identity is bound up in deciding where its loyalties lie, i.e. either with Berlin or Boston, it has lost its own sense of stable identity. Though for many years the offshore islands, the Blaskets and the Aran Islands in particular, provided "a locus of assured identity" (2000: 11) for the Irish people, O'Toole notes that looking to the periphery was "a dead give-away" (2000: 11) with regard to the wider sense of uncertainty tangible in the greater island of Ireland itself. Peter Hay writes that "[f]or conceptual credibility [...] the nation requires the reality of sharp and largely impervious boundaries" (2006: 27), in what Beer refers to as "rel[ying] upon the cultural idea of the island" (1989: 21). Fiona Polack, looking at the case of Tasmania, writes: "an island's boundaries provide the sort of fixed limits that make it a perfect microcosm of [...] national concerns [that are] less easily containable or comprehensible in other locations" (in Brinklow *et al.* 2000: 217). Hay comments that "my own island serves as a psychological sink into which the fears, self-loathing and insecurities of the larger nation are displaced" (2006: 27). Fintan O'Toole's explanation is based on the Irish example, but could be universal in its core emphasis on the microcosmic island:

> The desire to make the microcosm stand for the macrocosm, to make the little island stand as a metaphor for the big one of Ireland as a whole, sprung precisely from the sense that the identity of the big island was far too messy, unstable and complicated (O'Toole, 2000: 11).

For O'Toole, the islands of Ireland provided an adequate symbol of stability and cultural continuity for the larger, more confused mainland of Ireland, though most of this symbolic nature was myth-based and "just doesn't work" (2000: 11). However, O'Toole is quick to remind his reader that "there is not and never has been [...] a single Irish identity" (2000: 11). Ó Direáin's comments on Inis Mór emphasises the micro- and macrocosmic identity an island can have for an islander:

> le breathnú air ar bhealach amháin, oileán cúng, oileán sceirdiúil, fuar, gortach ó thaobh dreach-tíre, nó ó thaobh an talamh de [a bhí i m'oileánsa]. Ach ar an taobh eile, ní raibh teorainn ar bith le do chuid samhlaíochta, samhlaíocht ghasúr a bhí ag éirí suas san áit. Thar íar na spéire, d'fheicfeá tír na n-iontas [...] agus ansin ar an teaghlach fuair tú an rud céanna. Bhí an domhan thoir [...] níos gaire duit ná Gaillimh, nó Baile Átha Cliath (An Charraig Stoite, 12: 00 mins., 2003).[6]

An island is predominantly referred to in microcosmic terms: "a world in miniature" (Péron, 2004: 338); "fragments of an earth, once whole" (Gillis, 2004: 21). An island's microcosmic structure suggests wholeness, a finiteness that is thought to represent and to add to an island's isolationary nature. Baldacchino notes that "[a]t face value, an island's 'signature' is its obvious optic: it is a geographically finite, total, discrete, sharply precise physical entity which accentuates clear and holistic notions of location and identity" (2004: 272). However, such geographical boundedness is "often confused with closure [...] a facile but unwarranted assumption" (Kirch, 1986: 2). Until recently very little work had been carried out on examining the openness of the island space. Terrell (2004) stated that "isolation is not a defining characteristic of island life; to the contrary, it could be argued that islanders are generally more aware of, and in touch with, the worldwide web of human intercourse than others may be" (2004: 11). Hay correctly points out that hard-edges and the sea are two defining forces,

6   "From one perspective, it was, from the point of view of landscape, confined, bleak and cold. But on the other hand, there was no limit to your imagination, no limit to the imagination of a youngster growing up on the island. One saw a land of wonder over the horizon. And you experienced the same thing at home. The Orient [...] was closer to the island than Galway or Dublin".

though they are not as insulatory or as alienating as previously thought (2006: 22). Instead, as Gillian Beer posits, the edge of the island is a "shifting liminality" (2003: 33), or in Hay's words, "a mobile, fluid, or permeable boundary [...] a liberated zone; a site of possibility" (2006: 22). This possibility also has a relationship within utopian studies whereby utopia itself is thought to be a place of infinite promise and potential. Another tie between both island and utopian studies here concerns the fluidity and the flux suggested by the openness of the island terrain. Being less rigid, and thus more open to possibility, change and instability, the island is a zone "where things happen that could not happen anywhere else" (Jane Ledwell, 2002: 10).

Islands and Desire

Edmond and Smith highlight the academic, geographical, and cultural import of the island figure and of islands in general. They begin with some very interesting questions: "[w]ere islands the detritus of crumbling continents or the seeds of new ones? Did they constitute points of ending or of origin? But if, in geographic terms, islands have signalled loss as well as gain, their redactions have always been fertile" (2003: 1). Throughout both maritime and cultural history, islands have represented much more than their geographical locations and geological make-up might imply. Indeed, Edmond and Smith, citing Howe (2000: 10), note that: "European voyagers [...] often thought of islands in terms of paradise or utopia, either an ideal inhabited island or else an empty island on which to start again" (in Edmond and Smith, 2003: 1). This imaginativeness has led to the association of islands with desired utopian destinations as well as with the desire to be explored, owned, or colonised. Edmond and Smith recognise this factor, observing that "islands seem to be natural colonies. This is not just because of the desire to possess what is paradisal or utopian, but because islands, unlike continents, look like property [...] [the] unit of land which

fits within the retina of the approaching eye is a token of desire" (2003:
42). Conkling's sense of the visual desirability of an island is captured in his
description of the small island as a "lens for looking" (1997: 55), and this is
echoed in Robinson's portrayal of the sea around the Aran Islands.

> On the day of our arrival [in 1972] we met an old man who explained the basic
> geography: "The ocean", he told us, "goes all around the island". We let this remark
> direct our rambles on that brief holiday, and found indeed that the ocean encircles
> Aran like the rim of a magnifying glass, focussing attention to the point of obses-
> sion (1986: 10).

Obsession, desire and possession are words commonly associated with
small islands, and particularly so with the Aran Islands. The sea is often
depicted as possessing the Islands, framing them for the eye to behold.
Roderic O'Flaherty saw Aran "as in a sea-parenthesis" ([1684]1846), caught
and held by the force of the waves. While the strategic utility of Aran was
most valued between the sixteenth and nineteenth centuries, their literary and geo-cultural value was and continues to be immeasurable to this
day. From a geographical point of view, the "defining idea of an island
is its boundedness [as] boundedness makes islands graspable, able to be
held in the mind's eye and imagined as places of possibility and promise"
(Edmond and Smith, 2003: 2). It is the element or the promise of such
possibilities which entices many to island shores, while also providing the
ideal setting for much utopian fiction, encapsulating as it does a bounded
space, desired and feared in equal measure. Tied up with this imagery of
possession and promise, are the ways in which islands have become analo-
gous with descriptions of the human form and body, thus making islands
capable of representing images of both penetrability and isolation; island
can be used to suggest both separation and connection (Edmond and
Smith, 2003: 4). For writers such as Beer (1990) and Hamilton-Paterson
(1992), the link between the island figure and the female nurturing body
is an important one; both writers note the connection between a type of
"pre-natal" (Beer 1990: 271) image of a human foetus with that of an island,
surrounded as it is by the "amniotic sea, connected to the mainland by an
umbilicus" (Edmond and Smith 2003: 4). Nuala Ní Dhomhnaill's poem
"Oileán" / "Island" describes her lover's body as an island:

Oileán is ea do chorp	Your body is an island
I lár na mara móire.	In the middle of the great ocean.
Tá do ghéaga spréite ar bhraillín	Your limbs are spread on a bright sheet
Gléigeal os farraige faoileán.	Over a sea of gulls.[7]

Seán Ó Ríordáin's *"Oileán agus Oileán Eile"* / An Island and Another Island" suggests that *"[n]íl éinne beo nach bhfuair oileán, / Is trua a chás má thréig"*, seeing that individuals have personal (often internal) islands, with which they are entrusted.[8] Later in the poem, Ó Ríordáin examines how an individual can betray their islands:

Do scoiltis-se do thusa ceart	You split your true self
Le dúil sa tsaol,	because of worldly desire,
Ach is paidir fós an tusa sin	But that self remains a prayer
Ar oileán séin,	On an island,
A fhan go ciúin ag cogarnach	Whispered softly
Ar bheolaibh Dé	On the lips of God
Nuair do rincis-se go macnasach	While you danced with abandonment
Ar ghob an tsaoil.	On life's edge.[9]

Islands, Colonialism, Tradition and Modernity

The linkage with female in/penetrability also has implications for colonial circumstances, whereby the claims proffered by some colonists and critics that islands are more easily attainable and thus more *ownable* seems in some way to legitimise the colonial enterprise of is/land acquisition. However, though the notion of islands as havens and cultural safe-houses is one which remains prominent, Edmond and Smith remind their readers

7   In *Pharoah's Daughter* (1990: 40–43).
8   "No one is born without an island / Pity anyone who might desert it", in *Eireaball Spideoige* (1952: 80).
9   In *Eireball Spideoige* (1952: 81).

that "[i]slands are not pure: they are subject to breaching and incursion, both natural and cultural" (2003: 5). One might assume then that islands would constitute a significant focus of research and interest in postcolonial studies. However, this does not appear to be the case:

> [I]sland stories have tended to slip the nets of postcolonial theorising. Within a history of imperialism that has focused on the politics of territorial acquisition and the displacement or colonisation of large-scale populations, islands are figured as negligible, purely strategic sites. The dismissal of the colonial politics of the island is an act of historical repression that becomes explicit in situations such as the Cuban or Falklands crises, where the relationship between islands and their continental neighbours comes under scrutiny, registering the fear that the island, however fractional, may act as a site of ideological contamination to the mainland (Edmond and Smith, 2003: 5).

In the case of the Aran Islands, however, it was the ideological contamination of the mainland, and its consequences for the Islands, that most concerned its nineteenth- and twentieth-century visitors and writers. "After the antiquarians came the linguists, ethnographers, and folklorists, and then the writers, poets, film-makers and journalists" (Robinson, 1986: 8–9), all seeking to protect themselves and the Islands from the damaging forces of modernity. John T. O'Flaherty's account of the Islands is significant for its comparative nature and also for its suggestion of the need to place Aran on a pedestal equal to its importance:

> If the Islands of Aran had formed a portion of the Hebrides or Orkneys, or stood in view of any part of the British coast, they would, long since, have been made the theme of the statistic and sentimental tourist; but, though abounding with many particulars, valuable to the Antiquary, Historian and Philosopher, they have been hitherto neglected (1824).

It is critical to note that O'Flaherty's aim here, in comparing the British reverence for her islands with Ireland's indifference towards her islands, was to animate Irish people's imaginations and re-direct their gaze back to the West coast of Ireland, towards Aran. The trickle of early visitors quickly became a flood; Aran was put on the map. However, this may seem somewhat difficult to imagine given that transport links throughout

Ireland were still poor and underdeveloped at the start of the nineteenth century. To have accessed Aran, then, must have seemed like a difficult task. Though the majority of Irish offshore islands were largely impregnable up until the mid-nineteenth century, the Aran Islands were fortunate to have a semi-regular ferry service from 1863. The fact that there was also a regular train link between Dublin and Galway from 1851 was also significant as visitors could arrive in Galway and take the boat, docked a few yards from the train station, to the Islands on the same day.[10] This gives the lie to the myth propagated by cultural nationalists in the early twentieth century that the Aran Islands had remained virgin territory until their intervention. However, it was vital for Aran's earliest visitors to ignore their own knowledge that the Islands could not possibly have been untouched until their arrival. John. R. Gillis writes that "there is no culture in the world that can be said to be fixed and bounded, separate from other cultures" (Gillis, 2004: 118). The West had been very much awake before the re-discovery of Aran, but this was not what was needed for the projection of Aran as national ideal. The Gaelic League's posters from the 1890s proclaim the great awakening of Ireland's sequestered West, yet it was only the rest of Ireland that had been asleep. As Sheeran explains, "the '90s creation of Aran had infinitely more to do with the needs of urban, cosmopolitan intellectuals and less with the actual inhabitants of the place" (1994: 301).

Synge's presence on Aran, however, should not be considered in this particular vein, though this is consistently the approach taken throughout the majority of the literature regarding his decision to visit the Islands in the first instance. His self-awareness that his very presence on the Islands signalled a seachange in the modernisation of the Islands is highly significant. It also illustrates his personal understanding of his presence there, something remarkably lacking in the accounts of Yeats, Symons and

10   I am most grateful to Deirdre Ní Chonghaile for this information and for other bibliographical details. See also: Powell (1984), *Oileáin Árainn: Stair na nOileán anuas go dtí 1922* and Ní Chonghaile (2010), "Ní neart go cur le chéile: lámhscríbhínní ceoil a chruthaigh Petrie agus Ó Comhraí in Árainn in 1857".

Gregory. Noting the "absence of the heavy boot of Europe" (*The Aran
Islands*, 1992: 21) on Inis Meáin, Synge wore pampooties, or raw-hide
shoes to lessen his imprint on the landscape and also to blend in with the
island way of life. It was not Synge's desire to gain more from Aran than
he returned to it. This was also the case with Lawless. Synge's criticisms
of her show his own territorial underpinnings; yet these are somewhat
understandable, if not wholly reasonable. Nonetheless, in registering his
dismay with her alleged lack of knowledge about the Islands, he perhaps
illustrates his own frustration at not having had more time to spend there.
Leaving Galway for Inis Mór on his first visit to the Islands, Synge had a
copy of *Grania* and Loti's *Pecheur d'Islande* with him. However, Synge
would later condemn Loti in a fashion similar to his treatment of Lawless,
believing that Loti had in some way deceived people in giving fictional
accounts of occurrences that were made to appear as reality. Synge could
not comprehend why fiction would be the preferred method of literary
depiction of both Lawless and Loti in relation to Aran, and could certainly not understand the discrepancies and exaggerations of which he
found both authors guilty.

Exploration and Escape: Lawless and Synge

Hay notes that island boundaries, "rather than constituting movement-
constraining barriers [...] invite transgression; inspire restlessness; demand
to be breached" (2006: 23). Like Hay, Anderson finds that island boundaries
"impel [people] to explore and even to escape into the unknown" (2003:
47); for Synge and Lawless' work in particular, this is an apposite observation. Both Synge and Lawless had a keen awareness of the figure of the
island, not merely in its geographical qualities but also in its capabilities
as a refuge for themselves and their characters. This dual notion of exploration and escape is also relevant if one considers Yeats' advice to Synge
upon going to the Aran Islands; perhaps, as Kiberd has also noted, it was

Synge himself who needed to explore his own artistic sensibilities rather than simply explore the Islands. For Lawless on the other hand, the island may have figured as a refuge for all her artistic desires or perhaps it was a remote enough symbol for her to depict the often-isolated and separate tradition of female authorship. For Dening "each new intruder finds a freedom [in the island conditions of isolation and escape] it never had in its old environments" (1980: 32). This may be true of Synge, the interloper[11], and Lawless, the female outsider, and also for the island authors who may be considered a distinct group. Every artist, whether native or non-native, could be considered an intruder of sorts upon the terrains which he/she traverses, discovering and uncovering much about their art and themselves along the way. By immersing themselves, more often than not, in familiar terrain, authors like Liam Ó Flaithearta and Máirtín Ó Direáin had, without question, a seemingly easier task ahead of them than authors such as Lawless and Synge had.

However, it could also be argued that a level of detachment is necessary if one is to adequately portray a particular time and place, a detachment that is not readily available when one lives in a small and contained island community. Thus, for Ó Direáin and Ó Flaithearta, the task of being sufficiently outside of a tradition while simultaneously being inside of what that tradition represents in order to write about it is complicated from the outset. It is perhaps not surprising, then, that both authors used authorial devices which gave them the requisite distance from the subject(s) at hand: Ó Flaithearta created an Aran of his own in Nara, and Ó Direáin wrote about his beloved Inis Mór from the safe yet tortuous remove of Dublin city.

---

11   Kiberd notes that Synge describes himself as an interloper (1996: 107). However, in Kiberd's *Trieste Tropiques* (2000), the interloper is given a more positive connotation. Pádraig Standún, who was stationed, as parish priest, in Inis Meáin and Inis Oírr for twelve years, also describes himself as an interloper (1994: 309), but again, it is with a positive connotation in mind.

Aran Writers: Handling the Past and the Present

An evocative perspective from which to analyse and comprehend these shifts and changes from past to present and back again, is to look at literature by islanders themselves, particularly islanders who saw themselves as having a foot in both the island and the mainland, as well as island authors who remained on the islands for the greater parts of their writing careers. Liam Ó Flaithearta, having left Aran, was advised by his London editor to return to his island home and write simply and truthfully about life there. Máirtín Ó Direáin suffered an urban-based exile in Dublin in order to fully establish himself as a poet of merit. Dara Beag Ó Fátharta (born 1920), a native of Inis Meáin where he has spent all but a few months of his ninety years, continues the Aran poetic tradition in much the same style as Ó Direáin. Together, these three islanders have contributed to a tradition of poetry and prose which tells us much of what it is like to be insider and outsider, islander and emigrant, man and poet and author. However, perhaps the most important and interlocking strands running through Ó Flaithearta, Ó Direáin and Ó Fátharta's work are those which concern and address the symbolic and actual properties of "islandness" as both a condition and a reality and those which look at the physical and psychological isolation and freedom which the Islands' natural and metaphorical boundaries represent for them.

Islandness

To understand the complex issue of "islandness" one must firstly look at what island studies can tell us about this unique condition. Peter Hay's article, "A Phenomenology of Islands" (2006), raises some of the most challenging and pertinent questions which island studies must address if it is to establish itself in academic and cultural arenas. The article, taken

from the first volume (2006) of *Island Studies Journal* (<http://www.
islandstudies.ca/journal>), argues for the vital multi-disciplinary approach
which island studies offers, while also tackling the concerns which critics
of the discipline have raised regarding its validity as an academic and theoretical model. Hay highlights the three main "faultlines" (Hay 2006: 19)
which the discipline must address, accept and amend in order to strengthen
its growing academic position. These faultlines are identified as, (1) "the
nature of the island *edge*" (my emphasis) (2006: 19), (2) "the import for
questions of island memory" (2006: 19) and (3) "the appropriation of
island 'realness' by those for whom 'island' best functions as a metaphor"
(2006: 19). The latter two faultlines address issues raised in relation to
the utopian concern with the real and with memory. In utopian studies, memory is an ongoing process which is capable of symbolising and
representing a place situated in the past or the present. In island studies,
memory plays a similar role, although the memory often associated with
island studies is seen as fixed, and aligned with static pastness, a relationship which is represented as much more flexible in utopian studies. In
utopian studies, as Baccolini has advised (2007: 172), memory must strive
to free itself of becoming associated with stasis and traditionally conceived
notions about the past. One reason why memory in island studies has
become linked with the past has to do with change and modernity. As
an island becomes physically and culturally eroded over time, islanders'
memories of the pre-eroded island become fixed to the parts (actual and
intangible) of the island now lost. In particular, exiled islanders, and most
especially exiled island writers, find that their memories of their island
home cannot embrace the current or present situations and thus become
preoccupied with imaginatively reclaiming the lost or eroded elements
of what functioned as reality in their youth. This is especially clear in the
poetry of Máirtín Ó Direáin. In utopian studies, the opposite occurs; the
fragmented or lost past provides the impetus for the imagining of and
working towards a better future.

Islandness: Ó Direáin and Ó Flaithearta

A poignant illustration of this island memory is Ó Direáin poem *"Cá bhFuilid /* Where are They". Ó Direáin queries the whereabouts of the characters he had earlier immortalised in *"Cuimhní Cinn /* Remembrances" (1980: 23). In *"Cuimhní Cinn"* he suggested that the women in their heavy shawls and red-petticoats and the men in their home-spun clothes will live forever in his memory, until his death: *"[m]aireann a gcuimhne fós i m'aigne / Is mairfidh cinnte go dté mé i dtalamh".* There is an eerie silence in *"Cá bhFuilid",* however, when the poet asks *"Cá bhfuil fear an chreasa / [...] Cá bhfuil mná na gcótaí dearga?"* (1980: 204).[12] No reply or answer is forthcoming, though none is anticipated to begin with, and the poem ends solemnly and coldly. It is as if the people Ó Direáin is searching for are hidden from view, obfuscated by some veil of nostalgia; though current in the poet's memory the men and women of his childhood do not exist in the present. However, though in another equally sombre poem, Ó Direáin finds that some remnants of the past re-enter an individual's memory with the coming of old age. *"Greim Cúil an Dúchais /* The Grip of Nature" (1980: 146) introduces Ó Direáin's grandfather's cousin who is on his deathbed. The poet writes that *"déarfaí faoi do shórt / Go dtugais cúl le dúchas",*[13] but is quite astounded to find that as his relation lies dying it is *"i dteanga Dhónaill an tSrutháin / A bhís ag ráimhaillí faoi do mhuintir".*[14] It may be more a sign of the dementia or absent-mindedness of old age that enables Ó Direáin's relation to embrace his past and his people's language rather than an awareness of the need to return to the source. Nonetheless, Ó Direáin notes the power of the past, and of one's heritage and upbringing, especially in times of trials:

12   "Where is the man with the belt / Where are the women with the red skirts?"
13   "It was said of your sort / That you gave your back to your nature".
14   "... it was in the tongue [Irish] of Dónall of Sruthán [his grandfather] / that you were raving about your people".

I gcruthúnas go raibh cúig	Proof that there was a trick
Fanta fós i láimh an chine,	Still left in the people's hands,
Is gur nós leis an dúchas	And that it is nature's habit
Greim cúil a fháil ar deireadh.	To get the [upper] hand in the end.

A cynical reading of the poem might also uncover a more personal note on Ó Direáin's part: the poet wishing to acknowledge his own understanding of his having turned his back on his familial obligations to work the land or to stay on the island and add to the community there at the expense of his art. Perhaps Ó Direáin is comforting himself with the knowledge that, regardless of his being away from the island and its traditions and customs, he will remember his youth in the end, and death will be eased in the knowledge that he had returned to the source in other, more poetic ways. Ó Direáin believed from an early age that he was surrounded by poetry, and that words and meanings seeped into his vernacular from the environment around him. His move away from the island intensified this connection, while also highlighting the culture which had enriched his poetry:

> *Bhí an fhilíocht i mo thimpeall agus mé ag fás. Bhí an charraig oileánda ar ar tógadh mise ar mhuin na filíochta, gan bealach ag duine uaithi dá mb'áil féin leis é. Bhí sí sna brachlanna cúrbhánna a d'éiríodh de dhroim na mara glaise, i nglór na dtonn a bheireadh dúshlán carraige is trá agus bhí sí arís sa monabhar ciúin síoraí a níodh mallmhuir samhraidh is í ag súgradh go lách le ciumhais an chladaigh. Ach thar gach ní bhí sí i gcaint mo dhaoine (Dánta, 1939–1979, 1980: 13).*[15]

Ó hEithir (in Mac Con Iomaire, 2000; 1977) and Denvir (1991) also note a similar need to repatriate his thoughts and his art to the source in Liam Ó Flaitheartá's decision to write *Dúil*. Ó Flaitheartá's own memories of Inis Mór were growing weaker, and he clearly felt the desire to ground some of these remembrances in story-form. Desire is both the title and central

---

15　"I was surrounded by poetry growing up. The island on which I was raised was the essence of poetry with no escape from it, even if you wanted to. She [poetry] was in the ripples of foam that rose on the backs of ocean waves. She was in the sound of the waves that challenges rocks and strand. And she was again in the quiet murmur of a summer neap-tide, playfully caressing the seashore. But above all else, she was in the speech of my people".

theme of the 1953 publication; coupled with this, though rarely investigated, is the author's own desire to tease out the various ways in which each of the islanders depicted in the stories seek to satisfy their desires by immersing themselves in very ordinary, almost mundane sensations and comforts. In the opening story, *"Dúil"*, the young boy wishes to grasp the shafts of sunlight which he sees dancing on the floor. In *"Bás na Bó"* the heifer wishes to plunge to her death in order to be reunited with her stillborn calf. What is perhaps most interesting about *"Bás na Bó"*, however, is that its Irish does not appear as natural in syntax as that presented in the edition of *Dúil*. Indeed, as Daniels has investigated, and as which a close examination of both editions confirms, the 1953 edition is written, at times, in a more formulaic and less relaxed style than that presented in 1966. Ó Flaithearta's reasons for doing this are ill-defined and outside the scope of this book. However, it could be suggested that, this being his first full work in Irish, Ó Flaithearta wanted to present a more formal, professional and erudite version of the Irish language than the more relaxed style which would emerge in later years, particularly in interviews and commentaries on radio and television.

In *"An Beo"* a mother rejoices at the safe birth of another child, while her father dies in the next room; *"An Scáthán"* portrays the desire of the young girl for freedom from hard work and the heat of the sun. Ó Flaithearta's stories, and indeed their titles, emphasise his interest in animal life, particularly wild life: *"An Seabhac"*, *"An Chearc Uisce"*, and *"An Luchóg"*.[16] Other stories, not included in *Dúil*, include: "The Black Rabbit", "The Little White Dog", "Grey Seagull", and "The Wild Swan". A.A. Kelly notes that "[h]is first short story collection, *Spring Sowing* (1924), showed he could write lyrically of man and beast in natural surroundings, but a liking for struggle, an undercurrent of violence, remains an important characteristic in his work" (1976: 10). It is in such struggles, predominantly linked with the natural environment, that Ó Flaithearta makes best use of his animal characters, suffusing them with human characteristics, feelings and determination. However, it is Ó Flaithearta's concern with these miniature

16   "The Hawk", "The Water Hen" and "The Mouse".

characters, and also with the minuteness of their natural world that most illustrates the author's own personal intrigue with minute, intimate details, and with insight of the everyday.

Cahalan writes that "O'Flaherty was well prepared to see human existence as animalistic and had [due to his having grown-up in Inis Mór] excellent credentials to write about animals" (1991b: 53). In Ó Flaithearta's letters to his editor Edward Garnett (A.A. Kelly, ed., 1996), the author made frequent references to his interest in animals. Among the most interesting insights which these letters provide relate to how Ó Flaithearta found elements of his own self reflected in the animals, or how he imbued the animals with human characteristics, particularly the birds. In one letter, dated "July sometime, 1925" (1996: 124) Ó Flaithearta wrote to Garnett, quoting a proverb: "[t]he sandlark cannot have both beaches at the one time" (1996: 125). This remark precedes Ó Direáin's poem "*Mo Cheirdse / My Trade*" which compares his poetic trade with that of a fisherman's, casting his line "*idir dhá chladach /* between two shores" (1980: 131). Other, more personal poems of Ó Direáin's also communicate his dividedness, his liminal existence.

While Ó Flaithearta's remark might resonate on the plains of bilingualism and personal duality, Ó Direáin's clearly redirects the reader's mind from the larger island of Ireland back onto the smaller island of Inis Mór. However, Ó Flaithearta may well have been reflecting on his home and his youth upon writing to Garnett. While Cahalan is correct to point out that Ó Flaithearta "recalled [the proverb] while ruminating about his divided life" (1991b: 55), he fails to consider that the body of letters which preceded the comment highlights Ó Flaithearta's concern with the translation of some of his short stories and the length of time, and amount of money, involved in such work. Thus, it could be that, rather than providing an insight into Ó Flaithearta's relationship between home and elsewhere, the metaphor of the sandlark represents the difficulty of carrying out, one's artistic duty and of remaining true to one's linguistic background. However, Ó Flaithearta's ties with both Irish and English began at approximately the same time, and thus, perhaps, contradict the proverb: Ó Flaithearta's career was in fact built around travelling and mining both linguistic and cultural beaches. Nonetheless, he could not settle for too long a time in either language, and this is the most likely source for the analogy with the sea-bird. In another related example, Ó Direáin's poem "*A Fhaoileáin Uchtbháin* / White-Breasted Gull" (1980: 46) details the poet's desire to exchange his own identity with that of the seagull. Seeing the seagull's contentment at resting upon the seas between the island and the mainland, and comparing that with his own unhappy position between the island and the city, Ó Direáin asks for a trade:

A fhaoileáin uchtbháin	White-breasted gull,
Déan malairt liom fiú lá,	Take my place for a day,
Go gcuirfead díom crá	Till I shed my sorrow
[...]	
Go mbeidh lonnaí laga gan chás	And soft careless ripples
Ag déanamh láíocht	Press gently
Le mo bhrollach.	Against my breast.[17]

For Ó Direáin, the dangers of life on the oceans were minimal when compared with those faced by the exiled, urbanised poet.[18] It is also worth noting that the more solid beach of Ó Flaithearta's remark, and the more fluid and uncontained seascape of Ó Direáin's poem both provide shelter for the birds. To extend this image further still, it is important to consider that Ó Flaithearta's connection with the real and earthed nature of island life was his greatest backdrop, while Ó Direáin's imagination and his own craft were immersed in the less quantifiable, the more ethereal qualities of island life. Whereas Ó Flaithearta has time, through the lengthier vehicle of the short-story form to present the meat and bone stories with which generations have become familiar, Ó Direáin, with his more concise art of poetry, relies more on descriptive, yet cogent language, to unearth his feelings and emotions. Ó Direáin's stones are portable and mutable; Ó Flaithearta, in

---

17 Mac Síomóin and Sealy's translation (1984: 35).
18 In his later work, however, Ó Direáin shows a marked disgust with the seagulls of his poetry. This may seem inconsequential at this point; this noted, it is important to consider that the seagulls of his poetry were city gulls, which he described as fat, greedy and overly prone to defecating on passers-by.

his last visit to Inis Mór in 1980, sat upon a stone he recognised and was unsurprised to note that it had not changed and was easily identifiable.

> There they saw his childhood home, and he evoked the past for his companion and friends who came with them, apostrophising the rock that stood nearby: *"Bail Dhia ort, a chloch mhór; tá aithne agam ortsa"* ["The blessings of God on you, big rock, I know you"] (Costello: 1996: 106).

Conversely, Ó Direáin could not reconcile the changes and the imaginative and actual erosion which his beloved island and stones had undergone, and rejected the old and the new versions of the island (see *"Árainn 1947"*). These differences, however, may largely be representative of their respective natures; Ó Flaithearta was certainly more vociferous about the harsh realities of his upbringing, and it is understandable, as a result, to find that his interest in the realities of island life is more forcefully portrayed than Ó Direáin's.[19] Indeed, Ben Forkner has described Ó Flaithearta as "the most 'naturalistic' of the Irish realists" (1981: 670). Tied to this realism, however, was Ó Flaithearta's self-declared passion for coldness; in *Shame the Devil* Ó Flaithearta observed that "when a man is born on naked rocks like the Aran Islands, where the struggle for life against savage nature is very intense, the instinct for self-preservation is strong in him" (1934: 10). This nakedness is characteristic of his short stories in *Dúil*. The stripped-down nature of each of the eighteen stories might at first glance underscore their depth of narrative and theme. *"An Fiach / The Hunt"*, for example, is just two pages long; this brevity, however, belies the power and impact of the story in much the same way as the bare nature of some of the other stories belies the extent of their meaning. In getting to the heart of each story in an almost completely unadorned manner, Ó Flaithearta was able to achieve a naked, cold and blistering style of writing. However, this is not to suggest, as Crawford (1953) does, that Ó Flaithearta's stories are

---

19   However, Pegeen O'Flaherty-O'Sullivan recounts how her father used to comment that "'your own salt is sweeter than a neighbour's honey' and [that] Aran was his honey" (2004: 38), reinforcing the idea that her father's attitude to the island of his birth was not as bitter as often described in his novels and stories.

simply "black and white" (1953: 41). Writing in the wake of *Dúil's* publication, such a review must have been difficult for the author to take;
Breandán Ó hEithir confirms this in his radio lecture (1989) and in "Liam
Ó Flaithearta agus a Dhúchas" (1977). The only black and white aspects
of Ó Flaithearta's stories in *Dúil* relate to shades of light, and though
some stories are shorter than others, it is unjustified to state that they
are bland or simple as a result of this brevity. Other reviewers, Murphy
(1973) and O'Connor (1976) for example, were critical of Ó Flaithearta's
weaker English translations of the stories. While Ó Flaithearta considered
Ó Cadhain's collection *An Braon Broghach* as reflective of "the torments
and the beauty that are together in life" (1949: 30), he seemed unconvinced
that his own stories were similar to those of Ó Cadhain.

Daniels (1988) also considers much of this criticism, and, having studied both *Dúil* and many of the translations, comes to the conclusion, like
Kelly, that Ó Flaithearta's "better stories suggest more than they state"
(A.A. Kelly, 1976: 7). However, no critic to date has considered how the
size of each of *Dúil's* short stories mirrors the size of an island. Although
not every story in *Dúil* could be said to take place on an island, their concise
nature speaks to a miniature world, and the worlds of the stories and the
characters speak to contained worlds and existences; Ó Dubhthaigh does
note that islands are almost always near in the stories (1981: 60) but does
not expand on this observation. Daniels estimates that half of the short
stories in *Dúil*, which makes nine, have "island-like settings" (1988: 128).
This would account for the fact that the action of over half of the stories
takes place near or looking towards the sea. Edges, sea-shores, cliffs and
solitary rooms are all represented in *Dúil*. Each presents a stage between
the beginning of one element and the end of another: the cliff-face in
"Bás na Bó" symbolises the distance between the heifer and her calf on the
rocks below, and it also signifies an island's break away from its surrounding sea. However, the cliff-face also suggests other related incidents: the
now half-eroded structure of Dún Aengus in Inis Mór, with its missing

western-half having fallen onto the rocks and into the sea below;[20] the
incident, fresh in Ó Flaithearta's memory, of the landlord's cattle being
driven over the cliffs on Inis Mór in retribution for increasing rents on the
island; and also the many women on the island looking out across the sea
where their emigrant children now live. The drop from the cliff to the sea
below indicates the pain and the distance from the island to the sea and
from the island to the mainland. These spheres of action represent cut-off
points between life and death, between action and inaction and between
the island and the brooding sea.

Another consideration of the short stories in *Dúil* pertains to the
ways in which Ó Flaithearta uses the sea, amongst other things, to both
mask and reveal the island terrain. As might be expected, the descriptions
of the sea also mirror the angst, strife or contentment of the characters of
the stories. This textual pathetic fallacy is also found in *Grania*, and *The
Aran Islands*, where changes in the prevailing weather and in particular the
sea conditions often correspond with moments of liberating epiphany or
grim realisation. Invariably, the sea is black and fierce or calm and clear. It
is rarely, however, a benign presence.

Islandness: Lawless

In Ó Flaithearta's "*Uisce Faoi Dhraíocht* / The Enchanted Water", he introduces the reader to the various ledges of the island, and the variety of birds
which perch on the individual pieces of rock. Birds also appear in Lawless's
Grania, in Synge's *The Aran Islands*, as well as in Ó Direáin's poetry more
recently in the poetry of Dara Beag Ó Fátharta. They symbolise an existence
that can serve both island and mainland, travelling and surveying distances

---

20　This was discussed on the BBC 1 programme Coast: From the Air. Details of the
episode are found here: <http://www.bbc.co.uk/coast/programmes3/06_galway_
baltimore.shtml#txtimes>.

that the poet or writer cannot. Often they represent resilience; Lawless's use of birds in both *Grania* and in her poetry is marked by her interest in their relationship with the edge of the island. In the "Preface" to *With the Wild Geese* (1902), Stopford A. Brooke explains Lawless's fascination with The Wild Geese and also emphasises how her poetry allowed Lawless "to stand, when she wills, aside from her patriot grief and to see the misfortune of her country from an isolated point of view" (1902: xix). In an image akin to that of Ó Direáin's white-breasted seagull and also to that of Ó Flaithearta's sandlark, Brooke sees that "[a] true poet sits in the centre of things, among universal emotions" (1902: xix). In much the same way as the gull rests on the waves between the island and the mainland, or in how the sandlark flits between two shores, Lawless situates herself in the middle, in the interspace. There are, of course, echoes here of Grania's character, who finds herself trapped between allegiances to Honor and Murdough, between the freedom of the seas and the entrapment of the land. When Grania drowns, she drowns in the space between these two poles, between home and away. In "The Cormorant: Song" (1902: 85) Lawless presents the sturdy and resilient cormorant as capable of withstanding the tests of weather and time in order to retain his place on the waves:

> Now the seagull spreads his wing,
> And the puffin seeks the shore,
> Home flies every living thing,
> Yo, ho! the breakers roar!
> *Only the Cormorant, dark and sly,*
> *Watches the waves with a sea-green eye.*
>
> Under his bows the breakers fleet,
> All alone, alone went her;
> Flying alone through the blinding sleet,
> Flying alone through the raging sea [...].

In describing the cormorant in language similar to that used to describe a *currach*, or traditional Aran rowing canoe, Lawless draws parallels between the bird and the boat. The *currach* had for centuries provided the most efficient and hardy transport network between the Islands and the mainland, and the cormorant is one of the Islands' most recognisable sea-birds. Their blackness represents both their closeness to doom and danger and also the contrast between the blue of the sea and the darkness of the sea-floor. In *Grania* there are two references to cormorants, and in each case they signify the protagonist's disorientation while on the sea and her disillusionment with her lover while on land. Later in the novel, while Grania is hopelessly attempting to reach Inis Mór to seek help for her ailing sister, she imagines seeing a "black beak-like bow of the boat" coming towards her. Boats and boating language are integral to *Grania*'s narrative, and on most occasions, are described as being bird-like. Indeed, in one particular instance, Grania is likened to a bird about her father's hooker:

> Opposite, at the further end of the boat, the little red-petticoated figure of his daughter sat perched upon the top of a heap of loose stones, which served for the moment as ballast. [...] Hardly had the smaller boat pushed away from the larger one and regained its former place, before the little girl upon the ballast scrambled hastily down from her perch, [...] and went up to the boy as he stood there astonished, furious, red to the roots of his hair with anger and indignant surprise (1892: 7).

Islandness: Dara Beag Ó Fátharta

From a contemporary point of view, Dara Beag Ó Fátharta's poetry also utilises island birds to illustrate geographical features such as rocks, as well as placenames and also to symbolise new advances on the Islands. The best example of this is Ó Fátharta's use of the seagull as a metaphor for the aeroplane service between the three Aran Islands and the mainland of Indreabhán. Though some eighty years apart, it is noteworthy that birds continue to be useful symbols for conveying the bifurcated identity of islanders and visiting mainlanders alike. Ó Fátharta's poem "*An Aerstruip* / The Airstrip" (1990: 31) compares the daily flights between Inis Meáin and Indreabhán with that of the seagulls and sea-birds that also make the journey:

Ach anois tá na daoine chomh maith leo,	But now the people are just as agile,
Mar is féidir linn gluaiseacht más gá.	Because we can move if we need to.
[...]	
Nach ansiúd a bhéas an gliondar is croitheadh	It'll be there you'll see happiness and the
láimhe	shaking of hands
Roimhe dhaoine a thiocfas anall.	For the people who'll come from away.
Ach silfear na deora go fras ann	But the tears will flow there
I ndiaidh imeacht gan filleadh go brách.	When they leave without returning.

However, the final lines relating to emigration from Inis Meáin emphasise the impact that increased links and ease of access to the mainland have had on the depopulation of the island. This stated, without these essential services, neither tourist nor islander could survive on Aran. In another of Ó Fátharta's poems, "*Bróga Úrleathair* / Pampooties", published in his latest collection *Cloch na nGabhar*[21] (2003: 11), the poet writes about the pampooties, or raw-hide shoes that islanders wore up until the late 1970s. However, though Ó Fátharta has respect for the traditions of the island, and of the making of raw-hide shoes, he is also a realist:

Tagann daoine ón Rúis agus ón tSín,	People come from Russia and China,
Gearmánaigh is Francaigh –	the Germans and French –
Is cuma leo céard tá lena íoc	They don't mind how much they pay
Ach iad a fháil le tabhairt abhaile.	As long as they can purchase them and bring
	them home.
Tá athrú mór tagtha ar an saol,	Big changes have occurred,
Tá siad ag gabháil as faisean.	They are going out of fashion.
Iarraimse ar Dhia amach ó mo chroí,	I wholeheartedly ask God,
Gan iad a thabhairt ar ais dom.	Not to bring them back to me.

It should be explained that Ó Fátharta is one of the last people on Inis Meáin to wear traditional clothing. He wears the home-spun trousers and vest, and the *crios*, the multi-coloured belt that was distinctively patterned and thus easily attributable to particular families. He looks, to all intents and purposes like the people commemorated in Ó Direáin's poetry

---

21   "The Goat's Rock".

(see *"Cuimhní Cinn"* and also *"Cá bhFuilid"*) and those immortalised in Synge's descriptions of the colourful clothing of the men and women on the Islands.[22] He is often photographed and painted by visiting artists and documentary makers, and he is ever-willing to explain his decision to remain true to the island's traditions. Mary O'Malley of the *Irish Times* reported on the Aran Islands International Poetry Festival, held in Inis Mór in 1997: "'This is as close as I'll get to hearing Homer', said one visiting American poet as Aran Islands writer Dara Bheag (sic.) Ó Flatharta (sic.) finished his recitation. At that moment, a gap closed briefly and two traditions and two languages met".[23] The cover photograph of Bob Quinn and Liam Mac Con Iomaire's *Conamara: An Tír Aineoil / The Unknown Country* (1997) is of Dara Beag Ó Fátharta; he has come to represent Inis Meáin's perpetuation of the past-present. His homage to Synge in *"Aimsir Synge / Synge's Time"* (1990: 4) details the historical and personal importance of the writer. Documenting the harshness of the landlord system which Synge saw first hand, Ó Fátharta also celebrates the islanders' defiance in the face of such difficulties, and their allegiance to the Irish language.

Níl ár n-oileán ró-mhór, ná saibhir go leor,	Our island is not large or wealthy,
Is, ar ndóigh, dá mbeadh, né bheadh muide ann;	And if it were, we would not be there;
Ach an Béarla go tréan,	English would be strong and
Is an Ghaeilge i bhfad siar	Irish in the past,
Is molaimis go hard an Té a rinne.	We highly praise He who made it.
Is áit í a chruthaigh Dia le go dtógfadh sí an siol	God created the island to grow the seed
A bhí ruaigthe ar fán is ar seachrán.	That had been banished and was missing
Is tá an Ghaeilge ann faoi bhláth, is í i gcónaí ag fás	Irish flourishes here, always growing
Chomh tréan leis an lá a labhair Fionn í.	As strong as the day when Fionn spoke it.

22 Unsurprisingly, Dara Beag was asked to read *"Cuimhní Cinn"* for the documentary *"An Charraig Stoite"* (2003).

23 *Irish Times*, Friday, 15 August 1997, p. 12.

Place and Island Studies: Locating Islands and their People

A fundamental question which has been asked by many academics, both within and without island studies is: "why do so many people desire to make sense of islands; why so many declared islophiles?" (Hay, 2006: 31). For Hay the answer lies in the fact that "islands – *real* islands, real geographical entities – attract affection, loyalty, identification" (Hay, 2006: 31). However, to bring such attributes to bear on a particular phenomenon which is at the heart of Island Studies requires one to "take a bounded geographical entity and add an investment of human attachment, loyalty and meaning [in such a way as to arrive at] the phenomenon known as 'place'" (Hay, 2006: 31). Investing such personal emotions in a place – an island – surely requires that place to be in some way(s) unique, special or meaningful. However, what would happen if an island does not live up to or meet with the aspirations of those who invest in it such strong feelings and desires? It is possible that the myth or ideal may never fully live up to the actual or real that is so sought after, and thus we are in danger of creating, in effect, two separate islands instead of one if we fail to recognise the reality and the metaphorical implications of the island itself.

A brief overview of the texts and journals available to the island studies scholar shows a clear fascination within the discipline with ideas about "place". Baldacchino observes that "small islands are special because their 'geographical precision' facilitates a [unique] sense of place" (2005: 35). Thus, the ability of pinpointing and accurately locating the island gives the individual an assured locus of place from which to orient him/herself and, one would imagine, direct oneself to, or away from. However, also implicit in the observation from Baldacchino is the notion that this locating ability also allows the individual to know or to have a place whereupon to, quite literally, place his/her aspirations, geographical knowledge, and literary imaginations. For islanders themselves, however, there is without question a "heightened sense of place to which islandness conduces" (Hay, 2006: 31). In her *Collected Stories* (2004), Carol Shields notes that

[c]hildren born on [small] islands differ from Elsewhere children in that they are knowing of each rock and fencepost of their homeplace, of every field-corner and doorway, every spit of sand and beach pebble [...] [T]hey are able to look out across the widewater and observe the wonder and diversity of our earth-home. May it ever be so (2004: 428).

Place and Space: Ó Direáin

Ó Direáin was inherently aware of what Shields has described above; when he speaks of his life on Inis Mór, the island is not considered a large entity, but as a collection of rocks and fields, cliffs and shorelines. This awareness of the minutiae of life on a piece of land which is small in itself, if compared with the mainland, for example, provides the reader with an understanding of the intimacy with which an islander regards his/her home as well as with an appreciation of the knowledge of each intricate part of that island home. Ó Direáin's attachment to his island home is heightened through his use of the most essential components of the island itself (rock, stone, soil, and field). These elements symbolise both the starkness of island life and also the way in which these elements have combined to form the place described. As Riana O'Dwyer explains,

> [t]he experience of exile depends symbiotically on an identification with place. To really feel the otherness of a strange location, one must firstly identify closely with a familiar location as the norm. [...] This constitutes the construction of a narrative of belonging (1994: 63).

Ó Direáin began constructing a similar narrative upon leaving Inis Mór. As Ryan points out "[...] he reconstructs his island home [...] For Ó Direáin the island is almost a character in itself" (Ryan, 2002: 267), highlighting the way in which the poet embellishes and fleshes out this homeplace in such a way as to bring it to the level of an individual with distinct characteristics. However, in her subsequent book *Carraig agus Cathair*, Ní Riain notes that Ó Direáin may have never, really, left his island home;

"[b]'fhéidir nár fhág sé an baile riamh i ndáiríre, is é sin le rá thug sé leis é.
Ach, ar an taobh eile den scéal, b'fhéidir nárbh é Árainn fiú amháin a bhí i
gceist sa deireadh aige. Ba dhomhan dá chuid féin é a bhí cruthaithe aige"
(Ní Riain, 2002: 74).[24] Yi-Fu Tuan's concept of topophilia, describes the
"affective bond between people and place or setting" (Tuan, 1977: 4).[25]
For Ó Direáin, "[p]lace is everything. Describing, recreating, agonising
about Inishmore in much of his work provided the poet with a substi-
tute home" (Ryan, 2002: 268). In her socio-political study of Ó Direáin's
work in *Carraig agus Cathair* (2002), Ní Riain stresses the point that the
human condition of the island character was of less concern to the poet
than was the actual *islandness* of the life there, or the qualities which that
brought with it. Though some of Ó Direáin's poetry describes one person
or a particular group of people, for the most part he talks of the islanders
as a collective unit, and this serves to highlight the primary importance
which he placed on the island condition itself and the effect it had on the
individual or group. The effect which the islanders had on the island is
of only secondary importance as, for Ó Direáin, and Liam Ó Flaithearta
too, the island always came first. This primary interest, then, in the spatial
qualities of island life and islandness itself highlights much of what writers of the Irish Literary Revival and after believed in relation to island life
and its powerful hold upon a person, artist, and writer.

For Ó Direáin, however, there is another layer of understanding which
is necessary to investigate. The island which the poet (re)creates in verse
whilst in Dublin is a very different island to the one he left behind, in that
it takes on a position which it may not have had, had the poet not left for
the city. Throughout Ó Direáin's poetic compositions we find as much an
Árainn of the mind as an Árainn which is actual and mappable and real.
This recreation of his home place, through the vehicle of poetry, is an act
of spatial understanding, for the descriptions of the islands are rich with

24   "... [m]aybe he never really left home, that is to say that he took it [home] with him.
     However, on the other hand, it may not have been Árainn at all that he had in mind
     at the end. He had created a world of his own".
25   Ryan sees this as the term which "best sums up Ó Direáin's relationship with his
     island home" (Ryan, 2002: 268).

an awareness of, regard, and love for the islands as well as a consideration of what the island actually represents for Ó Direáin and his audience. By giving the main focus to the island and not to a particular islander, or group of islanders, Ó Direáin shows that distance provides some sort of emotional filtration system, whereby the observer can filter through the elements of his affection and identify the constituent components.

This process of identification is not unproblematic, however, and can lead to the growth of a chasm between what the poet desires and what that desired-for place actually represents. The end result, as in Ó Direáin's poetry, is that there comes into being two separate places: the island as a geographical entity, and the island as a symbolically manifested and emo-tionally charged space, one that is capable of containing all the imagined *and* real desires, hopes and dreams of the outsider who wishes to be the insider once again. As Isobel Ryan has noted, Inis Mór was the geographical entity in Ó Direáin's poetry and Árainn was the name of "the poetic island" (Ryan, 2002: 268). Ó Direáin's Árainn has, nonetheless, much in common with the actual or real island of Inis Mór. However, Árainn is brought closer to Dublin for the purposes of contrast and comparison on occasion by Ó Direáin, and at other times, it is made distant and vague; perhaps by imaginatively "moving" or displacing the island, the poet can show its inherent fluidity and its capacity to act as a liminal symbol between one place and another. Such inherent flexibility and liminality may well allude to Ó Direáin's creation of a third layer within the heretofore bifurcated space/ place stratagem, which is the creation and poetic growth of the interspace. The richness of his island life is in stark contrast with the life he has in Dublin; "[t]he built environment of the city is invisible and nameless when compared to both the natural and built environments of Inishmore" (Ryan, 2002: 268). Much of Ó Direáin's reflections on his previous existence as an islander focus on the work done on the land, how the seasons changed the place, and how the people responded to such changes, but in Dublin the ceaseless changes of urban life seem to go unnoticed and unchecked, and these changes seem to have little or no regard for the people who inhabit the city's environs. The communion between man and nature and between man and concrete is a theme which the poet investigates throughout this work, none more so than in "*Stoite* / Uprooted" (1980: 30):

Thóg fear seo teach	One man built a house
[...]	
A mhair ina dhiaidh	Which outlived him
Is a choinnigh a chuimhne buan	And kept his name alive
[...]	[...]
Beidh chuimhne orainn go fóill	We will be remembered yet:
Beidh carnán trodán	A stack of files
Faoi ualach deannaigh	Weighed down with dust
Inár ndiaidh in Oifig Stáit	Will survive in a government office.[26]

The stark contrast drawn in the poem between the natural world and that of the man-made world is one of Ó Direáin's most urgent themes. Seamus Heaney's poem "Digging" carries an echo of what Ó Direáin achieves in *"Stoite"*. When Heaney realises that he has "no spade to follow men like them", he concentrates on his own spade, his pen, and vows to dig with that intead (1998: 4). The name of the islander who built the wall in *"Stoite"*, will live on as a result of that process, but the name of the man remembered in the "stack of files" will not resonate with any such natural process, but only serve to gather dust in a bleak governmental building. Though Heaney's poem ends on a note of perserverance and continuation, Ó Direáin's does not, perhaps reflecting his own dissatifaciton with office work and with his divergence from the path of his ancestors. The two buildings mentioned in the extract from the poem above could not be more different: one is functional and bears the mark and the name of its owner and maker, the other holds no such mark of character and is unremarkable in use, save for holding files. The tangible life of the islander's home and the neglected state of the government office are also contrasted; Ó Direáin constantly alludes to the lifelessness of urban life and structures. The poet does do some digging of his own though; in *"Mo Leic / My Bedrock"* (1980: 178), Ó Direáin searches for some evidence of his island identity:

26   Mac Síomóin and Sealy's translation (1984: 13).

Is gnó dom féin fós	It is still my concern
Dul ar thóir mo leice,	To search for my bedrock,
Dul ag tochailt fúm	Digging below me
Sa chlais chúng	In the narrow trench
D'fhonn teacht uirthi	To find it.[27]

When he describes Árainn, the physicality and the animation of his themes, characters and settings are very much to the fore, while his descriptions of Dublin emphasise Ó Direáin's perception of what he regarded as the vapid nature of life there. In *"Deireadh Ré /* End of an Era" (1980: 51), Ó Direáin vents his frustration at the same society he decried in *"Stoite"*, noting also that his name is forgotten and his craft unknown on the busy streets of Dublin:

I measc na bplód gan ainm,	Among the nameless crowds;
Gan 'Cé dhár dhíobh é' ar a mbéal	"Who is he?" doesn't spring to their lips,
Ná fios mo shloinne acu.	My name to them unknown.

For Ó Direáin, however, one way in which he could create a home of sorts for himself in Dublin was to imagine a home based more on imaginary fragments than on physical characteristics. By recreating his island home, described in marked contrast to his Dublin life, Ó Direáin ultimately created a different type of home: a home of the mind. "[T]he Árainn of the poetry remains a distinct place which comes into being through the poetry and which cannot be relocated when the poet returns to the island later in life in search of the home he once knew [...] the poetry brings a version of home into being" (Ryan, 2002: 269). In some of Ó Direáin's later poetry, especially *"Neamhionraic Gach Beo /* The Essence is not in the Living" (1980: 189), "he writes that nothing in life stays with us for ever, even the island has 'left his poem'" (Ryan, 2002: 271). In the beginning he judges people in terms of whether they are the "essence of an island" or not, but at the end of the poem he says:

---

27   Collinge's translation (1985: 272).

Sleamhaíonn nithe neamhbheo	Unliving things slip
Siar ón mbeo go bhfágann é:	Away from life and leave it:
An amhlaidh sin a d'fhág	Was it thus
An t-oileán mo dhán,	The island left my poem,
Nó ar thugais faoi deara é?	Or did you notice?[28]

It seems apparent here that Ó Direáin is aware that he has, throughout the course of his writing career, created two separate islands in his work and imagination, one a "physical reality and [one] the mental construct" (Ryan, 2002: 270). However, as evidenced in his poem "Berkeley" (1980: 121), where Berkeley's theory "that all substance is really present only in the mind" (2002: 271) is played out, Ó Direáin seems to accept his own embracing of the mental construct ahead of the reality, and ultimately his decision to continue to engage with the former construct, which by that stage was more familiar and accessible to him than the "real" island he had left behind in his youth. "Ó Direáin believed in his early works that when he wrote about Inishmore he was writing about the island as it really was. However, as time went on, he realised that his Árainn and the Inishmore he grew up on and now visited were separate entities" (2002: 271). As Mícheál Mac Craith has recently noted:

> From the late 1960s on, a new gentleness permeates the poet's work. Hand in hand with a frank recognition that the guiding island of his poetic inspiration owes more to the realm of the imagination than to reality, Ó Direáin generously acknowledges the role of the city in fostering his creative talents. Instead of the polarized opposition of the earlier works, we now find reconciliation, unity, and a realization that the combination of his island and urban heritage had made the poet what he was (2001: 75).

Ó Direáin's unconscious realisation that the creation of an interspace between the city and the island was possible through his poetry, as well as through his own recognition of his rural-urban duality, came late in his writing career. Had he been able to accept such duality from the outset of his exile in Dublin, then his writing career and his relationship with the

---

28   Mac Síomóin and Sealy's translation (1984: 121).

island may well have developed in completely different ways. It is significant that, in later years, upon returning to Árainn, Ó Direáin finds that the island he so loved has disappeared and is in fact lost to him and for him. In *"Deireadh Ré"* he finds that the island has suffered a "metamorphosis" and he feels out of place there (Ryan, 2002: 272). Had Ó Direáin been able to embrace *both* the mental and the actual constructs of the island earlier in his career – possibly through his recognition of the vehicle of the interspace – then his dissatisfaction with the changes on Árainn may possibly have been lessened.

The changes that have led to a lack of familiarity with Ó Direáin's name and work on the island have come about as a result of the sweeping modernity which the poet himself sought to avoid by creating Árainn. It is a shock to his sensibilities that the modernity he fought against in his pastorally oriented poetry has crept into the island he wrote about as being the antithesis of the metropolitan lifestyle he found in Dublin. For the homecomer to return to his/her familiar terrain and to find that terrain changed significantly there is inevitably a sense of loss. Relph charts this loss when he writes that:

> [t]here is the common sensation of returning to a familiar place after the absence of several years and feeling that everything has changed [...]. Whereas before we were involved in the scene, now we are an outsider, an observer, and can recapture the significance of the former place only by some act of memory (Relph, 1976: 31, in Ryan, 2002: 273).

This act of (re)memory is an important concept; Ó Direáin realises in his later poetry that although *his* island is now lost there is the hope that his poetry will outlive him and will commemorate the island he once knew. Ó Direáin is also keenly aware that though his name and the place he describes in verse may not be known by the generations to come his craft will stand as his legacy and time itself will not erode the literary monument that is the poem.

Place and Space: Ó Fátharta and Ó Direáin and Ó Flaithearta

Dara Beag Ó Fátharta's poetry echoes Ó Direáin's thematic concerns with childhood, with the island as a character and as a natural element, as well as following in Ó Direáin's poetic footsteps with regard to the writing of elegies to islanders and notable visitors alike. Ó Fátharta's poetry celebrates and commemorates many islanders' contributions to the creation of a unique way of life on the islands, especially with regard to the construction of houses, roads and piers on the islands. His writing also focuses on the physical and psychological strength of the islanders, and in particular the men of the islands. Immediately evident in Ó Fátharta's poetry is the recurring use of cliff-edge imagery. Though this may seem natural enough given the island theme of much of the poetry, Ó Fátharta makes use of the boundary which the cliff provides for two main purposes: one metaphorical and one natural. In *Cloch an Fhaoileáin*, Ó Fátharta echoes both Synge and Ó Flaithearta's use of the cliff-face to designate an area of artistic freedom and potential.

In "*A Chéad Eitilt* / His First Flight" (*The Short Stories of Liam O'Flaherty*, 1966: 41) Liam Ó Flaithearta's young seagull goes to the edge of the cliff to brace himself for this first flight into the world, and it is possible to view this story as a thinly-veiled allegory for the author's own first steps into the world of mainland Ireland, or indeed, as a metaphor for the danger of leaving the island of one's birth, not knowing if the winds of artistic appreciation will be favourable. Máirtín Ó Direáin's poetry also makes much use of the imagery of cliff-faces and it is worth noting that, like Dara Beag Ó Fátharta and Ó Flaithearta, he represents them as places of both promise and possible danger. It is not difficult to see that the island's natural edge and imaginative edge, which all three writers adopt as a central theme, is one which says much about their own relationships with the island's isolationary and insulatory nature, and the resulting control and freedom which this geographical feature allows them as artists. Though islands can function as both open and closed spaces, they are usually regarded as geographically closed and potentially artistically open. The sea provides all three authors with a central image to explain this duality of penetrability and impenetrability. For Ó Direáin the sea can either hinder or help one's understanding of the island, but it is invariably portrayed as nature's way of isolating the island and its people from unwanted outsiders and influences and thus preserving the way of life there.

For Ó Flaithearta, however, the sea is a gateway to the outside world, though not always a welcome one. In "The Landing" (1966: 42) the power of the sea over the islanders is all-consuming and dangerous in the extreme, while in "Going into Exile" (1966: 98) the sea is the bridge which young islanders must traverse in order to achieve a more economically-sound existence for themselves in America and beyond. Similarly, the islanders in Ó Flaithearta's stories combine elements of the duality also represented by the sea; they are simple yet satisfied individuals who, nonetheless, often long for the exile which will separate them from their homes and the place which most aptly symbolises and explains their strong and determined natures. Ó Flaithearta subsequently referred to "the cliff-bound shores of Aran" in *Two Years* as "the school in which we, as boys, were taught our manhood; and it was the school also, where I especially was taught by my mother to appreciate the beauty of nature" (1930: 75). Here we see the author's awareness of his boundedness and isolation, but his sense of them as vital to his upbringing and understanding of the island condition as a positive personal and artistic force.

In Ó Direáin and Ó Fátharta also we see this deep understanding of the importance of their island home in helping them to develop as both men and as writers; in *"Cuimhní Cinn"* by Ó Direáin, as in *"Bróga Úrleathair"* by Ó Fátharta, we find remembrances of days of old and the way in which each member of the community had an impact on the young poets. Significant also, however, is the way in which the island itself formed an almost human figure for the three writers, especially for Ó Direáin, for his exile was far more permanent and painful than that experienced by Ó Flaithearta. Images of important structures on the Islands figure in all three writers' works; forts, piers, churches, ruins, homes, and schools all feature, and though this may be unsurprising, their importance is greatly amplified if one considers that at one stage or other each of these structures functioned as a refuge or a place of solitude and endeavour for the authors. By extension, the island mirrors the completeness and safety of these smaller structures, in that it functions as a safe and protected area for both artist and islander alike. The isolationary nature of the poetic and authorial enterprise is often mirrored in the writer's approach to his or her craft. Ó hÓgáin illustrates an extreme example of isolation for creative purposes whereby the early Irish poet removed himself to a dark chamber as an aid to inducing poetry (1990: 367). This also has resonance with the original import of "seer", which was attached to the poetic profession. The Irish word *"file"*, or poet, was initially invested with a similar meaning to "seer" in terms of insight and ability to see (Williams and Ní Mhuiríosa, 1979: 19). Thus, poetry often became both a vehicle from which to see and also a place within which to create.

In his poem *"Fís an Daill* / The Blind Man's Vision" (1980: 45), Ó Direáin introduces a neighbour of his from Inis Mór. The man was blind, but was fond of telling stories to anyone willing to listen; Ó Direáin notices that the group listening to him are mocking the blind man, clearly as a result of their own inability to imagine. In anger, the poet leaves the scene, and retorts: *"Is gur dhúras nárbh eisean / Ach iadsan a bhí dall".*[29] Blindness and, conversely, vision are two themes which Ó Direáin often employs throughout his poetry. Collinge notes that Ó Direáin's position as a mediator between "the long Gaelic tradition, and the bleak vision of younger contemporary poets" (1985: 380) was critical because he could offer insight for both sets of writers. However, Ó Direáin also felt himself isolated or imprisoned in his chosen language of Irish in the early 1960s. The toll of the English language's dominance was considerable, and Irish-language poetry and poet were suffering for their decision. Seán Ó Ríordáin, a contemporary of Ó Direáin's, felt this imprisonment, and recounted his linguistic conflict in his poem *"Cath* / Battle" (1964: 123). Ó Direáin's *"Teanga an Phríosúin* / Prison Language" (1980: 175) demonstrates on two distinct levels some aspects of the nature of the old Irish *file*, isolated in a cell creating poetry, and also elements of the contemporary Irish-language poet, isolated and entrapped by and in his chosen language:

29   "And I said that it was not he / But they who were blind".

Samhail agam cime	I liken myself to a prisoner
A chaith an fhaid istigh,	Who served a long term
[...]	
Tuigim don ghliomach sa phota stóir.	I understand the lobster in the pot.[30]

However, Ó Direáin rules out a return to Inis Mór as the solution to his
problem of isolation. Although it may have seemed like the natural choice
for the poet, his decision to stay in Dublin reflects a fundamental realisation
on the poet's part: Dublin was the reality and the island was the dream,
and the dream was the essence of his poetry. In *The Government of the
Tongue*, Seamus Heaney observes that "[t]he new place was all idea, if you
like; it was generated out of my experience of the old place but it was not
a topographical location. It was and remains an imagined realm, even if it
can be located at an earthly spot, a placeless heaven rather than a heavenly
place" (1989: 4). Heaney's remarks could have come from Ó Direáin, albeit
after forty years of believing in the importance of the idea rather than its
reality. The notion of slippage is significant here; the imagined gives way
to the real, the island is rejected in favour of the city and the poet, as fisherman, finds himself "*idir dhá chladach* / between two shores" (from "*Mo
Cheirdse* / My Trade", 1980: 131).

Idir dhá chladach	Between two shores
Atáid na héisc uaim,	Are the fish I seek
Idir dhá cleacht	Between two traditions
Mo dheis a chaill.	I have missed my chance.[31]

A recent initiative on Inis Mór, under the stewardship of *Mná Fiontracha*,
and supported by the Heritage Council of Ireland, collected folklore and
family histories on the island, and produced a book, *Ár nOileán: Tuile
's Trá* / Our Island: Ebb and Flow (2004). An article written for this book
by Niamh Sheridan, Máirtín Ó Direáin's daughter, includes some salient
considerations on the poet's later life and about how his view of the island
and the city changed with time.

---

30   Collinge's translation (Thesis, 1985: 384–385).
31   Collinge's translation (1985: 387).

Aran shaped my father – the people and the Islands nourished his genius. [...] he
had a great love for the people of Aran. He particularly loved the old people as he
would have sat in their kitchens many a time being allowed to listen and learn the
chat around him. I believe he got his gentleness and dignity from them. My father
loved Dublin and its people also (2004: 107, 109).

Using the Island: Metaphorical and Real Deployments of the Island in Aran Poetry

Though an Aran literary tradition certainly exists, it would be to over-
simplify things to bracket each author under the same headings. A focus
on the deployments of the island metaphor in the poetry of Ó Direáin
and in that of Ó Fátharta reveals important points of intersection and of
dissonance. Ó Direáin, like Ó Flaithearta, sees the shoreline as fixed but
penetrable through the vehicle of the imagination, while for Dara Beag
Ó Fátharta the cliff is the natural delimiter between Aran and the outside
world of Ireland: it is fixed, locatable and non-negotiable. One reason for
Ó Fátharta's exactness and understanding of the island as a more concrete and
less imaginary figure could simply be explained by his almost-undisturbed
habitation on the island of both his birth and his poetry. For Ó Direáin, his
island is as much an island of the mind as it is a fixed geographical reality,
and his poetry reveals far greater imaginative uses of the island figure, without doubt brought about by his exile from Aran. Another notable feature
of Ó Fátharta's poetry focuses on his appropriation of the island as not just
a separate sphere from the rest of mainland Ireland but also as a potential
utopian destination where much happens and where things are always just
about to happen. Though relying heavily on island myths of legend and
heritage, such as fairy forts and holy wells, the Inis Meáin of Ó Fátharta's
poetry provides us with an understanding of how islanders and insiders
genuinely believe and continue to perpetuate the image of the island(s) as
the places that the rest of the island of Ireland could and should strive to
be like again. This is also reflected in utopian studies and in the potential

for projecting our hopes and desires onto pure and locatable places; there is no need for the places to be unreal or non-existent as was formerly believed to be the case in utopian studies (Sargent, 2007) in order to bring about the changes we wish to see in our own worlds and realities. That the Aran Islands may function as some sort of utopian mirror of progress in Irish society and literature is a proposition well worth examining.

In choosing to concentrate on the island and its associated themes and elements, Ó Flaithearta, Ó Direáin and Ó Fátharta are not unusual. However, what is significant is that their treatment of the island highlights, at almost every mention, the value and importance which they place upon the island, singling it out as a vital character as well as a metaphor of substantial merit and usefulness. To suggest that Aran literature should be considered as a single, separate entity would seem to deny the interaction with and intertextual nature of island and "mainland" Irish literature; however, there needs to be a reappraisal of what, and where, island literature contributes to Irish literature as a whole, and a recognition of the importance of how the "island" has become such a weighty and valuable image and symbol in Irish literature and cultural identity.

Fixed Links and the Bridging Effect: A Comparison with Canadian Island Literature

It would appear that size is an important factor in a matter such as tourism. However, as Stephan Royle has also noted, the larger the island, the less like an island it becomes, and the more like a country or continent. Royle notes that though Australia is an island, its size bears little in common with conceptualisations of what an island should look like (2007b: 49–50). Similarly, with regard to bridges and other fixed links between islands and mainlands, the debate as to whether or not an island can remain an island if it is connected in such a physical and visible way with the mainland continues. Canada's Prince Edward Island [PEI], for example, became connected with the mainland of New Brunswick in 1997, though many islanders sought to have the plans for the Confederation Bridge rejected. As MacDonald explains:

> While it was difficult for many people to articulate, "islandness" was central to their (the islanders who opposed the building of the Bridge) sense of identity. A fixed crossing would, for many, make Prince Edward Island less of an island. And to be less of an island compromised, perhaps fatally, *the felt distinctiveness of the Island's culture* (my emphasis) (MacDonald, in Baldacchino (ed.), *Bridging Islands: The Impact of Fixed Links*, 2007: 40).

Royle questioned whether or PEI should have renamed itself Prince Edward Peninsula in 1997 (2001: 8). The example of PEI is used here to illustrate the difficult relationship which exists between islands and mainlands, between islanders and their own indefinable understanding of their island identity, and also with regard to the perceived betrayal or transgression of an island's fixed insular boundaries, integral to its own sense of *being an island*. Achill Island, off the coast of county Mayo, is also a fascinating island case-study. Bridged since 1887, many regard it as an extension of Newport/Mulranny, its nearest mainland town, and find it difficult to consider it still an island. Gössling and Wall explain that "[c]lear physical borders also constitute psychological borders, which aid the imagination of being isolated, and are thus attractions for visitors seeking to escape routines, stress and responsibility" (2007: 429). A fixed link, while destroying this sense of isolation, might also destroy the sense of having left "routines, stress and responsibility" behind on the mainland; a bridge, for example, joins both island and mainland and thus it could be argued that there is no clear understanding of where one ends and the other begins. Edward MacDonald articulates this succinctly, writing "[h]ow many people could 'get away from it all' to Prince Edward Island before 'it all' followed them? Overcrowding and over-packaging might destroy the very genuineness and distinctiveness of the experience that tourists sought" (in *Bridging Islands*, 2007: 40). In another telling initiative on the Island, many anti-link protestors attempted to persuade local government to build a tunnel between the Island and the mainland instead of a bridge. It would seem that the more visible structure (the bridge) was their greatest difficulty, and that a more covert-type structure (the tunnel) would be more accept-able. This is a very remarkable departure, and one which suggests much about the underlying issues surrounding the construction of the link. For islanders who ostensibly opposed the bridge for economic and cultural reasons, it would appear that this was a smokescreen for their genuine reasons for opposing the structure: a visible link between the Island and New Brunswick would erode their Island's islandness, its distinctiveness, and also, possibly, make the islanders themselves re-examine their island identity in the face of encroaching mainland penetration.

Poets across Seas: Prince Edward Island and the Aran Islands

The poets of Prince Edward Island share much with the poets of the Aran Islands. PEI's Brent MacLaine and Frank Ledwell's poetry speaks about edges, fields, shorelines, maps and the immemorial quality of the island. Ledwell's "John of the Island" was inspired by British Columbia's Tourist Board's omission of Prince Edward Island from their map of the locality:

> It is the place of my birth,
> [...]
> Rocking in the sea, a cradle.
> [...]
> Here I am at home.
> [...]
> I do not need a map to tell me
> I am here.
> [...]
> I hope my body will sink down here.
> I do not need a map (2006: 34–35).

Brent MacLaine's connection with the farming and agricultural communities of the island manifests itself in his poetry. In a poignant poem for

his musician daughter, his hopes for her are of remembrances rather than
future oriented dreaming:

> I would wish for you visions of these soft fields,
> [...]
> that, even as the space between the notes
> conveys a time and place from worlds apart,
> you will breathe again the air that gives them heart;
> [...]
> I would wish for you to pause a moment more and hear
> As well applause from artful waves welcoming the shore
> (from "To my Daughter, Aspiring Cellist", 2000: 84).

Jane Ledwell's essay "Afraid of Heights, Not Edges: Representations of
Shoreline in Contemporary Prince Edward Island Poetry and Visual Art"
(2002) brings to light some fascinating correlations between PEI poetry
and the Island's own geographical and cultural constitution. Ledwell notes,
however, that "[s]uch strongly human, individual, creative identification
with landscape is not without problems for the artist [...] the shoreline is
a place of uncertainty and instability" (2002: 3). The shoreline, Ledwell
continues, "is visibly a moveable, shifting space" (2002: 3) and this is how
the island becomes in the mind of the artist: fluid, malleable and undergo-
ing constant change from erosion, tidal changes and effects of weather and
habitation. Writing about Milton Acorn's poetry, Anne Compton notes
that "liminal spaces [islands] [...] disturb certainties" (Compton, 2002:
38).[32] While this is fundamentally correct, it is not negative in the sense that
certainties are fundamentally essential. As Baldacchino has commented, we
think we know islands, and therefore think that they are static, unchanging
and easy to define, almost one-dimensional objects. Islands, however, are far
more complex, and can encapsulate a multiplicity of identities, personalities
and cultures in any one example. Thus the need to demystify the strongly
held beliefs that people have in relation to the uni-dimensionality of the
island is growing apace.

---

32   "The most important Prince Edward Island poet of the 20th century" (Ledwell,
      2002: 3).

Being from Away: Islandness and Insider Perspectives

Islands, by their geological and cultural distinctiveness, can disturb or unsettle certainties. Geological erosion, though largely damaging or negative, visibly illustrates the ways in which the island changes, and yet highlights how the island retains its character in the face of such erosion and physical vicissitude. Cultural erosion is a little more difficult to illustrate, and is for the most part invisible. This invisible attrition seems more insidious. It signals a danger that coastal erosion manifests in the physical sense. For the exiled artist or author, these erosive processes are only rarely present in their work, predominantly due to the fact that the image of the island remains static in their imagination and the island of their youth lies unchanged and untouched by weather or by modernity. However, the exile does carry the form and structure of his/her island terrain with him/her and uses it as a yardstick with which to compare the foreign surroundings in which they find themselves. This latter terrain is always found wanting and cannot compare on any level, especially on the level of ordinariness and natural beauty, with that of the island. As Ledwell writes, "[i]n a poem called 'Exile', Thomas O'Grady documents the pangs of longing for home that do not strike 'until I walk this stony/ foreign shore'. Reflecting on how at home 'the russet strand gives way/ beneath soft feet', the poet's 'brittle bedrock/heart erodes' in sympathetic response" (Ledwell, 2002: 6). Artistic representations of exiles who return are an important facet of PEI's relationship with both shores. An attractive turn-of-phrase which Prince Edward islanders use concerns "being from away" or of "coming home from away". Often exiled islanders refer to themselves as "islanders away" to communicate their bifurcated identity. The vagueness of "away" is highly significant. It does not present another physical place, such as "mainland" might, but it does convey distance nonetheless. "Home" on the other hand conveys proximity, and though vague in the sense that it names a generic locale – much like "away", it emotes a stronger sense of place-based identity than that of "away". The very act of *going* home represents a conscious decision to travel, whereas *being* away connotes a sense of enforced exile, of being held in a place that is not desirable. *Going home* reflects free-will, whereas *being away* reveals unhappy separation from a familiar location. Just as the island is in constant flux and at the mercy of weather and tides and economic and cultural change, so too is the exile caught between the flows of staying and leaving, between return and retreat.

From an Irish perspective, a recent collaboration between photographer Jim Vaughan, poet Macdara Woods and various photographers from Clare Island resulted in the publication of the book *This Time, This Place* (2007). Similar collaborative projects by islanders and artists have emanated from Inis Mór (2004) and Tory Island (2002) with the support of writing groups and the Department of Community, Rural and Gaeltacht Affairs. These initiatives are both welcome and necessary to communicate the continuation of literary and cultural traditions on Irish islands and to support emerging and established writers and artists. Macdara Woods's poem "Fifteen Contacts" draws its inspiration from the accompanying photographs in *This Time, This Place*, and from the island community on Clare Island.

> Deep in the unknown
> Empty quarter
> Of that country
> [...]
> This is how we
> Came here
> Like the cormorant
>
> Inhabiting two species
> The water and
> The stone walls [...] (2007: 51–52).

Head Space:
The Island As a Place to Think, Create and Become

In a thought-provoking commentary, Ledwell examines the paintings
of PEI native Elaine Harrison. Ledwell finds that "[f]or Harrison, 'the
Island' has become less a headland [...] and more a 'head space'. [...] It's
not an island's – or a head's – size that matters. It's what one does with it.
The shoreline [...] may be a container, but it is not a limitation" (2002: 12).
The *head space* is a fascinating concept. John R. Gillis's *Islands of the Mind*
(2004) presents a corresponding method of seeing an island as offering a
place for mental and psychological space. Gillis expands upon this notion
by suggesting that the metaphorical power of *island*, as in the *islands of the
mind* vein of thought, might well be the fundamental metaphor within
western discourse. "[W]estern culture" Gillis writes, "not only thinks
about islands, but thinks *with* them" (2004: 1). Developing upon this,
however, it is possible to deduce that islanders think *within* islands, and
from *without* them as well. This metaphorical deployment of the island is
highly transportable, and is regularly employed as a means of reconnec-
tion with one's former homeplace. However, the island metaphor can also
be used to register a sense of "radical individualism, wherein the uniquely
gifted and courageous individual rises above the constraints imposed by
the mediocrity of the many" (Hay, 2006: 27). This noted, it is more often
the case that the opposite is true: the island can serve as "a metaphor for
a lost relationship between individual and community" (Hay, 2006: 27).
Edmond and Smith advance the argument on this correlation between the
island and the individual, writing that

> [i]n terms of the modern European understanding of human consciousness, there is
> also a suggestive congruence between islands and individuals. Islands have a marked
> individuality, an obstinate separateness that we like to think corresponds to our own.
> [...] they have been the setting where individuals can prove their self-sufficiency.
> Just as typically, however, they become the place where individuals are disabused
> of such a fantasy. [...] Islands, then, can perform as images of both separation and
> connection (2003: 4).

Synge and the Aran Islands:
The Perfect Head Space to Create *The Aran Islands*?

In John Millington Synge's *The Aran Islands* there are strong traces of
this nexus between the island and the individual, as well as an association
between levels of separation and connectedness with regard to the islanders and the outsider, Synge himself, and between Synge and the island
locale itself. The twin notions of separation and connection also relate to
the islanders' way of life and the mainland threat of modernity; or to put
it another way, there is a tangible sense of the islanders' position on the
outside of the sweeping modernity of the rest of Ireland, but also an awareness that modernity is creeping in, insidiously, without their approval or
desire. Though the Islands did rely and still do, on the movement of tourist and islanders alike between the mainland and the Islands, there is little
that can be done to prevent the spread of change and linguistic decay given
the degree of coming and going to and from the Islands. Synge, by his own
admission, is wary of his presence on the Islands, and of introducing the
first alarm clock to the islands (Kiberd, 2000: 88), bringing a time piece
to a place where time is unimportant and measured by the direction of the
wind and the opening and closing of southward or northward-facing doors
of the houses. The introduction of the clock seems at odds in a place where
time is only a vague concept. Aran and the West of Ireland were remarkable
for their apparent timelessness; for Leerssen this is a natural consequence
of being peripheral to a time-obsessed centre (1996b: 243).

Synge had been heading towards Aran all along. Synge's macrocosmic existence, like that of Ireland's, was too diverse, too unattached to
secure him any steady artistic base. On a personal level also, Synge had
been romantically jilted and wished to escape from that disappointment.
The safety of having a bounded and quantifiable location wherein to flee
encroaching modernity and failed artistic and romantic attempts would
have seemed particularly desirable for Synge. However, there was more
to his decision to go to Aran than either of these explanations impart. At
least one reason identified here is that Synge recognised the potential of

the island as both a physical and imaginative entity and sought to employ this potential for his own personal motives and for his art. The island acted as a visual and tangible frame for Synge, both in a physical and artistic way. Life is confined on an island, it has natural limits, and yet imagination transcends these limits, all the while using the island's natural edges and geographical character as his influence and primary testing ground. The surrounding sea provides the ultimate frame, however, and its many physical and metaphorical deployments throughout Synge's work focus attention on the sea's power but also on the element which it surrounds and isolates – the island.

Christina M. Gillis's identification of an "enisling narrative" (2008: 50) provides a helpful lens through which to view *The Aran Islands*. The inherent separateness of an island, encircled by the sea, is reflected in small island writing whereby "key events and confrontations [in the text are] like separate, bounded islands within the sea of story" (Fowles, 1978: 30). Synge's text is episodic, snapshot and Gillis suggests that this quality is characteristic of modern island literature in that:

> [in] collections of loosely connected "chapters", each an entity in itself [...] we do not find a long sustained narrative that might be likened to a journey from "coast to coast". Small islands do not have "coasts" in this sense. We do not begin at one defined spot and end at another. Rather we move around in a small island, experience parts that are themselves enisled (Gillis, 2008: 50).

This sense of moving around within the confines of an island, and of discovering yet smaller islands within small islands is also explored in *Grania*, whereby Grania inhabits several enisled, or islanded, spheres: woman, sea-captain, sister, farmer, and disillusioned lover. Synge also inhabits interlocking spheres; he is an outsider, a peripheral insider, an "interloper" (Kiberd, 2000), and a writer. His capacity as a photographer perhaps best illustrates his awareness of the small, intimate island. Indeed, the photographs themselves are enisled representations of a larger island, and his text, which incorporates some of these photos, further enisles them in his depiction of a small island in the West of Ireland. The concept of islands within islands is very strong here, as it is in *Grania* and also within many of Ó Flaitheartá's stories in *Dúil*. Ó Direáin, however, takes this one step further, in that he

imaginatively occupies the created island (Árainn) within the memory of
the real island (Inis Mór), and even enisles himself in his urban life by creating barriers around his daily existence, through the use of metaphors: files,
keys, business jargon and office buildings. *"Stoite"* may also be interpreted
as *"scoite"* or cut-off. The files on the desk constitute miniature and enisled
versions of peoples' lives, while also acting as a visual obstruction between
Ó Direáin's creative desires and his reality as an office clerk. The poet is
cut-off from his island by the realities of his working life in Dublin, and
isolated from urban existence, working behind files and responsibilities of
employment, he is further enisled in his own office space.

Franks has recently observed that individuals and writers who have
experienced alienation or some type of personal or situational isolation
may "seek out the farthest, smallest and most isolated of any archipelago"
(2006: 6). Lawless and Synge may well have sought out Inis Meáin for this
very reason. However, Ó Flaithearta and Ó Direáin's decision to employ an
island often similar to Inis Mór may appear to contradict Franks' remark,
in that the island is the largest Aran Island, it was not alienated or isolated
in the same way that the other two smaller Islands were, and it was the closest to the mainland. However, both writers were naturally attached to the
island of their birth and, as Ó Direáin pointed out in *Feamainn Bhealtaine*,
an individual's sense of scale and size is often fragmented into more man-
ageable portions of space and content. The labyrinthine quality of Aran's
landscape, with its limestone walls and patchwork quilt-like covering of the
island's terrain may help to make Ó Direáin's explanation even clearer. Every
stone-enclosed field designates boundaries between different peoples' land,
and often designates village borders. Thus, people associate certain island
villages with certain families, thus enisling parts of the island from other
sections of the same island, and creating separate spheres of island life. Inis
Mór continues to be divided imaginatively between the westernmost half
of the island and the easternmost half, and this would have been similar in
Ó Flaithearta's and Ó Direáin's time. So, in effect, Inis Mór was two small
islands within one large island. A contemporary example of this "islands
within islands" scenario is reflected in Deirdre Ní Chonghaile's *agallamh
beirte* or verse dialogue, entitled *"An Ceann Thoir agus An Ceann Thiar"*

(2008).[33] *An ceann thiar*, or the westerly head, represents old, traditional Inis Mór, and *an ceann thoir*, or the easterly head, embodies the more modern elements of island life. *Thiar* represents pastness, and *thoir* symbolises advancement and progress. An extension to this is when islanders comment that they were *"thiar i gConamara"*, or back (West) in Conamara and *"thoir i nGaillimh"*, or (East) in Galway. The connotations of old and new continue to linger in the directions.

Ó Flaithearta and Ó Direáin grew up quite removed from the metropolis of Cill Rónáin (Kilronan), the capital of Inis Mór and of the Aran Islands as a whole.[34] As Ó hEithir has noted, English flourished in Cill Rónáin because of the strong military and professional presence there. Ó Flaithearta and Ó Direáin's island was a place of simplicity and smallness in its most intimate and positive form. This is reflected in Ó Direáin's delight in mundane objects such as potatoes, soil and stones. Ó Flaithearta's animal and human stories also relate to simple, ordinary events, and yet a complexity and depth of meaning are implicit in both writers' work. *Dúil* centralises everyday activities such as sea-weed gathering, periwinkle-picking and farming, and yet each activity reflects the frustrations or the desires of the various characters in the stories. Synge observed that "[e]very article on these islands has an almost personal character, which gives this simple life [...] something of the artistic beauty of medieval life. [...] they seem to exist as a natural link between the people and the world that is about them" (*The Aran Islands*, 1992: 13–14). This nexus between the island and the objects and activities of the islanders serves to foreground the deep sense of communion between land and individual which all four authors considered in this book have observed and documented in their work.

Péron's stimulating work on how the outsider graphs and charts the island's terrain in order to gain a more rounded and intimate knowledge of the landscape is an interesting way in which to plot Synge's familiarisation

---

33   Deirdre Ní Chonghaile kindly allowed me access to this *agallamh beirte*, and also explained the subtle differences between both halves of the island.

34   Brendan Behan, for example, referred to Cill Rónáin as "Aran's Big Smoke" (Ó hEithir, 1991: 5).

with Aran, and his remarkable relationship with the topography and natural life on Aran. The cosmopolitan chaos of his life up until his first visit to Aran in 1898 was surely immense. The island environment, then, must have significantly appealed to the writer; the sturdiness and the tranquillity it promised to provide too tempting to ignore.

Grania: Lawless's Woman of Aran

The *island as head space* hypothesis may well have appealed to Lawless. Seeing Grania as an islanded character, solitary, alone and resilient, Lawless was unquestionably aware of the correlation between islands and isolated figures. However, as is clear from Lawless's own diary entries from her visits to the West of Ireland and the Aran Islands, the author was keenly aware of her own need to escape the confines of her own gender-ordained role and the necessity of finding somewhere different wherein she could be herself and also explore her creative calling.

From the outset of *Grania: The Story of an Island*, Grania is closely identified with the landscape around her. Grania is an islander, but as her mother is from the mainland of Galway, the protagonist is often depicted as being more of an outsider than an insider. As Grania spends a large part of the novel on the sea in her father's Galway hooker, this position best exemplifies her dual identity: she is at home between both island and mainland, in her interspatial position on the sea. At other times, however, Grania is associated with the more rugged and isolating features of the island, rather than with the more liberating aspects which the open waters represent:

> Inishmaan was much more than home, much more than a place she lived in, it was practically the world, and she wished for no bigger, hardly for any more prosperous one. It was not merely her own little holding and cabin, but every inch of it that was in this peculiar sense hers. It belonged to her as the rock on which it has been

born belongs to the young seamew. She had grown to it, and it had grown to her. She was a part of it, and it was a part of her (*Grania*, 1892: 103).

It could be argued that it is at points in the novel when Grania exercises her dominance over both the land and the men in her life that she is most like the island; when she despairs of her lot and dreams of being free from the chains of servitude and social standing, she is most like the fluid and ever-changing seas around her island. Though the novel both begins and ends with Grania in the waters between Galway and Inishmaan, the largest part of the novel finds her struggling with life on the obstinate climate of "the rock" (*Grania*, 103) of Inishmaan. "If all humans are themselves islands, as the poet has suggested, then this tall, fiercely-handsome girl was decidedly a very isolated, and rather craggy and unapproachable, sort of island" (104). Thus Grania was enisled within Lawless' novel. When Lawless was asked whether or not Grania was based on some woman she knew, she replied: "[a] Grania [...] I have never known in that rank of life. The idea is taken from something a good deal higher up in the social scale" (quoted in Hansson, 2007: 74). Aligning the character of Grania with a woman of social standing such as Lawless herself was surely a bold move for the writer. It is likely that in portraying Grania as a spirited young woman, constrained by the male-dominated structure of island life, and held back by her ailing sister Honor and by the island's geographical distance from the mainland, Lawless was attempting to give voice to her own frustration at being hemmed in by literary and societal restrictions. Another reading may find, however, that in Grania's dogged fight to make Murdough love her and provide for her and her family Lawless is critiquing women for their lack of self-sufficiency and self-belief. Thus, any attempt at understanding Grania results in a plurality of possible answers; and it is this plurality, or at least duality, that makes *Grania* such a powerful statement of the significance of the interspace as both a literary trope and an actual condition of existence. When Grania drowns at the end of the novel, she does so in the interspace between both the island and the mainland and also between the life of a struggling islander and that of a liberated, self-sustained mainland woman. As Hansson explains: "[...] since she can neither go back to Inishmaan and marriage with Murdough Blake nor leave the island for a life elsewhere, she is caught in a double bind where the only place she can be truly herself is in the border zone of the Atlantic. Her death by drowning is not so much a tragedy, then, as the only possible solution [...]" (2003: 128). At the end of the novel, the sea speaks to Grania and asks her to choose between one space or another:

> "Look well at me", it seemed to say, "you have only to choose. Life up there on those stones! Death down there upon these – there, you see, where the surf is licking the mussels! Choose – choose carefully – take your time – only choose!" (*Grania*, 1892: 202–203).

Perhaps the most interesting aspect of *Grania* is Lawless's interest in the land and the place itself rather than the people who constitute it. By eliminating any discourse with issues that might be read as engaging with debates on the West of Ireland as some sort of cultural holy-grail, Lawless is free to explore the actual West, with its geographical specificity and its topographical detail to the fore. Lawless can be seen, then, to give voice not just to Grania's character, and her own personal agenda, but also to the West of Ireland's natural and physical character. By liberating the West from the dialogue of Revivalists and cultural nationalists, Lawless frees the West's potential as a place in its own right, instead of one that has become appropriated to meet other ends. However, this complicates our understanding of what is to be central and what is to be peripheral, and disrupts the neat balance that has previously existed in relation to how the West of Ireland was viewed: "[t]he map that introduces the novel is of the Aran islands alone, without any relation to mainland Ireland, England or any centre of which the islands could be the periphery, which further complicates the notion of the West as 'other'" (Hansson, 2003: 129–130). This sense of dislocation should not be unfamiliar; Lawless's interspace rejects orderly geographical polarities just as it rejects received societal norms, and this is another example of where Lawless's own personal voice can be heard in the text.

Reflections

As the passing years widened the distance, the land the immigrants had left acquired charm and beauty. Present problems blurred those they had left unsolved behind; and in the haze of memory it seemed to these people they had formerly been free of present dissatisfaction. It was as if the Old World became a mirror into which they looked to see right all that was wrong with the New. The landscape was prettier, the neighbours more friendly, and religion more efficacious; in their frequent crises when they reached the limits of their capacities, the wistful reflection came: This would not have happened here (Handlin, 1973: 232).

The concept of the West of Ireland as a mirror for the nation is important. Maurice Goldring writes that "the writers of the Revival could see their ideal alive [in the Irish countryside], the image of Ireland they wanted to fashion, a rural society directed by a new aristocracy – the aristocracy of the mind" (1982: 66). The related use of the "image" and of imagery itself also highlights the importance of the mirror concept. However, a smaller, less widely discussed use of this concept is the island as mirror, and in particular, Aran as the West of Ireland's most employed cultural and linguistic mirrors. An island frames experience, in that an island has geographical limits, edges, shores, cliffs. Experience is contained on an island. In this way, the Aran Islands were Ireland's best cultural and literary gauge from the early nineteenth century onwards. However, the reflected images were often interpreted to suit various causes, and personal and artistic agendas. For many, the image of the Islands as colonial outposts was ignored in favour of the Islands as utopian destination. For islanders, particularly Ó Flaithearta and Ó Direáin, the Islands were both real places and imagined spaces, and though both linguistic issues pertaining to colonisation of the Islands and metaphorical creations of the Islands as elsewhere are present in their work, it is in their descriptions of the borderlines and interspaces of home that both best excel.

CHAPTER 6

Conclusions
Conclúidí

Mar a bhí / As it Was

Aran's past is one of Ireland's greatest literary, cultural, geographical and social archives. Some excellent work has previously been carried out on aspects of the cross-comparative nature of the Islands' literature (see Cahalan, 1999; Kiberd, 1979, 2000). The Islands themselves represent a multi-layered experiential and historiographical text. The literature of Aran's past has enabled a present-day understanding of the Islands' significance, and has also allowed more recent generations of writers to weave their literary works into the greater tapestry laid out before them.

The works of Lawless, Synge, Ó Flaithearta and Ó Direáin continue to resonate with a new wave of scholars and readers. It is also apparent that a greater understanding of the art of writing and of the importance of inspiration and location at the time of production is vital for a fuller appreciation of both old and new texts of Aran's literary canon. We can now say with greater conviction and clarity how and why these writers cast their gaze upon Aran. The Islands were a much more natural choice of destination and thematic location for Synge and Lawless than previously credited. Synge was drawn to Aran rather than being sent there; Lawless was seeking a space which, up to then, had not been claimed or occupied in literature by a woman of her background. For Ó Flaithearta and Ó Direáin it was not so much a matter of choosing so much as a matter of being linked to the rocks, stones and earth of the Islands from birth. They had an almost umbilical connection with Aran, representative of both the filial bond between parent and child as well as the metaphorical, cultural link between island and mainland. The attraction and magnetic appeal of the three limestone rocks in the mouth of Galway Bay was felt not just by outsiders or visitors. Ó Flaithearta returned to familiar ground throughout his literary career, and Ó Direáin sought refuge in the safe environs of his imagined island ("*An Gad Stoite* / The Cut Cord", 1980: 161).

Go bhfuil gad imleacáin an chine	Your race's umbilical cord
In bhur bpáirtse stoite	Has been cut off
Is meabhraím murach fál na toinne	And I remember that were it not for the wall of sea
Is iargúlacht mo chine	And my people's isolation
Go mbeinnse mar atá sibhe	That I would be like you
Gan inné agam mar chiste.	Denied the treasures of yesterday.

Lawless's *Grania* takes a revolutionary step forward in marking the territory of Aran as representative of both secure home and potentially-unstable freedom. In the character of Grania Lawless sought to blur the lines between the traditional matriarchal and patriarchal positions, seeking more than a neat juxtaposition of male and female roles. She wished to address the constant struggle of a female who was outside of the socially determined boundaries of her gender, in a place itself concurrently geographically and psychologically restricting to and liberating for the protagonist. Ultimately, it transpired that both Lawless and Grania suffered because they refused to conform to the mores of their gender and class. Perhaps in a pre-sentiment of her own fate, Lawless chose for Grania to lose herself in the interspace between rejection and acceptance. Synge made careful attempts not to destabilise his artistic backdrop to any detrimental extent, and thus, did not endeavour to colour his work with heavy-handed opinions on the Islands or the inhabitants. His role as a primarily uninvolved, distanced observer contrasts remarkably with Grania's direct participation in both plot and consequence. Lawless was holding a mirror up to patriarchal society, hoping to illuminate the plight of her fellow writers and matriarchs, whereas it could be argued, Synge was more concerned with using the Aran Islands as a mirror for the Irish nation, but, more personally, as an indicator of his own artistic development.

The island as it appears in Ó Flaithearta and Ó Direáin is imaginatively preserved. In reality, we understand that though this was once the way everything was, it no longer appears as such on the Islands. However, this does not have an injurious effect on the work itself, or indeed on how tourists or subsequent generations of authors use the island as theme and location. This is highly interesting in its own right, and had much to do with the utopianisation of the island territory throughout history, and particularly so in the Irish context. Mythologised, hyper-described and catalogued, the Aran Islands represent vastly different and differing symbols and locations to various observers and commentators, islander and non-islander alike. There are energies, creative, imaginary and tangible, surrounding our impressions of islands, and of the power that islands possess in allowing us to revisit and reengage with our past, our own thought-processes and also our future-oriented positions. The Aran Islands have for centuries been employed as touchstones for Ireland's uncontaminated past, and as markers of continuity, creativity and endurance for Ireland's ceaseless forward-facing motion. As Ireland's, and Aran's futures look more uncertain than at any other time in recent memory, it is apposite to re-examine these geo-cultural markers for some understanding of where we have come from and where we are going.

Mar atá agus mar a bheas / As It Is and Will Be: An Aran Renaissance?

Much of this book has concentrated on the Aran Islands of the past, and on the treasures of yesterday. The present situation with regard to literature and culture on the Islands is one of resurgence and hope. Though the Aran Islands International Poetry Festival has not taken place since 1998, and the Synge School on Inis Meáin has not featured since 1999, a renewed interest in our past has led many island- and non-island-based writers and researchers to begin the reinvigoration of the literary, artistic and musical heritage of the Islands. The cross-island cooperation that is today being developed will help to sustain writing and cultural interactions for the uncertain days to come on Ireland's most famous and desired Islands. The current renaissance of Aran writing provides a valuable opportunity for scholars and writers to collaborate in pursuit of a more comprehensive understanding of what islandness means today, and how the figure of the island has impacted upon writers and individuals since Lawless and Synge, Ó Flaithearta and Ó Direáin's time. If islanders envisage their islands as limitless sites for viable cultural and social projects, then the time has come for the people, the writers, the artists, and the musicians of the Aran Islands to stake their place in the pages waiting to be written in the next instalment of the Islands' history.

Bibliography

Primary Texts

Lawless, E. (1892) *Grania: The Story of an Island*, London: Smith, Elder and Co.
Mac Síomóin, T. and Sealy, D., eds (1984) *Máirtín Ó Direáin: Selected Poems / Tacar Dánta*, Dublin: The Goldsmith Press.
Ó Direáin, M. (1961) *Feamainn Bhealtaine*, Baile Átha Cliath: An Clóchomhar Teo.
Ó Direáin, M. (1980) *Máirtín Ó Direáin: Dánta 1939–1979*, Baile Átha Cliath: An Clóchomhar Teo.
Ó Flaithearta, L. (1953) *Dúil*, Baile Átha Cliath: Sáirséal agus Dill.
Ó Flaithearta, L. (1966) *Dúil*, Baile Átha Claith: Sáirséal agus Dill.
Synge, J.M. (1907) *The Aran Islands*, Dublin: Maunsel & Co.
Synge, J.M. (1992) *The Aran Islands*, London: Penguin [edited and introduced by Tim Robinson]

Secondary Texts

Agnew, J. and Duncan, J., eds (1990) *The Power of Place: Bringing Together Geographical and Sociological Imaginations*, Boston MA: Unwin Hyman.
Anderson, B. (1991) *Imagined Communities: Reflections on the Origin and Spread of Nationalism*, London: Verso.
Anderson, M-L. (2003) "Norfolk Island: Pacific Periphery", *Island*, 92, 47–53.
Arrowsmith, A. (2000) "Plastic Paddy: Negotiating Identity in Second-generation 'Irish-English' Writing", *Irish Studies Review*, 8: 1, 35–43.
Ashcroft, B. (2001) *On Postcolonial Futures: Transformations of Colonial Culture*, London: Continuum.

Ashcroft, B., Griffiths, G. and Tiffen, H., eds (1989) *The Empire Writes Back: Theory and Practice in Post-Colonial Literatures*, London: Routledge.

Baccolini, R. (2007) "Finding Utopia in Dystopia: Feminism, Memory, Nostalgia, and Hope", in Griffin, M.J. and Moylan, T., eds, *Exploring the Utopian Impulse: Essays on Utopian Thought and Practice*, Bern: Peter Lang, 159–190.

Baccolini, R. and Moylan, T., eds (2003) *Dark Horizons: Science Fiction and the Dystopian Imagination*, London: Routledge.

Baldacchino, G. (2004) "Editorial Introduction", *Tijdschrift voor Economische en Sociale Geografie*, 95: 3, 269–271.

Baldacchino, G. (2004) "The Coming of Age of Island Studies", *Tijdschrift voor Economische en Sociale Geografie*, 95: 3, 272–283.

Baldacchino, G. (2005) "Islands – Objects of Representation", *Geografiska Annaler*, 87: 4, 247–251.

Baldacchino, G., ed. (2007) *A World of Islands: An Island Studies Reader*, Malta: Agenda Academic Press.

Baldacchino, G., ed. (2007) *Bridging Islands: The Impact of Fixed Links*, Canada: Acorn Press.

Banim, M. (1896) "Here and There Through Ireland", in Ó hEithir, B. and Ó hEithir, R., eds, *An Aran Reader* (1991), Dublin: Lilliput Press, 73–83.

Bassnett, S. (1993) *Comparative Literature: A Critical Introduction*, Oxford: Blackwell.

Beer, G. (1989) "Discourses of the Island" in F. Amrine, ed., *Literature and Science as Modes of Expression*, Dordrecht: Kluwer Academic, 1–27.

Beer, G. (2003) "Island Bounds", in Edmond, R. and Smith, V., eds, *Islands in History and Representation*, London: Routledge, 32–42.

Belanger, J. (2000) "The Desire of the West: The Aran Islands and Irish Identity in *Grania*", in Litvack, L. and Hooper, G., eds, *Ireland in the Nineteenth Century: Regional Identity*, Dublin: Four Courts Press, 94–107.

Bell, D. (1995) "Picturing the Landscape: *Die Grune Insel*, Tourist Images of Ireland", *European Journal of Communication*, 10: 1, 41–62.

Benitez-Rojo, A. (1992) *The Repeating Island: The Caribbean and the Postmodern Perspective*, Durham, North Carolina: Duke University Press.

Bhabha, H. (1994) *The Location of Culture*, New York: Routledge.

Bloch, E. (1995) *The Principle of Hope*. Trans. Neville Plaice *et al.* Cambridge, MA: MIT Press.

Bloch, E. and Ritter, M. (1976) "Dialectics and Hope", *New German Critique*, 9, 3–10.

Bloch, E., Halley, A. and Suvin, D. (1970) "Entfremdung, Verfremdung: Alienation, Estrangement", *The Drama Review*, 15: 1, 120–125.

Boehmer, E. (1995) *Colonial and Post-Colonial Literature: Migrant Metaphors*, Oxford: Oxford University Press.

Bongie, C. (1998) *Islands and Exiles: The Creole Identities of Post/Colonial Literature*, Stanford: Stanford University Press.

Böss, M., and Maher, E., eds (2003) *Engaging Modernity: Readings of Irish Politics, Culture and the Literature at the Turn of the Century*, Dublin: Veritas Publications.

Bourgeois, M. (1913) *John Millington Synge and the Irish Theatre*, London: Constable and Company.

Bourke, A. (2006) "Re-Imagining the Gaeltacht: Maps, Stories and Places in the Mind", in Wyndham, A.H., ed., *Re-Imagining Ireland: How a storied island is transforming its politics, economy, religious life, and culture for the twenty-first century*, University of Virginia Press, 82–98.

Bramsbäck, B., ed. (1990) *Homage to Ireland: Aspects of Culture, Literature and Language*, Uppsala: Acta Univ. Usaliensis.

Breathnach, C. (1992) *An Fearann Breac*, Baile Átha Claith: Coiscéim.

Breathnach, C[iara]. (2005) *The Congested District Board of Ireland, 1891–1923: Poverty and Development in the West of Ireland*, Dublin: Four Courts Press.

Brinklow, L. (2008) "A 'Subterranean River' to the Past: The Importance of Inheritance in Creating Island Identity in the Fiction of Alistair MacLeod", in Novaczek, I., ed., *Culture and the Construction of Islandness*, Charlottetown, Prince Edward Island, Canada: Institute of Island Studies Press, 10–16.

Brinklow, L., Ledwell, F. and Ledwell, J., eds (2000) *Message in a Bottle: The Literature of Small Islands*, Charlottetown, Prince Edward Island, Canada: Institute of Island Studies Press.

Brown, T. (2004) *Ireland: A Social and Cultural History, 1922–2002*, London: Harper Perennial.

Buck, C.D. (1949) *Dictionary of Selected Synonyms in the Principal Indo-European Languages: A Contribution to the History of Ideas*, Chicago: University of Chicago Press.

Buttimer, A. and Seamon, D., eds (1980) *The Human Experience of Space and Place*, New York: St. Martin's Press.

Cahalan, J.M. (1991a) "Forging a Tradition: Emily Lawless and the Irish Literary Canon", *Colby Quarterly*, 27: 1, 27–39.

Cahalan, J.M. (1991b) *Liam O'Flaherty: A Study of the Short Fiction*, Boston: Twayne Publishers.

Cahalan, J.M. (1999) *Double Visions: Women and Men in Modern and Contemporary Irish Fiction*, New York: Syracuse University Press.

Carpenter, A., ed. (1974) *My Uncle John: Edward Stephen's Life of J.M. Synge*, London: Oxford University Press.

Carpenter, A. (1977) *Place, Personality and the Irish Writer*, Buckinghamshire: Colin Smythe.

Carroll, C. and King, P., eds (2003) *Ireland and Post-Colonial Theory*, Cork: Cork University Press.

Cassirer, E. (1946) *The Myth of the State*, London, Oxford University Press.

Chambers, W. (1927) "Modern Literature in Gaelic", *The Irish Statesman*, 19 November, 252.

Chambers, I. and Curti, L., eds (1996) *The Post-Colonial Question: Common Skies, Divided Horizons*, London: Routledge.

Childs, P. and Williams, P. (1998) *An Introductory Guide to Postcolonialism*, New York: Prentice-Hall.

Clarke, T. (2002) *Islomania*, London: Abacus Books.

Comerford, R. (2003) *Inventing the Nation*, London: Hodder Arnold.

Compton, A. (2002) "The Ecological Poetics of Milton Acorn's Island Poems", in Compton, A., ed., *Milton Acorn's The Edge of Home: Selected Poems*, Charlottetown, Prince Edward Island, Canada: Institute of Island Studies Press, 22–42.

Conkling, P. (1997) "Islands in Time", in Little, C., *Art of the Maine Islands*, Camden, Maine: Down East Books.

Connerton, P. (1989) *How Societies Remember*, Cambridge: Cambridge University Press.

Connolly, C. (2001) "Theorising Ireland", *Irish Studies Review*, 9: 3, 301–315.

Connolly, C., ed. (2003) *Theorizing Ireland*, UK: Palgrave.

Coogan, T.P., ed. (1986) *Ireland and the Arts*, London: Namara.

Corkery, D. (1931) *Synge and Anglo-Irish Literature*, Cork: Cork University Press.

Costello, P. (1996) *Liam O'Flaherty's Ireland*, Dublin: Wolfhound Press.

Crawford, J. (1953) "Liam O'Flaherty's Black and White World", *Irish Press*, 1 August, 4.

Crichton Smith, I. (1986) *Towards the Human*, Midlothian: Macdonald Publishers.

Cronin, J. (2003) "Liam O'Flaherty and *Dúil*", *New Hibernia Review*, 7: 1, 45–55.

Cronin, J. (2004) "O' Flaherty, Liam (1896–1984)", *Oxford Dictionary of National Biography*, Oxford University Press, available at: <http://www.oxforddnb.com/view/article/40868>.

Crouch, D. and Parker, G. (2003) "Digging-up Utopia? Space, practice and land use heritage", *Geoforum*, 34, 395–408.

Curran, B. (2007) *Lost Lands, Forgotten Realms: sunken continents, vanished cities and the kingdoms that history misplaced*, USA: Book-mart Press.

Dames, N. (2001) "Austen's Nostalgics", *Representations*, 73, 117–143.

Daniel, J.O. and Moylan, T., eds (1997) *Not Yet: Reconsidering Ernst Bloch*, London: Verso.

Daniels, W. (1988) "Introduction to the Present State of Criticism of Liam O'Flaherty's Collection of Short Stories: *Dúil*", *Éire/Ireland*, 23, 122–135.

Davis, T. (1914) *Essays, Literary and Historical*, Dundalk: Tempest.

de Bhaldraithe, T. (1968) "Liam O'Flaherty – Translator (?)", *Éire/Ireland*, 3, 149–153.

de Paor, L. (1998) "An Scéalaíocht" in Ní Annracháin, M. and Nic Dhiarmada, B., eag., *Téacs agus Comhthéacs: Gnéithe de Chritic na Gaeilge*, Corcaigh: Cló Ollscoil Chorcaí, 8–34.

Deane, S. (1992) "Brian Friel: The Name of the Game", in Peacock, A.J., ed., *The Achievement of Brian Friel*, Great Britain: Colin Smythe Limited, 103–113.

Deane, S. (1996) *Strange Country: Modernity and the Nation: Irish Writing Since 1790*, New York: Clarendon Press.

Dening, G. (1980) *Islands and Beaches: Discourse on a Silent Land, Marquesas 1774–1880*, Melbourne: Melbourne University Press.

Denvir, G. (1991) *An Dúil is Dual*, Gaillimh: Cló Iar-Chonnachta.

Denvir, G. (1997) "Decolonizing the Mind: Language and Literature in Ireland", *New Hibernia Review*, 1: 1, 44–68.

Dorgan, Theo (2002) "Twentieth-century Irish-language poetry", *Archipelago*, <http://www.archipelago.org/vol7-3/dorgan.htm>.

Dudley Edwards, R. (1977) *Patrick Pearse: The Triumph of Failure*, London: Gollancz.

Dunlop, F., ed. (1995) *Aurel Kolnai: The Utopian Mind and Other Papers*, London: Athlone.

Eagleton, T. (1995) *Heathcliff and the Great Hunger: Studies in Irish Culture*, London: Verso.

Eagleton, T. (1990) *Nationalism, Colonialism and Literature*, Minneapolis: University of Minnesota Press.

Edmond, R. and Smith, V., eds (2003) *Islands in History and Representation*, London: Routledge.

Farren, S. (1976) "Culture and Education in Ireland", *Compass: Journal of the Irish Association for Curriculum Development*, 5: 2, 24–38.

Fennell, J. (2007) "Church, state, and unfettered capitalism: three Irish-Gaelic dystopias", *Utopian Studies*, 18: 3, 379–390.

Fitting, P. (2004) *Imaginary Communities: Utopia, the Nation, and the Spatial Histories of Modernity* by Wegner, P.E., reviewed in *Science Fiction Studies*, 30: 1, available at: <http://www.depauw.edu/SFs/review_essays/fitting89.htm#fitting89>

Flannery, E. and Mitchell, A., eds (2006) *Enemies of Empire: New Perspectives on imperialism, literature and historiography*, Dublin: Four Courts Press.

Fleming, D. (1995) *A Man Who Does Not Exist: The Irish Peasant in the Work of W.B. Yeats and J.M. Synge*, Michigan: University of Michigan Press.

Forkner, B., ed. (1981) *Modern Irish Short Stories*, New York: Penguin.

Foster, J.W. (1977) "Certain Set Apart: The Western Island in the Irish Renaissance", *Studies*, 261–274.

Foster, R.F. (1988) *Modern Ireland: 1600–1972*, London: Penguin.

Foster, R.F. (2000) "Good Behaviour: Yeats, Synge and Anglo-Irish Etiquette", in Grene, N., ed., *Interpreting Synge: Essays from the Synge Summer School 1991–2000*, Dublin: Lilliput Press, 41–56.

Foucault, M. (1982) "Space, Knowledge, and Power: Interview with Paul Rainbow", in Hayes, K.M., ed. (2000) *Architecture Theory Since 1968*, MIT Press, 428–439 [See also Hayes, 2000].

Franks, J. (2006) *Islands and the Modernists*, Jefferson, North Carolina: McFarland & Company.

Friberg, H. (1990) "Women in Three Works by Liam O'Flaherty: In Search of an Egalitarian Impulse" in Bramsbäck, B., ed., *Homage to Ireland: Aspects of Culture, Literature and Language*, Uppsala: Acta Univ. Usaliensis.

Friel, B. (1980) *Translations*, London: Faber.

Friel, B. (1986) "Extracts from a Sporadic Diary", in Coogan, T.P., ed., *Ireland and the Arts*, London: Namara, 51–61.

Gandhi, L. (1998), *Postcolonial Theory: A Critical Introduction*, New York: Columbia University Press.

Gerstenberger, D. (1964) *John Millington Synge*, New York: Twayne Publishers.

Gibbons, L. (1996) *Transformations in Irish Culture*, Cork: Cork University Press.

Gillis, C. (2008) "Enisling Narratives: Some Thoughts on Writing the Small Island", in Novaczek, I., ed., *Culture and the Construction of Islandness*, Charlottetown, Prince Edward Island, Canada: Institute of Island Studies Press, 50–56.

Gillis, J. (2004) *Islands of the Mind: How the Human Imagination Created the Atlantic World*, New York: Palgrave Macmillan.

Goldberg, D.T. and Quayson, A., eds (2002) *Relocating Postcolonialism*, Oxford: Blackwell.

Goldring, M. (1982) *Faith of Our Fathers: The Formation of Irish Nationalist Ideology 1890–1920*, Dublin: Repsol Publishing.

Goodwin, B., ed. (2001) *The Philosophy of Utopia*, Essex: Frank Cass Publishers.

Gössling, S. and Wall, G. (2007) "Island Tourism", in Baldacchino, G., ed., *A World of Islands: An Island Studies Reader*, Malta: Agenda Academic Press, 429–453.

Graham, B., ed. (1997) *In Search of Ireland: A Cultural Geography*, London: Routledge.

Graham, C. (1994) "Liminal Spaces: Post-colonial Theories and Irish Culture", *Irish Review*, 16, 29–43.

Graham, C. (2001) "Blame it on Maureen O'Hara: Ireland and the Trope of Authenticity", *Cultural Studies*, 15: 1, 58–75.

Graham, C. (2001) *Deconstructing Ireland: Identity, Theory, Culture*, Edinburgh: Edinburgh University Press.

Graham, C., ed. (1999) *Ireland and Cultural Theory: The Mechanics of Authenticity*, Basingstoke: Macmillan Press.

Grant Duff, M.E. (1904) *Notes from a Diary, 1892–1895*, London: J. Murray.

Greene, D.H. and Stephens, E.M. (1959) *J.M. Synge; 1871–1909*, New York: Macmillan.

Greene, D. (1971) "Synge in the West of Ireland", *Mosaic*, 1, 1–9.

Grene, N., ed. (2000) *Interpreting Synge: Essays from the Synge Summer School 1991– 2000*, Dublin: Lilliput Press.

Griffin, M.J. and Moylan, T., eds (2007) *Exploring the Utopian Impulse: Essays on Utopian Thought and Practice*, Bern: Peter Lang.

Grubgeld, E. (1986) "The Poems of Emily Lawless and the Life of the West", *Turn-of-the-Century Women*, 2, 35–41.

Grubgeld, E. (1987) "Emily Lawless's *Grania: The Story of an Island* (1892)", *Éire: Ireland*, 22: 3, 115–129.

Grubgeld, E. (1997) "Class, Gender, and the Forms of Narrative: The Autobiographies of Anglo-Irish Women", in Shaw Sailer, S., ed., *Representing Ireland: Gender, Class, Nationality*, Florida: University Press of Florida, 133–153.

Hackett, E. and Folan, M.E. (1958) "The ABO and RH Blood Groups of the Aran Islanders", *Irish Journal of Medical Science*, 6: 390, 247–261.

Hall, S. (1996) "When was the 'Post-Colonial?' Thinking at the Limits", in Chambers, I. and Curti, L., eds, *The Postcolonial Question: Common Skies, Divided Horizons*, London: Routledge, 242–60.

Hamilton, H. (2010) *Hand in the Fire*, London: 4th Estate.

Hamilton-Paterson, J. (1992) *Seven-Tenths: The Sea and Its Thresholds*, London: Hutchinson.

Handlin, O. (1973) *The Uprooted*, Boston: Little Brown and Co.

Hansson, H. (2003) "Writing the Interspace: Emily Lawless's Geographical Imagination", in Böss, M. and Maher, E., eds, *Engaging Modernity: Readings of Irish Politics, Culture and the Literature at the Turn of the Century*, Dublin: Veritas Publications, 121–141.

Hansson, H. (2007) *Emily Lawless 1845–1913: Writing the Interspace*, Cork: Cork University Press.

Harmon, M., ed. (1972) *J.M. Synge: Centenary Papers 1971*, Dublin: Dolmen Press.

Harvey, B. (1991) "Changing Fortunes on the Aran Islands in the 1890s", *Irish Historical Review*, 27: 107, 237: 249.

Hay, P. (2006) "A Phenomenology of Islands", *Island Studies Journal*, 1: 1, 19–42.

Hayes, K.M., ed. (2000) *Architecture Theory Since 1968*, MIT Press [See also Foucault, 1982].

Heaney, S. (1989) *The Government of the Tongue: Selected Prose, 1978–1987*, USA: Farrar Straus and Giroux.

Heaney, S. (1998) *Opened Ground: Poems 1966–1996*. London: Faber and Faber.

Hedderman, B.N. (1917), *Glimpses of My Life in Aran*, London: Simpkin, Marshall, Hamilton, Kent & Co.

Higgins, A. (1972), *Balcony of Europe*, New York: John Calder.

Holm, B. (2000) *Eccentric Islands: Travels Real and Imaginary*, Minneapolis: MN, Milkweed.

Howe, S. (2000) *Ireland and Empire: Colonial Legacies in Irish History and Culture*, Oxford: Oxford University Press.

Hutchinson, J. (1987) *The Dynamics of Cultural Nationalism. The Gaelic Revival and the Creation of the Irish Nation State*, London: Allen and Unwin.

Jameson, F. (1974) *Marxism and Form: Twentieth Century Dialectical Theories of Literature*, Princeton: Princeton University Press.

Jeans, P.D. (2004) *Seafaring Lore and Legend: A Miscellany of Maritime Myth, Superstition, Fable and Fact*, USA: McGraw-Hill Companies.

Jordan, E. (2004) "Pastoral Exhibits: Narrating Authenticities in Conor McPherson's *The Weir*", *Irish University Review*, 34: 2, 351–368.

Joyce, J. (1914) *Dubliners*, London: Grant Richards Ltd. Publishers.

Kearney, R. (1997) *Postnationalist Ireland: Politics, Culture, Philosophy*, London: Routledge.

Kearney, R. (1988) *Transitions: Narratives in Modern Irish Culture*, Dublin: Wolfhound Press.

Kearney, R., ed. (1985) *The Irish Mind: Exploring Intellectual Traditions*, Dublin: Wolfhound Press.

Kearns, K.C. (1976) "The Aran Islands: An Imperiled Irish Outpost", *Proceedings of the American Philosophical Society*, 120: 6, 421–438.

Kelly, A.A., ed. (1996) *The Letters of Liam O'Flaherty*, Dublin: Wolfhound Press.

Kelly, A.A., ed. (1976) *Liam O'Flaherty: Short Stories*, Dublin: Wolfhound Press.

Kelly, A.A., ed. (1999) *Liam O'Flaherty: The Collected Stories, Volume 1*, New York: St. Martin's Press.

Kiberd, D. (1979) *Synge and the Irish Language*, London: Macmillan.
Kiberd, D. (1993) *Idir Dhá Chultúr*, Baile Átha Cliath: Coiscéim.
Kiberd, D. (1996) *Inventing Ireland: the Literature of the Modern Nation*, London: Vintage.
Kiberd, D. (1997) "Modern Ireland: Postcolonial or European?", in Murray, S., ed., *Not on Any Map: Essays on Postcoloniality and Cultural Nationalism*, Exeter: University of Exeter Press, 87–105.
Kiberd, D. (2000) "Synge's Tristes Tropiques: *The Aran Islands*", in Grene, N., ed., *Interpreting Synge: Essays from the Synge Summer School 1991–2000*, Dublin: Lilliput Press, 82–110.
Kiberd, D. (2005) *The Irish Writer and the World*, Cambridge: Cambridge University Press.
Kiely, D.M. (1994) *John Millington Synge: a biography*, Dublin: Gill and Macmillan.
Kirby, P., Gibbons, L. and Cronin, M., eds (2002) *Reinventing Ireland: Culture, Society and the Global Economy*, London: Pluto Press.
Kirch, P.V. (1986) "Introduction: The Archaeology of Island Societies", in Kirch, P, V., ed., *Island Societies: Archaeological Approaches to Evolution and Transformation*, Cambridge: Cambridge University Press, 1–5.
Kumar, K. and Bann, S., eds (1993) *Utopias and the Millennium*, London: Reaktion Books.
Latham, R. (2002) *Scraps of the Untainted Sky: Science Fiction, Utopia, Dystopia* by Moylan, T., reviewed in *Science Fiction Studies*, 29:1, available at: <http://www.depauw.edu/SFs/review_essays/latham86.htm>
Lawless, E. (1914) *The Inalienable Heritage and Other Poems*, Suffolk: Richard Clay and Sons.
Lawless, E. (1909) *A Point of View*, Suffolk: Richard Clay and Sons.
Lawless, E. (1906) *A Garden Diary: September 1899 to September 1900*, London: Methuen & Co.
Lawless, E. (1904) *Maria Edgeworth*, London: Macmillan.
Lawless, E. (1902) *With the Wild Geese*, London: Ibister.
Lawless, E. (1899) "North Clare – Leaves from a Diary" *Nineteenth Century*, 46, 131–41.
Lawless, E. (1894) *Maelcho: A Sixteenth Century Narrative*, New York: Appleton and Co.
Lawless, E. (1890) *With Essex in Ireland*, New York: Lovell and Co.
Lawless, E. (1888) *Hurrish: A Study*, London: Blackwood.
Lawless, E. (1882) "Iar-Connaught: A Sketch," *Cornhill Magazine*, 45, 319–33.
Ledwell, F. (2006) *The Taste of Water*, Canada: Acorn Press.

Ledwell, J. (2002) "Afraid of Heights, Not Edges: Representations of the Shoreline in Recent Prince Edward Island Poetry and Art", available at <http://bisd.hollandc.pe.ca/islands7/>

Leerssen, J. (1986) *Mere Irish and Fíor-Ghael: Studies in the idea of Irish nationality, its development, and literary expression prior to the nineteenth century*, Amsterdam: John Benjamin's Publishing Company.

Leerssen, J. (1996) *Remembrance and Imagination: Patterns in the Historical and Literary Representation of Ireland in the Nineteenth Century*, Cork: Cork University Press.

Lefebvre, H. (1991) *The Production of Space*, Oxford: Blackwell.

Levitas, R. (1990) *The Concept of Utopia*, New York: Syracuse University Press.

Levitas, R. (2007a) "The Imaginary Reconstitution of Society: Utopia as Method", in Moylan, T. and Baccolini, R., eds, *Utopia Method Vision: The Use Value of Social Dreaming*, Bern: Peter Lang, 47–69.

Levitas, R. (2007b) "Looking for the blue: The necessity of utopia", *Journal of Political Ideologies*, 12: 3, 289–306.

Levitas, R. (2007c) "The Archive of the Feet: Memory, Place and Utopia", in Griffin, M.J. and Moylan, T., eds, *Exploring the Utopian Impulse: Essays on Utopian Thought and Practice*, Bern: Peter Lang, 19–42.

Litvack, L. and Hooper, G., eds (2000) *Ireland in the Nineteenth Century: Regional Identity*, Dublin: Four Courts Press.

Lloyd, D. (1993) *Anomalous States: Irish Writing and the Post-Colonial Movement*, Dublin: Lilliput Press.

Lloyd, D. (2003) "After History: Historicism and Irish Postcolonial Studies", in Carroll and King, eds, *Ireland and Postcolonial Theory*, Cork: Cork University Press, 46–62.

Logan, J., ed. (1994) *With Warmest Love: Lectures for Kate O'Brien 1984–1993*, Limerick: Meelick Press.

Lonergan, P. and O'Dwyer, R., eds (2007) *Echoes Down the Corridor: Irish Theatre – Past, Present, and Future*, Dublin: Carysfort Press.

Loomba, A. (1999) *Colonialism/Postcolonialism*, London: Routledge.

Loti, P. (1913) *Pecheur d'Islande*, Boston: Ginn.

Lynch, P.A., Fischer, J. and Coates, B., eds (2006) *Back to the Present: Forward to the Past, Irish Writing and History since 1798*, Amsterdam: Rodopi.

Lyons, F.S.L. (1963) *Ireland Since the Famine*, London: Fontana Press.

Lucchitti, I. (2009), *The Islandman: The Hidden Life of Tomás O'Crohan*, Reimagining Ireland: 3, Bern: Peter Lang.

Mac Con Iomaire, L. (2000) *Breandán Ó hEithir: Iomramh Aonair*, Gaillimh: Cló Iar-Chonnachta.

Mac Conghail, M. (1984) "Dia agus an Diabhal: Comhrá le Máirtín Ó Direáin", *Comhar*, 43: 10, 3–7.

Mac Conghail, M. (1988) "Poet of the Bright Thread: The Poetry of Máirtín Ó Direáin", *Irish University Review*, 18: 2, 181–190.

Mac Craith, M. (1984) "Sólás na Ceirde", *Comhar*, 43: 10, 13–18.

Mac Craith, M. (1993) *Oileán Rúin agus Muir an Dáin: Staidéar ar Fhilíocht Mháirtín Uí Dhireáin*, Baile Átha Claith: Comhar Teo.

Mac Craith, M. and Macleod, M. (2001) "Home and Exile: A Comparison of the Poetry of Máirtín Ó Direáin and Ruaraidh MacThòmais", *New Hibernia Review* 5:2, 72–81.

Mac Mathúna, L. agus Nic Eoin, M., eag. (2000) *Teanga, Pobal agus Réigiún: Aistí ar Chultúr na Gaeltachta Inniu*, Baile Átha Cliath: Coiscéim.

Mac Murchaidh, C., ed. (2004) *Who Needs Irish: Reflections on the Importance of the Irish Language Today*, Dublin: Veritas.

MacDonald, E. (2007) "Bridge Over Troubled Waters: The Fixed Link Debate on Prince Edward Island, 1885–1997", in Baldacchino, G., ed., *Bridging Islands: The Impact of Fixed Links*, Canada: Acorn Press, 29–46.

MacLaine, B. (2000) *Wind and Root*, Canada: Signal Editions.

MacLaine, B. (2004) *These Fields Were Rivers*, New Brunswick, Canada: Goose Lane Editions.

MacLeod, A. (1999) *Island: The Collected Stories*, Toronto: McClelland and Stewart.

Maguire, P.A. (2002) "Language and Landscape in the Connemara Gaeltacht", *Journal of Modern Literature*, 26: 1, 99–107.

Marchbanks, P. (2006) "Lessons in Lunacy: Mental Illness in Liam O'Flaherty's *Famine*", *New Hibernia Review*, 10: 2, 92–105.

Marin, L. (1993) "Frontiers of Utopia: Past and Present", *Critical Inquiry*, 19: 3, 397–420.

Markey, A. (2006) "The Discovery of Irish Folklore", *New Hibernia Review*, 10: 4, 21–43.

Matthews-Kane, B. (1997) "Emily Lawless's *Grania:* Making for the Open", *Colby Quarterly*, 33: 3, 223–235.

Mays, M. (2005) "Irish Identity in an Age of Globalisation", *Irish Studies Review*, 13: 1, 3–12.

McCall, G. (1994) "Nissology: A Proposal for Consideration", *Journal of the Pacific Society*, 63: 17, 99–106.

McCoy, G. (2003) "*Ros na Rún*: Alternative Gaelic Universe", available at: <http://www.ultach.dsl.pipex.com/resources/RosnaRun.publishedpaper.doc>

McLeod, J. (2000) *Beginning Postcolonialism*, Manchester: Manchester University Press.

McMahon, E. (2003) "The Gilded Cage: From utopia to monad in Australia's island imaginary", in Edmond, R. and Smith, V., eds, *Islands in History and Representation*, London: Routledge, 190–203.

McNeillie, A. (2002) *An Aran Keening*, Dublin: Lilliput Press.

Meistersheim, A. (2001) *Figures de l'île*, Ajaccio: DCL Éditions.

Messenger, J. (1964) "Literary vs. Scientific Interpretations of Cultural Reality in the Aran Islands", *Ethnohistory*, 11: 1, 41–55.

Mná Fiontracha, eag. (2004) *Ár nOileán: Tuile 's Trá*, Gaillimh: J.C. Printers.

Montague, J. (1982) *Selected Poems*, Ontario: Exile Editions Limited.

More, T. (1975 [1516]) *Utopia*. Trans. Robert M. Adams. New York: W.W. Norton.

Moore-Gilbert, B. (1997) "Crises of Identity? Current Problems in Possibilities in Postcolonial Criticism", *The European English Messenger*, 1: 2, 35–43.

Moylan, T. (1986) *Demand the Impossible: Science Fiction and the Utopian Imagination*, New York: Methuen.

Moylan, T. (2000) *Scraps of an Untainted Sky: Science Fiction, Utopia and Dystopia*, Colorado: Westview Press.

Moylan, T. (2004) *Utopian Audiences: How Readers Locate Nowhere* by Roemer, K., reviewed in *Science Fiction Studies*, 31: 3, available at: <http://www.depauw.edu/SFs/review_essays/moylan94.htm>

Moylan, T. (2007a) "Realizing Better Futures, Strong Thought for Hard Times", in Griffin, M.J. and Moylan, T., eds, *Exploring the Utopian Impulse: Essays on Utopian Thought and Practice*, Bern: Peter Lang, 191–222.

Moylan, T. (2007b) "Irish voyages and visions: pre-figuring, re-configuring Utopia", *Utopian Studies*, 18: 3, 299–324.

Moylan, T. and Baccolini, R., eds (2007) *Utopia Method Vision: The Use Value of Social Dreaming*, Bern: Peter Lang.

Moylan, T. (2008) "Making the Present Impossible: On the Vocation of Utopian Science Fiction", *5th Ralahine Utopian Studies Workshop*, April.

Murphy, B. (1994) "Past Events and Present Politics – Roy Foster's 'Modern Ireland'", in O'Ceallaigh, D., ed., *Reconsiderations of Irish History and Culture*, Dublin: Léirmheas, 80–84.

Murphy, M. O'R. (1973) "The Double Vision of Liam O'Flaherty", *Éire-Ireland*, 8:3, 20–25.

Murphy, P. (2003) "J.M. Synge and the Pitfalls of National Consciousness", *Theatre Research International*, 28: 2, 125–142.

Murphy, P. (2007) "Paradise Lost: The Destruction of Utopia in *The Beach*", in Griffin, M.J. and Moylan, T., eds, *Exploring the Utopian Impulse: Essays on Utopian Thought and Practice*, Bern: Peter Lang, 243–256.

Murray, J. (1866) *Handbook for Travellers in Ireland*, London: John Murray Publishers.

Murray, S., ed. (1997) *Not on Any Map: Essays on Postcoloniality and Cultural Nationalism*, Exeter: University of Exeter Press.

Nash, C. (1999) "Irish Placenames: Post-Colonial Locations", *Transactions of the Institute of British Geographers*, 24: 4, 457–480.

Ní Annracháin, M. and Nic Dhiarmada, B., eag. (1998) *Téacs agus Comhthéacs: Gnéithe de Chritic na Gaeilge*, Corcaigh: Cló Ollscoil Chorcaí.

Ní Chonghaile, D. (2010) "Ní neart go cur le chéile: lámhscríbhínní ceoil a chruthaigh Petrie agus Ó Comhraí in Árainn in 1857", in Ó hUiginn, R., eag., *Léachtaí Cholm Cille XL: Foinn agus Focail*, Maigh Nuad: An Sagart.

Ní Dhomhnaill, N. (1990) *Pharaoh's Daughter*, Meath: Gallery Press.

Ní Riain, I. (2002) *Carraig agus Cathair: Ó Direáin*, Baile Átha Cliath: Cois Life [See also Ryan, I. (2002)].

Nic Dhiarmada, B. (2007) "Aspects of utopia, anti-utopia, and nostalgia in Irish-language texts", *Utopian Studies*, 18: 3, 365–378.

Nic Congáil, R. (2010) *Úna Ní Fhaircheallaigh agus an Fhís Útóipeach Ghaelach*, Dublin: Arlen House.

Nic Eoin, M. (2004) "'Severed Heads and Grafted Tongues': The Language Question in Modern and Contemporary Writing in Irish", *Hungarian Journal of English and American Studies*, 10: 1–2, 267–281.

Nic Eoin, M. (2005) *Trén bhFearann Breac: An Díláithriú Cultúir agus Nualitríocht na Gaeilge*, Baile Átha Cliath: Cois Life.

Nic Pháidín, C. (1998) *Fáinne an Lae agus an Athbheochan, 1898–1900*, Baile Átha Cliath: Cois Life.

Nic Pháidín, C., ed. (1991) *An Chaint sa tSráidbhaile: Breandán Ó hEithir*, Baile Átha Cliath: Comhar Teo.

Norstedt, J.A. (1980) *Thomas MacDonagh: A Critical Biography*, Charlottesville, North Carolina.

Norquay, G. and Smyth, G., eds (2002) *Across the Margins: Cultural Identity and Change in the Atlantic Archipelago*, Manchester: Manchester University Press.

Novaczek, I., ed. (2008) *Culture and the Construction of Islandness*, Charlottetown, Prince Edward Island, Canada: Institute of Island Studies Press.

Nutley, S. and Cross, M. (1999) "Insularity and Accessibility: the Small Island Communities of Western Ireland", *Journal of Rural Studies*, 15: 3, 317–330.

Ó Buachalla, B. (1967) "Ó Cadhain, Ó Céileachair, Ó Flaithearta", *Comhar*, 25, 69–75.

Ó Cadhain, M. (1948) *An Braon Broghach*, Baile Átha Cliath: An Gúm.

Ó Ciosáin, N., ed. (2005) *Explaining Change in Cultural History: Historical Studies XX III*, Dublin: UCD Press.

Ó Conaola, D. (1979) *An Gaiscíoch Beag*, Baile Átha Claith: An Gúm.

Ó Conaola, D. (1988) *Amuigh Liom Féin*, Inis Oírr: An Ceardshiopa Teo.

Ó Conaola, D. (1990) *Night Ructions*, London: Forrest Books.

Ó Conaola, D. (1992) *Misiún ar Muir / Sea Mission*, Inis Oírr: An Ceardshiopa Teo.

Ó Concheanainn, P. (1993) *Inis Meáin, Seanchas agus Scéalta*, Baile Átha Cliath: An Gúm.

Ó Conchubhair, B. (2000) "Liam Ó Flaithearta agus Scríobh na Gaeilge: Ceist Airgid nó Cinneadh Chonradh na Gaeilge?", *New Hibernia Review*, 4: 2, 116–140.

Ó Conghaile, M. (1988) *Conamara agus Árainn 1880–1980*, Gaillimh: Cló Iar-Chonnachta.

Ó Conghaile, M. (1993) *Gnéithe d'Amhráin Chonamara ár Linne*, Gaillimh: Cló Iar-Chonnachta.

O'Connell, J.W. (1994) "Interlude: History and the Human Kingdom", in Waddell *et al.*, ed., *The Book of Aran*, Galway: Tír Eolais, 71–75.

O'Connor, B. (1993) "Myths and Mirrors: Tourist Images and Nacional Identity", in O'Connor, B. and Cronin, M., eds, *Tourism in Ireland: A Critical Analysis*, Cork: Cork University Press, 68–85.

O'Connor, B. and Cronin, M., eds (1993) *Tourism in Ireland: A Critical Analysis*, Cork: Cork University Press.

O'Connor, F. (1956) "A Good Short Story Must be News", *New York Times Book Review*, 10 June, Section 7: 1.

O'Connor, J. (2010) *Ghost Light*, London: Harvill Secker.

Ó Criomhthain, T. (1937) *The Islandman*. Trans. Robin Flower. Dublin: Talbot Press.

Ó Dubhthaigh, F. (1981) *Dúil Uí Fhlaithearta*, Baile Átha Cliath: Foilseacháin Náisiúnta.

O'Dwyer, R. (1994) "A Ghost Where Her Memory Revisited" in Logan J., ed., *With Warmest Love: Lectures for Kate O'Brien 1984–1993*, Limerick: Meelick Press, 63–77.

O'Faolain, S. (1977) "*Dúil*", in Jordan, J., ed., *The Pleasures of Gaelic Literature*, Dublin: Mercier, 111–119.

O'Farrelly, A. (2010 [1902]) *Smaointe ar Árainn / Thoughts on Aran*. Trans. Ríona Níc Congáil. Dublin: Arlen House.

Ó Fátharta, D. (1990) *Cloch an Fhaoileáin* [Privately published].

Ó Fátharta, D. (2003) *Cloch na nGabhar*, Baile Átha Cliath: Coiscéim.

O'Flaherty, J.T. (1824), "A Sketch of the History and Antiquities of the Southern Isles of Aran, lying off the West Coast of Ireland; with Observations on the Religion of the Celtic Nations, Pagan Monuments of the Early Irish, Druidic Rites, &c.", in *Transactions of the Royal Irish Academy*, Dublin.

O'Flaherty, L. (1923) *Thy Neighbour's Wife*, London: Jonathan Cape.

O'Flaherty, L. (1927) "Writing in Gaelic", *The Irish Statesman*, 17 December, 348.

O'Flaherty, L. (1929) *Return of the Brute*, London: Mandrake.

O'Flaherty, L. (1929) *A Tourist's Guide to Ireland*, London: Mandrake.

O'Flaherty, L. (1930) *Two Years*, London: Cape.

O'Flaherty, L. (1934) *Shame the Devil*, London: Grayson and Grayson.

O'Flaherty, L. (1935) *Skerrett*, London: Victor Gollancz.

O'Flaherty, L. (1966) *The Short Stories of Liam O'Flaherty*, London: Four Square Press.

O'Flaherty, L. (1981 [1924]) *The Black Soul*, Dublin: Wolfhound Press.

O'Flaherty, R. ([1684]1846) *A Chronological Description of West or H-iar Connaught*, [edited with notes and illustrations by James Hardiman], Dublin.

O'Flaherty, T. (1934) *Aranmen All*, Dublin: Hamish Hamilton.

O'Flaherty, T. (1935) *Cliffmen of the West*, London.

O'Flaherty-O'Sullivan, P. (2004) "Agallamh le Pegeen iníon le Liam Ó Flaithearta", in Mná Fiontracha, eag., *Ár nOileán: Tuile 's Trá*, Gaillimh: J.C. Printers, 35–42.

Ó Flaithearta, L. (1949) "An Braon Broghach" [léirmheas], *Comhar*, 8: 5.

Ó Giolláin, D. (2000) *Locating Irish Folklore: Tradition, Modernity, Identity*, Cork: Cork University Press.

Ó Gráda, C. (1999) *Black '47 and Beyond: The Great Irish Famine in History, Economy and Memory*, New Jersey: Princeton University Press.

O'Grady, T. (2005) "The Passing of a Cultural Moment" – Obituary of Máire Bn. Uí Fhátharta, *Irish Times*, 7 March.

Ó Gráinne, D. (1989), "Mo Chomhráití le Máirtín Ó Direáin", *Comhar*, 48: 12, 10–24.

Ó hAnluain, E. (1984) "Fearann Coimirce m'Aislinge", *Comhar*, 43: 10, 20–25.

Ó hAnluain, E., eag. (2002) *Ón Ulán Ramhar Siar*, Baile Átha Claith: An Clóchomhar Teo.

Ó hEithir, B. (1977) "Liam Ó Flaithearta agus a Dhúchas", in Ó hEithir, B., *Willie the Plain Pint agus an Pápa*, Baile Átha Cliath: Cló Mercier, 65–76.

Ó hEithir, B. (1977) *Willie the Plain Pint agus an Pápa*, Baile Átha Cliath: Cló Mercier.

Ó hEithir, B. (1984) *Over the Bar*, Dublin: Ward River Press Ltd.

Ó hEithir, B. (1988) "Mise, Máirtín agus an Hound of the Baskervilles", *Comhar*, 47: 5, 27–28.

Ó hEithir, B. (1989) *An Nollaig Thiar*, Baile Átha Cliath: Poolbeg.

Ó hEithir, B. and Ó hEithir, R., eds (1991) *An Aran Reader*, Dublin: Lilliput Press.

Ó hÓgáin, D. (1990) *Myth, Legend and Romance: An encyclopaedia of the Irish folk tradition*, London: Ryan.

Ó hUiginn, R., eag., *Léachtaí Cholm Cille XL: Foinn agus Focail*, Maigh Nuad: An Sagart.

Ó Laoire, L. (2004) "Níl sí doiligh a iompar/No load to carry: A personal response to the current situation in Irish", in Mac Murchaidh, C., ed., *Who Needs Irish: Reflections on the Importance of the Irish Language Today*, Dublin: Veritas, 46–63.

O'Leary, P. (1994) *The Prose Literature of the Gaelic Revival, 1881–1921: Ideology and Innovation*, Pennsylvania: The Pennsylvania State University Press.

O'Malley, A. (2003) "Re-*Translations*, or, Can the Postcolonial Construct a Home? A Reading of Brian Friel's *The Communication Cord*", *EnterText*, 2: 2, 68–83.

O'Malley, M. (1997) *Irish Times*, 15 August, 12.

O'Mara, J. (1982) *Gerald of Wales: The History and Topography of Ireland*, London: Penguin Books.

Ó Ríordáin, S. (1952) *Eireaball Spideoige*, Baile Átha Cliath: Sáirséal – Ó Marcaigh.

Ó Ríordáin, S. (1964) *Brosna*, Baile Átha Cliath: Sáirséal agus Dill.

Ó Searcaigh, C. (2000) *Ag Tnúth leis an tSolas*, Gaillimh: Cló Iar-Chonnachta.

O'Sullivan, P., ed. (1976) *A World of Stone: Life, Folklore and Legends of the Aran Islands*, Dublin: O'Brien Educational Publishers.

O'Toole, F. (2000) *The Clod and the Continent: Irish Identity in the European Union*, available at: <http://www.ictu.ie/download/pdf/essay1.pdf>

O'Toole, F. (1998) *The Lie of the Land: Irish Identities*, Dublin: New Island.

Ó Torna, C. (2000) "Cruthú Constráide agus an Turas Siar: An Ghaeltacht i dtús an Fichiú hAois", *Aimsir Óg*, 1, 51–64.

Ó Torna, C. (2005) *Cruthú na Gaeltachta 1893–1922*, Baile Átha Cliath: Cois Life.

Ó Tuama, S. (1978) *Filí Faoi Sceimhle: Seán Ó Ríordáin agus Aogán Ó Rathaille*, Baile Átha Cliath: Oifig an tSolathair.

Patten, E. (1999) "With Essex in India? Emily Lawless's Colonial Consciousness", *European Journal of English Studies*, 3: 3, 285–297.

Peacock, A.J., ed. (1992) *The Achievement of Brian Friel*, Great Britain: Colin Smythe Limited.

Péron, F. (2004) "The Contemporary Lure of the Island", *Tijdschrift voor Economische en Sociale Geografie*, 95: 3, 326–339.

Pochin Mould, D. (1972) *The Aran Islands*, Devon: David and Charles Publishers Limited.

Polack, F. (2000) "Writing and Rewriting the Island: Tasmania, Politics, and Contemporary Australian Fiction", in Brinklow, L., Ledwell, F. and Ledwell, J., eds, *Message in a Bottle: The Literature of Small Islands*, Charlottetown, Prince Edward Island, Canada: Institute of Island Studies Press, 215–230.

Pordzik, R. (2001a) "A Postcolonial View of Ireland and the Irish Conflict in Anglo-Irish Utopian Literature since the Nineteenth Century", *Irish Studies Review*, 9: 3, 331–346.

Pordzik, R. (2001b) *The Quest of Postcolonial Utopia: A Comparative Introduction to the Utopian Novel in the New English Literatures*, New York: Peter Lang Publishing.

Powell, A. (1984) *Oileáin Árann: Stair na n-Oileán anuas go dtí 1922*, Dublin: Wolfhound Press.

Price, A., ed. (1962) *J.M. Synge: Collected Works, Volume II, Prose*, Oxford: Oxford University Press.

Prút, L. (1982) *Máirtín Ó Direáin: File Tréadúil*, Maigh Nuad: An Sagart.

Quayson, A. (2000) *Postcolonialism: Theory, Practice or Process*, Cambridge: Polity Press.

Quigley, M. (2003) "Modernity's Edge: Speaking Silence on the Blasket Islands", *interventions*, 5: 3, 382–406.

Quin, E.G., ed. (1984) *Dictionary of the Irish Language*, Dublin: Royal Irish Academy.

Rees, C. (1996) *Utopian Imagination and Eighteenth-Century Fiction*, London: Longman Group Limited.

Relethford, J.H. (1988) "Effects of English admixture and geographic distance on anthropometric variation and genetic structure in 19th-century Ireland", *American Journal of Physical Anthropology*, 76: 1, 111–124.

Relph, E. (1976) *Place and Placelessness*, London: Pion.

Ritchie, J.E. (1977) "Cognition of Place: The Island Mind", *Ethos*, 5: 2, 187–194.

Robinson, L., ed. (1947) *Lady Augusta Gregory: Journals 1916–1930*, New York: Macmillan.

Robinson, T. (1986) *Stones of Aran: Pilgrimage*, London: Penguin.

Robinson, T., ed. (1992) "Place / Person / Book: Synge's *The Aran Islands*", *The Aran Islands*, London: Penguin, vii-1.

Robinson, T. (1995) *Stones of Aran: Labyrinth*, London: Penguin.

Robinson, T. (2003) "The Irish Echosphere", *New Hibernia Review*, 7: 3, 9–22.

Rose, G. (1993) *Feminism and Geography: the Limits of Geographical Knowledge*, Cambridge: Polity Press.

Rousseau, J-J. and Herder, J.G. (1986) *On the Origin of Language: Two Essays*, Chicago: University of Chicago Press.

Royle, S.A. (1983) "The economy and society of the Aran Islands in the early 19th century", *Irish Geography*, 16, 36–54.

Royle, S.A. (1986) "A dispersed pressure group: Comhdháil na nOileán, the Federation of the Islands of Ireland", *Irish Geography*, 19, 92–95.

Royle, S.A. (1999) "From Dursey to Darrit-Uliga-Delap: an insular odyssey", *Irish Geography*, 32: 1, 1–8.

Royle, S.A. (2001) *A Geography of Islands: Small Island Insularity*, London: Routledge.

Royle, S.A. (2003) "Exploitation and celebration of the heritage of the Irish islands", *Irish Geography*, 36: 1, 23–31.

Royle, S.A. (2007a) "Islands off the Irish Coast and the 'Bridging Effect'", in Baldacchino, G., ed., *Bridging Islands: The Impact of Fixed Links*, Canada: Acorn Press, 203–218.

Royle, S.A. (2007b) "Island Spaces and Identities: Definitions and Typologies", in Baldacchino, G., ed., *A World of Islands: An Island Studies Reader*, Malta: Agenda Academic Press, 33–56.

Royle, S.A. (2010) "'Small Places like St Helena have Big Questions to Ask': The Inaugural Lecture of a Professor of Island Geography", *Island Studies Journal*, 5: 1, 5–24.

Ruppert, P. (1987) *Reader in a Strange Land: the Activity of Reading Literary Utopias*, Georgia: University of Georgia Press.

Ryan, I. (2002) "Poetic Place and Geographical Space: An Analysis of the Poetry of Máirtín Ó Direáin", *Irish Studies Review*, 10; 3, 267–275 [See also Ní Riain, I. (2002)].

Saddlemyer, A. (2007) "Synge's *The Aran Islands*", *New Hibernia Review*, 11: 4, 120–135.

Said, E.W. (1978) *Orientalism*, London: Routledge & Kegan Paul Ltd.

San Juan, Jr., E. (1998) *Beyond Postcolonial Theory*, London: Palgrave.

Sangiorgi, S. (2007) "Invitation to Utopia: Values, Communities, and Landscapes in Western Theme Parks", *3rd Ralahine Utopian Studies Workshop*, May.

Sargent, L.T. (1976) "Themes in Utopian Fiction in English Before Wells", *Science Fiction Studies*, 3: 3, available at: <http://www.depauw.edu/SFs/backissues/10/sargent10art.htm>

Sargent, L.T. (1994) "The Three Faces of Utopianism Revisited", *Utopian Studies*, 5:1, 1–37.

Sargent, L.T. (2001) "Utopianism and National Identity", in Goodwin, B., ed., *The Philosophy of Utopia*, Essex: Frank Cass Publishers, 87–106.

Sargent, L.T. (2007) "Choosing Utopia: Utopianism as an Essential Element in Political Thought and Action", in Griffin, M.J. and Moylan, T., eds, *Exploring the Utopian Impulse: Essays on Utopian Thought and Practice*, Bern: Peter Lang, 301–318.

Sargent, L.T. (2010) *Utopianism: A Very Short Introduction*, Oxford: Oxford University Press.

Sargisson L. and Levitas, R. (2003) "Utopia in Dark Times: Optimism/Pessimism and Utopia/Dystopia", in Baccolini, R. and Moylan, T., eds, *Dark Horizons: Science Fiction and the Dystopian Imagination*, London: Routledge, 13–28.

Sargisson, L. and Sargent, L.T., eds (2004) *Living in Utopia: New Zealand's Intentional Communities*, United Kingdom: Ashgate Publishing.

Saul, G. (1963) "A Wild Sowing: the Short Stories of Liam O'Flaherty", *Review of English Literature*, 4, 108–113.

Sayers, P. (1936) *Peig*, Dublin: Talbot Press.

Sayers, S. (2004) "Irish Myth and Irish National Consciousness", *Irish Studies Review*, 12: 3, 271–281.

Schaer, R. and Sargent, L.T. (2000) *Utopia: The Search for the Ideal Society in the Western* World, Oxford: Oxford University Press.

Schama, S. (1995) *Landscape and Memory*, London: HarperCollins.

Selvon, S. (2000) *An Island is a World*, Toronto: TSAR Publications.

Sheeran, P. (1976) *The Novels of Liam O'Flaherty: A Study in Romantic Realism*, Dublin: Wolfhound Press.

Sheeran, P. (1988) "*Genius Fabulae*: The Irish Sense of Place", *Irish University Review*, 18: 2, 191–206.

Sheeran, P. (1994) "Aran, Paris and the Fin-de-Siècle", in Waddell *et al.*, ed., *The Book of Aran*, Galway: Tír Eolais, 299–305.

Sheridan, N. (2004) "My Father Dr. Máirtín Ó Direáin", in Mná Fiontracha, eag., *Ár nOileán: Tuile 's Trá*, Gaillimh: J.C. Printers, 107–110.

Shields, C. (2004) *Collected Stories*, London: Fourth Estate.

Short, J.R. (1991) *Imagined Country: Society, Culture and Environment*, London: Routledge.

Sisson, E. (2004) *Pearse's Patriots: St. Enda's and the Cult of Boyhood*, Cork: Cork University Press.

Smyth, G. (2001) *Space and the Irish Cultural Imagination*, UK: Palgrave.

Standún, P. (1994) "The Aran Islands Today: A Personal View", in Waddell *et al.*, ed., *The Book of Aran*, Galway: Tír Eolais, 307–313.

Standún, P. (2004) *Eaglais na gCatacómaí*, Gaillimh: Cló Iar-Chonnachta.

Stokes, W. (1868) *Life and Labours in Art and Archaeology of George Petrie*, London.

Synge, J.M. (1905) *Riders to the Sea*, London: Elkin Mathews.

Synge, J.M. (1971) My Wallet of Photographs: the Collected Photographs of J.M. Synge. Arranged and Introduced by Lilo Stephens. Dublin: Dolmen Press.

Terrell, J.E. (2004) "Islands in the River of Time", Islands of the World VIII International Conference 'Changing Islands – Changing Worlds': Proceedings, available at: <www.giee.ntnu.edu.tw/island>

Thomas, S. (2007) "Littoral Space(s): Liquid Edges of Poetic Possibility", Journal of the Canadian Association for Curriculum Studies, 5: 1, 21–29.

Tiffen, C. and Lawson, A. (1994) De-Scribing Empire: Post-colonialism and Textuality, London: Routledge.

Titley, A. (1991) An tÚrscéal Gaeilge, Baile Átha Cliath: An Clóchomhar Teoranta.

Tóibín, C. (2005) "New Ways to Kill Your Mother", in Tóibín, C., ed. (2005) Synge: A Celebration, Dublin: Carysfort Press, 1–13.

Tóibín, C., ed. (2005) Synge: A Celebration, Dublin: Carysfort Press.

Tracy, R. (1998) The Unappeasable Host: Studies in Irish Identity, Dublin: UCD Press.

Tuan, Y.F. (1977) Space and Place: The Perspective of Experience, Minneapolis: University of Minneapolis Press.

Tymoczko, M. (1998) Translation in a Postcolonial Culture, Manchester: St Jerome Publishers.

Tymoczko, M. and Ireland, C., eds (2003a) Language and Tradition in Ireland: Continuities and Displacements, Boston: University of Massachusetts Press.

Tymoczko, M. and Ireland, C. (2003b) "Editors' Introduction: Language and Identity in Twentieth Century Ireland", Éire/Ireland, 38, 4–22.

Waddell et al. ed. (1994) The Book of Aran, Galway: Tír Eolais.

Watkins, C. (1985) The American Heritage Dictionary of Indo-European Roots, Boston: Houghton-Mifflin.

Weale, D. (1991) "Islandness", Island Journal, Maine Island Institute, 8, 81–82.

Wegner, P.E. (2002) Imaginary Communities: Utopia, the Nation, and the Spatial Histories of Modernity, Berkeley: University of California Press.

Wegner, P.E. (2007) "Here or Nowhere: Utopia, Modernity, and Totality", in Griffin, M.J. and Moylan, T., eds, Exploring the Utopian Impulse: Essays on Utopian Thought and Practice, Bern: Peter Lang, 113–130.

Whelan, K. (1992) "The Power of Place", Irish Review, 12, 13–20.

Whelan, K. (2002) "The Memories of 'The Dead'", Yale Journal of Criticism, 15.1, 59–97.

Whelan, K. (2003). "Between Filiation and Affiliation: The Politics of Postcolonial Memory", in Carroll and King, eds, Ireland and Postcolonial Theory, Cork: Cork University Press, 92–108.

Williams, J.E.C. agus Ní Mhuiríosa, M. (1979) *Traidisiún Liteartha na nGael*, Baile Átha Cliath: An Clóchomhar Teo.

Williams, R. (1978) "Utopia and Science Fiction", *Science Fiction Studies*, 5: 3, available at: <http://www.depauw.edu/SFs/backissues/16/williams16art.htm>

Winston, B. (1999) "Documentary: How the Myth was Deconstructed", *Wide Angle*, 21: 2, 70–86.

Woods, M. (2007) *This Time, This Place*, Dublin: Impress.

Wyndham, A.H., ed. (2006) *Re-Imagining Ireland: How a storied island is transforming its politics, economy, religious life, and culture for the twenty-first century*, University of Virginia Press.

Yeats, W.B. (1962) *Explorations*, New York: Macmillan.

Yeats, W.B. (1968) "Preface", *J.M. Synge: Collected Works, Volume III*, London: Oxford University Press.

Young, R. (1995) *Colonial Desire: Hybridity in Theory, Culture and Race*, London: Routledge.

Theses

Brewer, B.W. (1982) *Emily Lawless: An Irish Writer Above All Else*, Unpublished Thesis (PhD), The University of North Carolina at Chapel Hill.

Burke, A. (2008) *Performing Ethnography: The Photograph as Measure of Difference on the Aran Islands*, Unpublished Thesis (PhD), University of Ulster.

Collinge, D. (1985) *"Rock, Stone and Shore: The Poetry of Máirtín Ó Direáin, 1939–1979. A Translation and Critical Analysis"*, Unpublished Thesis (PhD), University College, Dublin.

Costello-Sulllivan, K.P. (2004) *Troubling Synonymies: Britishness and the nineteenth-century novel*, Unpublished Thesis (PhD), Boston College.

Fernandez Pajares, H. (1999) *Miniature Worlds: The Literature of the Irish Islands*, Unpublished Thesis (MA), NUI Galway.

Grubgeld, M.E. (1983) *Private Geographies: Land and Life in the Irish Literary Renaissance – Emily Lawless, George Moore, and J.M. Synge*, Unpublished Thesis (PhD), The University of Iowa.

Hampton, J.B. (1999) *Voices Outside the Irish Renaissance*, Unpublished Thesis (PhD), Southern Illinois University at Carbondale.

Harvey, A.D. (2007) *Irish Realism: Women, the novel, and national politics, 1870–1922*, Unpublished Thesis (PhD), University of California, Los Angeles.

Linn, W. (1971) *The Life and Works of the Honourable Emily Lawless: First Novelist of the Irish Literary Revival*, Unpublished Thesis (PhD), New York University.

Meredith, R.B. (1999) *Reviving Women: Irish Women's Prose Writing, 1890–1920*, Unpublished Thesis (PhD), Queen's University of Belfast.

O'Callaghan, J. (2004) *Politics, Policy and History: History Teaching in Irish Secondary Schools 1922–72*, Thesis (MA), University of Limerick.

Ryan, I. (1994) *Máirtín Ó Direáin: Oileánach agus Fear Cathrach*, Published Thesis (PhD), University College Cork.

State Publications

Dáil Éireann, *Debates*, vol. 87, 2 June 1942, Cols. 761–762.

Radio Interviews

"Breandán Ó hEithir ag caint le Máirtín Jaimsie Ó Flatharta", Inis Mór, Árainn, 9 Márta 1989. Cartlann Raidió na Gaeltachta.

Film

"An Charraig Stoite" (2003).

Mac Dara Ó Curraidhín (Stiúrthóir/Léiritheoir), Alan Titley (Scríbhneoir).

Index

Reimagining Ireland

Series Editor: Dr Eamon Maher, Institute of Technology, Tallaght

The concepts of Ireland and 'Irishness' are in constant flux in the wake of an ever-increasing reappraisal of the notion of cultural and national specificity in a world assailed from all angles by the forces of globalisation and uniformity. Reimagining Ireland interrogates Ireland's past and present and suggests possibilities for the future by looking at Ireland's literature, culture and history and subjecting them to the most up-to-date critical appraisals associated with sociology, literary theory, historiography, political science and theology.

Some of the pertinent issues include, but are not confined to, Irish writing in English and Irish, Nationalism, Unionism, the Northern 'Troubles', the Peace Process, economic development in Ireland, the impact and decline of the Celtic Tiger, Irish spirituality, the rise and fall of organised religion, the visual arts, popular cultures, sport, Irish music and dance, emigration and the Irish diaspora, immigration and multiculturalism, marginalisation, globalisation, modernity/postmodernity and postcolonialism. The series publishes monographs, comparative studies, interdisciplinary projects, conference proceedings and edited books.

Proposals should be sent either to Dr Eamon Maher at eamon.maher@ittdublin.ie or to ireland@peterlang.com.

Vol. 1   Eugene O'Brien: 'Kicking Bishop Brennan up the Arse':
          Negotiating Texts and Contexts in Contemporary Irish Studies
          ISBN 978-3-03911-539-6. 219 pages. 2009.

Vol. 2   James P. Byrne, Padraig Kirwan and Michael O'Sullivan (eds):
          Affecting Irishness: Negotiating Cultural Identity Within and
          Beyond the Nation
          ISBN 978-3-03911-830-4. 334 pages. 2009.

Vol. 3   Irene Lucchitti: The Islandman: The Hidden Life of Tomás
          O'Crohan
          ISBN 978-3-03911-837-3. 232 pages. 2009.

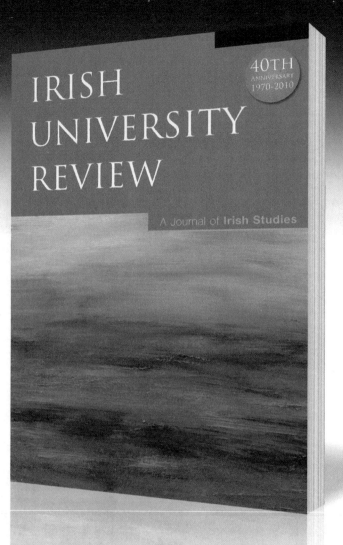

IRISH
UNIVERSITY
REVIEW

40TH
ANNIVERSARY
1970-2010

A Journal of **Irish Studies**

Established in 1970, the **Irish University Review** is the leading journal of Irish literary
studies. It publishes the best current criticism and scholarship, an extensive review
section, and the IASIL annual bibliography of Irish Studies.

The 'special issues', published annually, and devoted to the work of a particular
author, or a topic of current interest in Irish Studies, have shaped and defined the field.

To find out more, and for details of how to subscribe, please visit our website.

www.irishuniversityreview.ie